Tova Younger

Hands-on How-to's for the Home and Heart

Thoughts and techniques to enhance your life

book publishing services that are simply, Tov!

First edition Adar 5771
Second edition Tishrei 5772
Third edition Sivan 5772
Paperback edition Adar 5779

Published by
Tovim Press, LLC

HANDS-ON HOW-TO'S
FOR THE HOME AND HEART
Copyright 2019 Tova Gale Younger
ISBN: 978-0-9994786-8-4

No part of this book may be reproduced
IN ANY FORM, PHOTOCOPYING OR COMPUTER
SYSTEMS – for sales or business purposes.

Sharing information herein via photocopying sections, but not through email or internet, at no charge, is greatly encouraged and appreciated. When doing so, include:

Reproduced with permission from
HANDS-ON HOW-TO'S
FOR THE HOME AND HEART

For more information, or any comments or questions
please contact the publisher/author

1 323 285 7303 * 972 8 928 5589
ytovay@gmail.com

This book is dedicated to my father and his family.

לעילוי נשמת

אבי מורי ר' שמואל בן ר' יהודה דוד ז"ל
שנפטר כ"ו טבת תשס"ט

ומשפחתו
ר' יהודה דוד בן ר' טוביה שו"ב הי"ד
גיטל בת ר' חיים יעקב הי"ד

פערל לאה בת ר' יהודה דוד הי"ד
שיינדל בת ר' יהודה דוד הי"ד
אסתר רחל בת ר' יהודה דוד הי"ד

שנהרגו ונשרפו במלחמת הנאצים ימ"ש
עם כל היהודים מעיר ריישא

ה' באב תש"ב
ת.נ.צ.ב.ה.

Rabbi Zev Leff

Rabbi of Moshav Matityahu
Rosh HaYeshiva—Yeshiva Gedola Matityahu

D.N. Modiin 71917   Tel: 08-976-1138   Fax: 08-976-5326

בס"ד

הרב זאב לף

מרא דאתרא מושב מתתיהו
ראש הישיבה—ישיבה גדולה מתתיהו

טל 08-976-1138   פקס 08-976-5326   71917 ד.נ. מודיעין

Dear Friends,

Giving good advice is not limited to professional advisors alone but rather it is a fulfillment of the *mitzva* of *Gemillas Chassadim* which is incumbent on every Jew. This is the dimension of kindness one fulfills with his mind and speech, not with his body and material possessions. There is also a Torah commandment forbidding one from giving bad advice and thereby conceptually 'putting a stumbling block in front of the blind.'

I know the Youngers, who reside in Kiryat Sefer which is in close proximity to Moshav Matityahu, to be a fine Torah family who excellently represent the finest ideas and ideals of Judaism.

Mrs. Younger has committed to writing a plethora of good sound advice and practical tips and suggestions. The book "Hands-on How-to's for the Home and Heart" contains material that will be useful and helpful, some on a practical level, some inspirational and some sound guidance.

I congratulate her on her efforts and am sure she will be rewarded richly by *HaShem Yisborach* for the *Gemillas Chassadim* this book generates.

Sincerely,
With Torah blessings

Rabbi Zev Leff

Read what these people have to say about
HANDS-ON HOW-TO'S FOR THE HOME AND HEART
listed alphabetically within group

"What a pleasure to read a book that is both readable, useful and as good as most *sifrei mussar* in actually helping young and not so young mothers make positive changes both in their inner and outer lives as they discover a relaxed, *hashkafically* sound and PRACTICAL approach to their role in one easy read. I recommend this book as a perfect gift to your favorite new mother, or any woman on your list who would welcome a lift for body and soul."

Rebbetzin Tziporah Heller
Author, Lecturer

"It's a great book; combination of what every Jewish mother needs to navigate her life. It has something for everyone; even unique recipes! I enjoy reading it again and again."

Rebbetzin Tova Juravel
Storytyme Tapes

"It is a pleasure to read Mrs. Younger's book, the product of many successful years in the school of motherhood. She shares her tips, her positivity and her strength as a Jewish mother connected to her Father in Heaven. I highly recommend this book."

Rebbetzin Malka Kaganoff
Author, Lecturer

"We readers are the fortunate beneficiaries of Tova Younger's many talents. Her decades of creative homemaking and childrearing, her expertise in investigating and garnering tips and techniques to enhance the home and her literary skills – brought together in a fascinating, informative and useful guidebook.

From tips for pink eye to better *knaidlach*. From economical vacation ideas to the secret of making Amazing Croutons. From dieting, sleep aids or multiple practical use for razor blades; it's all there and much more.

Refreshingly imaginative and innovative, yet sensible and workable, enjoy your first read and then keep this book handy for valuable reference."

Rebbetzin Yehudis Samet
Author, Lecturer

"This is an incredible handbook that includes both the *hashkafa* as well as practical tips to run a Jewish Household. Both the novice as well as the experienced will be able to turn over and over again to this book to get *chizuk* and practical ideas to make the running of the household a smoother process. This book has something for everyone and will make a perfect gift."

Rebbetzin Shira Smiles
Author, Lecturer

"An alternate title for this great book might be, *How to Become a Tzaddekess within Your Comfort Zone*. It's a 'positive thinking' book, but much more, and very palatable as you go along.

I wouldn't have expected any less, having been exposed to Tova Younger's fresh, uplifting, original and very happy style as editor of the defunct Yated Ne'eman International Edition. Here, too, she guides the reader in self improvement in so many areas: Meaningful davening through very practical tips that are easy to incorporate in your daily rapport with *HaShem*; efficiency tips in so many areas, like doing chessed for others and not losing out.

This book cannot be read in one sitting and certainly not because it is boring or sermonizing. On the contrary, because it is so downright interesting, stimulating and has such great ideas, you will have to digest each precious page, internalize and put them into practice, like the handbook it is.

This book encompasses everything, from the kitchen sink straight to Heaven. In "Train Your Brain" she quotes the Bubby who was asked which modern convenience she considered indispensable. "The kitchen faucet…" she replied.

How does she take it from there? Her first 'appliance' is *tefilla*; the second is your brain, with very practical advice on directing your thoughts, improving your memory.

And I add – by keeping this invaluable handbook at hand for a daily spiritual 'fix', you will learn how to fix whatever needs fixing in your life as a Jewish woman, wife, mother."

Rebbetzin Sheindel Weinbach
Noted Author

"In this invaluable book, Tova Younger presents time tested techniques for solving everyday situations in the home and heart. From relationship issues to parenting to *shalom bayis* to self-improvement... Tova approaches each topic with a combination of common sense and creativity. Tova's writing reflects fresh honesty, clarity and a wealth of experience. This book is a 'must have' in every Jewish home."

Miriam Hendeles
Music Therapist, Author

"I like this book! Wow. This book contains lots of information VERY important for people to hear. You should have abundant *siyata d'Shmaya* and *hatzlacha*."

Yocheved Krems
Proofreader and Copyeditor Diamond Editing

"...spilling over with tiny gems..."

Yael Mermelstein
Author *Second Chances*

"Thank you for sharing this book with me, Tova! Page after page is chock-full of life-wisdom, helpful tips and inspiration!"

Sara Chava Mizrahi
Editor

...and from other delighted readers

"*Hands-on How-to's for the Home and Heart* is important for every Jewish home. It's easily readable and adaptable, covering many important topics from *davening* to re-cycling. The techniques and tips for creating a Jewish home are so valuable! I look forward to referring to it daily and to sending a copy to my daughter."

Naomi Obie, Seattle, Washington

"Once you pick it up, you just can't put it down!"

N.W., Brooklyn N.Y.

"It's so great to keep on hand to reference from. I don't remember ever seeing such a practical book like this, with such a wide variety of ideas in one compilation. You have given people a true treasure. The home and heart aka the Jewish woman. It will be a great companion for Jewish women in so many different stages in life. Thank you so much for sharing this with me."

M.R., London, England

"Full of *simchas hachaim*; everything sounds like lots of fun!"

T.H., Kiryat Sefer

"I always said you could be a good lawyer; you didn't disappoint me. With this book, you offer straight shooting advice to any reader. *Yaasher Koach!*"

Mrs. Stimler, Ramat Beit Shemesh; author's mother

Table of Contents

Introduction — 16

For the Heart

Hakaras HaTov –
Change Your Life with Gratitude — 21
Kavana – Put More into Your *Davening* — 27
Igeress HaRamban – An Appreciation — 34
Shmiras Haloshon – Tailor Your Talk — 36
Pathways to *Chessed* — 41
Get More Done, with *Chessed* — 48
Conversing with *Kavod* — 52
Use Your Phone –
For Fun and (Spiritual) Profit — 59
Ascribe Positive Motives — 65
Make Change Part of Your Routine — 71
How to be a Loveable Child — 74
Train Your Brain — 78
Da'as Torah – It's for Me and You! — 85

For the Home

Organize Now!	93
Try a Point Chart… Get Results!	98
It's Clean up Time!	102
Shabbos – Lighting Right on Time	105
Pesach Tips – Even for Procrastinators	112
Homework, Not Hardwork	118
Times Tables – Gift of a Lifetime	123
Games for the Gang	127
Family Time, Family Fun!	132
Make a Happy Birthday!	141
Join the Cut-Down-on-Candy Club!	147
Re-use with Relish	152
Love Laundry Day	157
Delight in Doing the Dishes	165
If You Can Read, You Can Sew	169
Be the Hostess with the Mostest	177
Be the Best Guest	182
Moving Day	187
Re: References	190
Simcha Savings	199
Grandparenting – Make it Grand!	205

Handy Tips

Babysitting Basics	215
Car and Travel	217
Children – Keep Them out of Trouble!	218
Careful with Computers	223
Diet – It can be Delicious	224
Health and Hygiene	227
Household Help	232
Kashrus – Keep it Clear in the Kitchen	233
Make it Modest	235
Miscellaneous Matters	237
Nursing – it's a Natural	239
Paper Towels/Wipes	242
Razor Blades	243
Shabbos Kodesh	244
Sholom Bayis	245
Shopping Successfully	249
Simply Superb *Simcha*	251
Sleep Aids	253
Speech Therapy	254
Teenage Trials	255

Recipes   (* Kosher for Pesach!)   258

Challah	263
Amazing Croutons	267
Israeli Salad*	268
Techina	269
Falafel Balls	269
Spicy Tomato Dip*	270
Ketchup*	270
French Fries*	271
Doughless Potato Knishes	271
Kishka Kugel	272
Pickle-y or Spicy Eggplant*	272
Beans in Tomato Sauce	274
Cabbage Salad*	274
String Beans	275
Beet Salad*	275
Tuna Quiche*	276
Gregarious Grains	276
Mixed Vegetable Soup*	278
Tomato Soup*	278
Onion Soup*	279
Lentil Soup	279
Mushroom-Barley Soup	280
Chicken and Potatoes*	280
Chicken Soup*	281
Knaidlach*	282

Zucchini Kugel	282
Chicken Salad*	283
Hamburgers/Meatballs*	283
Cholent	284
Goulash/Stew*	285
Sloppy-Joe*	285
Pizza	286
Pizza Wheels	287
Spinach/Zucchini Pie*	287
Tomato Quiche	289
Cornflake Quiche	289
Easy Lasagna	290
Lo-Cal Cheese Cake	291
Cheese Danishes	291
Pancakes	292
Banana Ice Cream*	293
Perfect Popsicles*	294
Jello Sherbet*	295
Egg Kichels	295
Mandelbroit	296
Crackers	296
Scones	297
Oat Bars	297
Cocush Cake	298

1-2-3-4 Cookies	299
Cookie Cutter Cookies	300
Apple Crumble	300
Chocolate Chip Cookies	301
No-Marg Chocolate Chip Cookies	301
Biscuits	301
Pesach-dik Cookies*	302
Bubby's Oatmeal Cookies	302

Dedication

Reflections on the Life of My Father	303
My Children's Bubby A"H: Extraordinary *Mesiras Nefesh*	316

Appreciation

Thank You, Mommy!	319

Epilogue

Count and Save Your Words	325
Sing a Song	326
The *Dreidel's* Message	328

Glossary 331

Introduction

Dear Readers,

You may wonder, as you skim through this book, "Who are you and what are your credentials?" So, allow me to introduce myself. A few years ago, I became what I happily refer to as a "Bubby with a baby." Although this description is not uniquely mine, it is not a title shared by many! It means that I have spent decades raising children and running a home, responding to crises and challenges on a continual basis. Due to my trepidation in making too many errors along the way, I have continuously sought guidance from many available sources. I have sifted through a plethora of books, newspapers, magazines and solicited input from friends, family, speakers; even professionals. In addition, my penchant for finding a use for **everything** and economizing whenever possible, led me to pick up and develop many novel approaches to problem solving. Armed with all of this material, it was only natural for me to turn around and share.

Communicating my ideas and experiences has always been an important part of my life; whatever worked for me was passed on whenever possible. The feedback I received greatly encouraged me. I discovered that I was able to help others, many of whom had normal issues to deal with, but did not enjoy reading all the material I was chomping away at.

In this book, I strive to get to the point quickly, while maintaining clarity. Bear in mind that different ideas will appeal/apply to you in different stages of life and in various circumstances. We can apply the rule of thumb, "Don't compare; it will make you either vain or bitter" equally to ourselves as we mature and face different challenges during the vicissitude of our lives. Our job is to do what we can, when we can, to the best of our ability, not to wallow in guilt over what is too late to change. Take the lessons and move on. And when in doubt, consult!

The ideas herein are designed to raise our consciousness on many issues which can help us fulfill our role in life. Truly, we are here to serve *HaShem* and that is the ultimate reason for performing *mitzvos*. For example, speaking properly and getting along with others are all part of "Love your fellow as yourself." Ideally, we should be motivated only by our desire to fulfill *mitzvos*. But while we work on reaching that very high level, we can and should enjoy the process and have patience until we can eventually benefit from the fruits of our labor. Clearly, I barely scratch the surface on the many subjects found herein. My hope is that the tools presented will help you directly or motivate you to research further. There are many wonderful books on each of these topics.

The ideas in this book are universal, but clearly geared toward women. For this reason, the study of Torah is not emphasized. But we must never forget that women do get a complete reward for this tremendous mitzva and mainstay of the world, by encouraging and supporting the Torah study of their husbands and sons. Sometimes it is done by preparing treats for them, other times it involves sending them out and remaining home alone. Other times, it can be done through donations of time, money or other resources, perhaps at some sacrifice to ourselves. But the study of *Torah*, and its observance, is the true goal; we must never lose sight.

Please note. All of the stories and quotes that appear in these pages are not exact transcriptions. I have tried to be true to the ideas, but have used a writer's license for the sake of clarity and, in some cases, privacy.

Now I would like to express my gratitude…

I joyfully begin with thanks to *HaShem* for so much *bracha* I have been *zoche* to in my life. Now, I wish to convey my tremendous gratitude to *HaShem* for enabling me to reach the realization of my dream; publishing this book.

My husband has patiently endured all of my novel attempts at getting things done, from dinner to laundry and more. His motto is, "I'll try anything once," and he gives me the freedom to experiment continuously. On top of that, I discovered an analytical side to him, as he agreed to help edit my work. His command of the English language and his critical thinking have helped me reformulate many sections enabling me to communicate my ideas in a way that hopefully you, the reader, will find more palatable. And without his technical help, this book would not have seen the light of day.

My father, *z"l*, and my mother, *yblct"a* have been amazing role models. Throughout my lifetime they have been constantly teaching me and directing me in so many areas of life. May *HaShem* grant my mother many more, happy, healthy years, in which she can continue to guide me daily.

My mother-in-law and her family, *a"h*, my brother and sisters-in-law, have all helped me in many ways. My children and their families have also taught me in the school of life. They have given me much guidance in so many areas, including encouragement with my writing career. Special mention goes to my daughter Penina Leah, as she helped me with this book both directly and indirectly. I thank you all and hope I will continue to learn from you.

I can never sufficiently thank my eighth-grade teacher, Mrs. Kokis. The lessons she imparted to my class changed my entire life. I must also thank Mrs. Bucell, *a"h*, my tenth-grade teacher, who made a big impression on me as well.

I owe so much to another group as well; amazing authors and speakers that have given me so much. I am very indebted to them, and many others who have influenced and educated me. Thank you, thank you!

I would like to thank **all** of my "teachers"; the many people whom I have encountered and from whom I have learned. I have noticed that when I come across someone walking with a very fine posture, I am reminded to keep my head up. Conversely, if I pass someone rather bent, I am again reminded to stand straight. Thus, I have found that it is truly possible to learn from each person; there is either something to imitate or to avoid! May I also share this tidbit? There are rules for guests and rules for hosts; but the guests should not read the hosts' rules, and the hosts should not read the guests' rules. We simply must daven, perhaps with our morning *bracha* of "Who gave the heart the understanding to distinguish between day and night," that we be worthy of learning the proper lesson.

I owe a very big thank you and acknowledgment to the various publications that have printed articles of mine. Some of the chapters in this book have appeared in different edited versions in Aish.com, Binah, The Jewish Press, *Mishpacha* and *Yated* International; I am grateful for their encouragement and for the opportunity they afforded me to share my ideas.

And finally, my deep gratitude goes to the wonderful people who read my book and edited or wrote lovely approbations. Please note, they did not review the final copy.

It has been said that it is worthwhile for a speaker to speak, even if only one person will be inspired, and even if that one person is the speaker herself. Although it may seem odd, I have learned a lot from what I have written! Certainly the adage, "It's easy to talk the talk, it's hard to walk the walk," has been borne out here. As I reread what I have written, I am reminded of and inspired anew in my desire to fulfill my goals, while realizing that incorporating change is far from easy.

My *tefilla* to *HaShem* is that my ideas and techniques help whoever reads them. I welcome any feedback and wish all much *hatzlacha*. Thank you for reading my book!

Tova Younger

For the Heart

Hakaras HaTov
Enhance Your Life with Gratitude

A popular speaker once told of two interesting phone calls she received, one after the other. The first caller wanted to let off steam. "I can't believe this weather! It's raining and everyone's home; I don't know how I will keep them occupied…" A few minutes later, the phone rang again; a different mother was on the line. "Wow! Did you look out the window? Rain! We haven't had any in months! I'm getting the children all dressed and going out! I think we'll take a bus and enjoy the scenery."

What is the secret of the second mother's outlook? I want to suggest that she has developed a certain manner of thinking and acting. She takes a situation, finds in it an element for which she can be grateful and runs with it. She uses any event to its fullest capacity, a gift from *HaShem*. After all, do we not learn that whatever *HaShem* does is for the best and that we must thank Him for it? This second mother is clearly operating in such a mode and doing so successfully.

How important is this attitude? I once heard Rebbetzin Esther Jungreis *a'h* speak, and among the inspiring thoughts she shared with her audience was the importance of *hakaras hatov*. "We are *Yehudim*," she pointed out. "From the word

Yehudah, the root of which means to thank." Gratitude is our essence.

Yes, we must thank. Thank *HaShem*, that is. For **everything**. Why is gratitude so important that our national identity is based on it? First of all, because it is proper to do so, logically speaking. We are in this world, living it up as in a five-star hotel, with an amazing, functioning body. We have eyes to enjoy gorgeous scenery, family, pictures and books! We have millions of taste buds to relish our food! Ears to take pleasure in all kinds of sounds: nature, singing, instruments and voices! And so much more! Not only must we express our thanks because it is proper behavior, but because it is important for **us**. It's a major part of our job here on earth, improving ourselves and coming closer to *HaShem*.

In chapter eight of the *sefer Mesilas Yesharim*, Rabbi Moshe Chaim Luzzatto discusses the manner of acquiring *z'rizus,* – zeal – for performance of *mitzvos*. We can become zealous, he informs us, by realizing both the great value of *mitzvos* and our tremendous responsibility in their performance. He subsequently emphasizes that we can strengthen ourselves by concentrating on all the wonderful things *HaShem* does for us during the course of our lives. The more we consider all of these benefits, the more we will be aware of our great debt to *HaShem*. We will thus realize that since we cannot repay *HaShem* in any way, the least we can do is perform His *mitzvos*, simply as an act of appreciation.

He continues, pointing out how all people, according to his or her station in life, have much to be thankful for. Certainly if we have our health and livelihood, we must thank *HaShem* for that. However, even those of us challenged with illness and/or hardship must be grateful to *HaShem* for keeping us alive and sustaining us despite these challenges.

Furthermore, the *Chovos Halevovos* explains that we can be thankful even for our trials and tribulations, which are all for our benefit. Of course, one must work hard on oneself to reach such a level.

We know that the Torah is full of examples of *hakaros hatov*, ranging from *Noach* thanking *HaShem* for keeping him alive during the flood, to *Moshe Rabbeinu* not striking the Nile River, which had saved his life. Our *Tanach* is replete with many more such examples.

When we read biographies of great people, especially *Rabbonim* and *Gedolim*, a common theme is *hakaros hatov* to all kinds of people and even animals. There is a stirring story told about Rav Gustman, *zt"l*, a *Rosh Yeshiva*, who was always careful to water his plants personally. He did so because herbs and vegetables had sustained him during the war.

Our challenge is to inculcate this *middah* within ourselves. By acting out our *hakaros hatov* on various levels toward everyone we interact with, we can build up to truly feeling gratitude to *HaShem*. It's relatively easy to work on this, since gratefulness is an internal quality that is not dependent on others. We can be proactive and express gratefulness whenever we like; anything at all is a stimulus.

~> ***Warning!*** ~> Do not fall into the trap of waiting for others to thank you for whatever you have done. You might be greatly disappointed. Just work on your *hakaros hatov* and who knows? As you model this *middah*, they may catch on.

Here are some ideas on how to get into the mindset of **thinking** gratitude:

🐾 Begin by removing the "they owe me" attitude. Tell yourself again and again, until you truly believe it, "No one owes me anything." That includes, but isn't limited to, your spouse, parents, children and neighbors.

🐾 Gratitude begins upon awakening. *Modeh ani*! Good morning! You are alive! *Baruch HaShem*! Are you pain free? Yes; *B"H*! Can you get out of bed on your own – many people cannot, so – *B"H*! And so on, throughout the day. If you answered "no" to these questions, delve further to find something for which to be grateful. It may be medication, a nurse or everyone's *tefillos* on your behalf. Think and you will zero in on the kindness *HaShem* is sending your way.

🐾 As you begin any *tefilla* or recite any *bracha*, such as for food, take a minute to truly thank *HaShem* for something, preferably related to the *tefilla*, but not necessarily.

🐾 Try to look at the world anew, as if you are marveling at it for the first time. Imagine a blind fellow, unable to see since the day he was born, who gets amazing news when he visits his doctor. "Here is this new medicine. You can only take it once a day, but right after swallowing this pill you will be able to see for an hour. Enjoy!" Take a few minutes to imagine his reaction. I think every waking minute would be spent planning what to see and read and do during that precious hour. And we can see all day! Vary this exercise by thinking of other abilities you have. The ability to speak, sing, hear, taste, walk and feel; even to think. Unfortunately, we hear of so many people with various challenges. There is a dual purpose for that. We must *daven* for them, yet we must also use our aroused feelings to appreciate what we have.

🐾 Further develop your *hakaros hatov* by delving into every detail of anything from which you benefit. Enjoying an orange? Cup of coffee? Peanut butter? Rabbi Avigdor Miller, *zt"l*, teaches that we can contemplate in detail how brilliantly *HaShem* has designed the world. Consider the many people we must be grateful to for even these "simple" luxuries. Think about all the workers and processes that were involved in enabling you to enjoy any item. You'll create an extensive list of people to whom you can feel grateful. Thank *HaShem* for guiding it all.

🐾 As you interact with anyone and everyone, try to think of something for which to thank them. Neighbors, cashiers, city workers, bus drivers; everyone will be glad to get a smile and a thank you.

🐾 Don't neglect your family. Your husband and children will greatly benefit from daily gratitude; it's as important as a daily vitamin!

🐾 And don't forget your mother-in-law and other extended family members. Think: multi-vitamin.

👣 Take this one step further. Train yourself to say, "I just wanted to thank you for being my devoted life partner, such a considerate neighbor, accurate cashier. For keeping our city clean, driving safely, teaching my children."

👣 In cases where particularly great kindnesses were done for you, express yourself with more specific details.

👣 Think of people who have helped you in some way in the past. Pick up the phone or write a note and thank them. A teacher, an old mentor or friend, employee, roommate.

👣 Using someone's pool? Please do not take it for granted. It may seem like nothing to you, especially if you do not own a pool, but the cost of doing such *chessed* can be high. People give up use of their pool, that is obvious, but also their yard. Sometimes the street gets blocked up with cars. There can be lots of phone calls to handle, mess left around, towels, bathing caps, and more. Whether you use someone's pool once or frequently, belonging to a good friend or someone who posts hours, they deserve a big thank you. Apply this when using someone's home, car, or really anything, because we really do not know the entire cost of someone's *chessed*.

👣 Your parents have done, and perhaps are still doing, so much for you. Try to regularly think of different things for which you can thank them. Dip into your memory banks and make use of what you find there. Drawing a blank? In your next conversation, steer the discussion towards your youth. Chances are your parents will have many memories of what they did for you. As they mention small recollections here and there, latch on to them and say thank you!

👣 Need more opportunities? Create situations with your loved ones so that you can thank them afterwards. Ask for advice, borrow something or make some small request. Now you have fresh grist for the mill. Or realize that whatever success you have in life, although you may not wish to think of it this way, very likely can be attributed to what your parents (and/or siblings) have done. Even if you have negative feelings toward them, you can, with some effort, reframe and cultivate feelings of gratitude. A friend of mine confided in me that she has always been disappointed in her mother's lack of interest in her life. Then someone suggested that perhaps because of that she was able to grow in her *Yiddishkeit*, which she admitted was correct. She realized that she could tell her mother on some occasion, "Mom, I really have to thank you for raising me in a way that gave me tools to grow in my spiritual development," or some such idea. Of course, if her mother is antagonistic to her growth, she can rather say "Mom, raising my children makes me aware of how much I have to thank you for all you did for me. Your investment in me enables me to give to my children."

🖐 As you converse with friends and family, be alert. If they have given you any news or encouragement, you can thank them. Just keep looking for opportunities and you will find them. The idea is to deliberate on this theme and keep your eyes open and your brain performing.

🖐 Although words and notes are appreciated, gifts and actions can speak louder than words. My mother has stopped driving and has become the recipient of rides from many kindhearted people. She loves starting her day baking; it really energizes her. Then she enjoys gifting bags of cookies to many of those who help her. We can each find our own way to reciprocate and put our words into action.

🖐 When people thank us, our reaction is a desire to do more. The same holds true with our relationship to *HaShem*. The more we thank Him, the more *bracha* He wants to give us.

Rabbi Avigdor Miller states that one reason *HaShem* afflicts us is simply to hear from us. When we fill our day with praises to Him, He has no need to get our attention.

Thanking all kinds of people is an exercise that *HaShem* provides to strengthen our *hakaros hatov* muscles. We can alter a tendency to find fault or complain by developing a positive outlook. We can better enjoy our lives. And after all, if we cannot thank those who we clearly see helping us, how can we hope to truly thank *HaShem*?

Kavana
Put More Into Your Davening!

We all know the feeling. We open our *siddurim*, hoping to get into some *kavana-dik davening*. We start with high hopes and perhaps succeed a bit initially, when suddenly, before we know it, we are at the end of the section and don't really know how we got there! Did we say the *tefilla* or not? Did we latch on to those powerful words? Did we utilize what we learned about various *tefillos* and *pesukim*?

I found that although I was working on my *kavana*, I just couldn't apply what I was learning. Studying books on *tefilla* greatly inspired me, but I couldn't always connect while *davening*; I was plagued with mind-wander.

I am happy to announce that I am now in remission. Not cured, but lots of successes.

I would like to share the development of my achievement, especially since working on my *davening* has also taught me how vital our *tefillos* are. We have a lot to accomplish. How can we succeed without utilizing our most potent tool?

A couple of years ago, I called a *Tehillim Gemach* and asked for an assignment. I wanted to be part of finishing the *sefer Tehillim* on a daily basis. "But give me something easy," I requested. I wanted to commit to something and keep it.

Her response made me want to laugh and cry. "Take *kuf-yud-tes*, (119)?" she said, matter-of-factly. Huh? Did she hear me? I said **easy**. Well either she had or hadn't; perhaps it was the language barrier. Although I think my Hebrew is pretty clear, I occasionally experience communication mix-ups. A quick perusal of the *perek* however, revealed that it wasn't so hard, just long; 176 *pesukim,* in alphabetical order, eight *pesukim* per letter! Boldly, I decided that this was a challenge that I would accept. I would endeavor to say this lengthy chapter daily!

As I took the plunge and began, I was so thankful that I had. What can I say? If you are not familiar with this chapter of *Tehillim*, check it out. It is replete with one request and praise after the other, all easy to understand, at least on a *p'shat* (surface) level. I found I was really "getting into it." I was also happy to notice that it was listed in the beginning of my *Tehillim* as a propitious chapter to recite for sons to learn Torah. Since that is my heartfelt desire, I was doubly glad that I had undertaken the assignment.

One day I had a thought, a scheme which would make use of the alphabetic arrangement. The idea was to concentrate momentarily on a particular child, relative or person(s) in need, for each letter. Armed with my twenty-two selections, I was off and running, *davening* for each of them on a daily basis. At first I had to consult a list, but after a short while, the one-to-one correspondence was firmly entrenched in my mind. Despite all this, I cannot claim that I was regularly concentrating on the meaning of the words. At least, however, I was cutting down a bit on "mind-wander," since my brain had to think about each person, however briefly.

One year later, still struggling with concentrating on other parts of *davening*, something clicked. "*Ashrei*, recited thrice daily, is also alphabetically arranged. Why not *daven*, briefly again, for each of these twenty-two loved ones while reciting *Ashrei*?" Thought and done. Wow! For the first time in my life, I was actually concentrating on each *pasuk* in *Ashrei*! No, not on each of those people, but on the *pasuk* itself. Upon analysis, it seemed that this is what was happening: My mind was being pulled out of the wandering mode and forced into an active-thinking mode. I knew that at the start of each *pasuk* I had to remember someone. I did, and moved on to the *pasuk* itself instantaneously. It may sound illogical, but that is what occurred.

After about a week of amazing *Ashreis,* I thought, 'Why not try this with the rest of *davening*?' Yes. That is what put me into remission, which actually means reduction. I didn't **eliminate** mind wander and the *kavana* doesn't come by itself, even with playing this word game. I still have to make an effort to concentrate. But what an improvement! Additionally, after just a few weeks of using this system, not even 100% of the time, my *davening* was transformed. Even when I find myself "lazy" or thinking, 'I can concentrate all by myself' and neglect to use my technique, there is a change. Clearly, an important divide has been crossed.

Although I tried to share this idea with friends, it sounded a bit complicated, not to mention far-fetched. People appeared to be reluctant to invest in a thought process that had developed naturally for me. Formulating a one-to-one correspondence which would only improve *kavana* a month hence was just much too convoluted and impractical. And some found it distracting to think about other people. See *Kavana* tips for a simplified approach.

Does this entire idea sound too incredible, improbable, silly or worse? Let me share this precious tidbit from a wonderful book, *A Touch of Wisdom, a Touch of Wit*, by S. Himelstein, page 46 (reprinted with permission from Artscroll.) Clearly, using a gimmick such as my suggestion is not such a new idea.

Rabbi Yaakov Yitzchak, the Yehudi Hakadosh, would say: "Whenever I get up to pray, I always imagine that there are ten Cossacks surrounding me with swords in their hands, ready to slay me on the spot if I don't pray properly."

As I began concentrating on my *davening* with greater frequency, I started studying more *sefarim* including *Rav Schwab on Prayer* and Rabbi Avraham Feuer's *Shemoneh Esrei*. I also began using the Artscroll Interlinear *Siddur* and *Pathways to Prayer* by Rabbi Mayer Birnbaum. They are full of insights that continue to enhance my *davening*. I also began to incorporate many additional ideas, culled from many sources. They have helped me even further.

KAVANA TIPS

🐾 Ascertain that you are presentable, just as when you have an important meeting; actually, you do. Wash your hands.

🐾 As you begin each *pasuk* or even each line or phrase, think BRIEFLY about the first letter. Mentally determine its *gematriah*, consider its sound or just name the letter itself. Any variation can work; the point is to get your brain to stop and think. Try it and you will be amazed.

🐾 Before you begin the actual *tefilla*, *daven* briefly in your own words, for *HaShem*'s help. I read of a *Rav* who used to do this specifically before *bentching*, having in mind that the phone and doorbell should not ring. Ask *HaShem* to assist you so that you can concentrate.

🐾 If you are *davening* at home, do so in an area with as few distractions as possible; away from telephones, doorbells and where others may be conversing.

~> **Reminder!** ~> When in a room with someone who is *davening* or *bentching*, DO NOT TALK!

🐾 Slow down. This will have an amazing impact on your *davening*. Try to *daven* at the same speed with which you speak or mimic the manner in which the *chazzan davens*. Yes, you will need a little more time to *daven*, but surprisingly, not that much more; surely you will agree, "It's worth it!"

🐾 Don't *daven* by heart. Don't even begin until you are at the right page and ready to recite the first word. Wait a second to turn each page before continuing. Close your *siddur* only when you finish *davening*.

🐾 Rabbi Avigdor Miller recommends working on one

small area at a time. "Every day you pick just one little part, let's say one *bracha* and make up your mind: On this *bracha* I'm going to put in all my thoughts, I don't care how long it takes."

🐾 Before saying a *bracha*, take a second to think about the full meaning of the first few words: "Source of all blessing," "We personally relate to," "Master of all; was, is, always will be," "All-powerful, watches over us individually," "King of the world." Check the end of the *bracha* as well; we ought to know what we plan to say before we begin! If you are saying *Birchos HaShachar* and someone is answering amen (a wonderful *zechus* for all!) use the few milliseconds during which they say amen to prepare for the following *bracha*.

🐾 Stop and think. Go through the six constant *mitzvos,* abbreviated: Believe in *HaShem*, no other, know His Oneness, love *HaShem*, fear *HaShem*, don't let yourself be misled. Select any *pasuk* and/or some thought of *hakaros hatov.* Think about what the section/*bracha* means, and what you plan to focus on. Any thought that strengthens your feelings of dependence on *HaShem* will do. Mentally review the phrase or thought before reciting each paragraph and/or right before making a *bracha*. Try it with each closing *bracha* of the 19 *brachos* in *Shemoneh Esrei*. Start and you'll develop a fantastic habit that really forces you to stop and concentrate.

🐾 Make up your mind to just focus. (Excerpted from *Conversations with Yourself*, by Rabbi Zelig Pliskin, reprinted with permission from Artscroll.) "Minds tend to wander. One tool to bring yours back is to say to yourself, 'Just focus.' When you give your mind instructions to 'Just focus,' your mind might just follow your instructions."

🐾 Visualize. I saw this idea in the fantastic book, *Battle Plans* by Rebbetzin Heller/Rigler, all about fighting the *Yetzer Hara*. I decided to apply it to my *davening*. Equipped with this concept, I found it easy to picture *Avrohom Aveinu* going to the *akeida* and the scene at the splitting of the sea, both beautifully described in detail in the morning *davening*. As I accustomed myself to look for images, loftier sections came to life as well. I could "see" *chassidim* dancing for *HaShem* and angels gathering for praises. Most importantly, in the *Shema* and *Shemoneh Esrei*, with forethought, each section easily brought a multi-faceted portrait to my mind.

🐾 Rebbetzin Vichna Kaplan, *a"h*, the founder of *Bais Yaakov* in America and one of the star pupils of Sara Schenirer, (initiator of the *Bais Yaakov* movement in Poland,) was speaking with some students about their *bentching Birkas HaMazon*. "How can it be," she asked, "that we *bentch*, go on to the next activity and a few minutes later, ask our friend or child, 'Did I *bentch*?'" When I heard this and realized how true it was, I set my mind to thinking while I *bentched* or *davened* a particular paragraph, "Remember! You are saying these powerful words! Don't wonder later whether or not you said them!" This is especially useful for additions such as *retzei* on *Shabbos*, *v'sein tal u'matar* in the winter and the like.

🐾 Use the largest print you can find. Point to each word with your finger. Decide to concentrate on the meaning of *HaShem*'s name each time you say it.

🐾 Keep track of your progress in a notebook or on a post-it note kept in your *siddur*. If your mind wanders a lot, count how many paragraphs you **did** concentrate on. When you reach the point where you mostly concentrate, keep track of the number of times your mind wanders. Note your growth. Feel free to garner rewards (could be a treat or earn taking time to indulge in something for which you do not normally take time off) or penalties. Be creative! For example, caught yourself thinking off-topic thoughts? Stop, spend a minute reading a *davening* tip and return to your *davening* – but not during *Shema* or *Shemoneh Esrei*, of course.

🐾 The *Vilna Gaon, zt"l*, writes, "If your mind strays while praying, do not give up trying to concentrate. As soon as you realize you are not concentrating on what you are saying, at that very moment begin concentrating." (Quoted from Rabbi Zelig Pliskin, *Gateway to Happiness*.)

🐾 Ready for more? Try this: There are really two types of the *shva* vowel, *na* and *nach*. *Shva na* makes the letter sound like its own syllable; with *shva nach* the letter is slurred, attached to the previous letter. The grammar rules are somewhat complicated; thankfully there are many *siddurim* with some type of notation on the vowel to indicate which it is. Artscroll, for example, has a dash on top of the *shva na*. I have seen some *siddurim* that have an enlarged *shva* for the *shva na*. If you have never paid attention to this, start now! You will slow yourself down nicely and will be pronouncing your words more correctly.

🐾 Select one or more *brachos* of *Shemoneh Esrei* to concentrate on daily, so that you cover the entire *tefilla* weekly or monthly. That is, either concentrate on three or four *brachos* a day or devote a day or two to each *bracha*. Number the *brachos* in your *siddur* to facilitate the process. You may want to read some sort of detailed commentary prior to or during your *davening* related to the selected *brachos*. This will actually do wonders for your concentration even on the other *brachos*.

🐾 Work on yourself to feel total dependence on *HaShem*. Turn to Him as a starving person begging for a slice of bread.

🐾 Use a stopwatch periodically to see how much time you spend on davening *Shemoneh Esrei*. As your concentration improves, delight in the extra seconds added to your *tefilla*.

🐾 I heard that at a *Siyum HaShas* a few years ago, the *chazzan* paid in the area of $40,000 for the privilege of leading the *davening*!! Occasionally before I *daven*, I think of this idea. I imagine I just paid that money and am standing in front of about 100,000 people... I am catapulted into an excellent concentrating mood!

Experiment with some or all of these tips at your own pace and see what works for you.

May all your *tefillos* be answered *l'tova*.

Igeress HaRamban
An Appreciation

Today we live in such a competitive society, where everyone seems to have their abilities and assets on display. We don't have to go into your home; we just get the address and we know your status. Or we pass by and see the lawn and other trimmings that give us a clear indication of what is inside. Maybe we see you drive by and that vehicle of yours tips us off. Some, wishing to leave nothing to chance, sport a $3,000 watch to get the message across. Even without intention, everyone's standard of living seems to be in everyone else's face.

There is a challenge here for each of us. For "have nots": How can we get a handle on feelings of jealousy and anger that can be aroused? We learn that anger can cause a person to lose all benefit of this world! Equally important, for the "have-its": How can we deal with feelings of superiority, which can lead to feeling proud? Concerning an arrogant person, *HaShem* says, "He and I cannot live in this world together." It is clear; no matter what your status, you have what to work on.

Enter *Igeress HaRamban, Letter of the Ramban,* an ethical letter which the great Nachmanidies wrote for his son in the fifteenth century. As you read it, you will learn what it takes to work on ridding yourself of these forbidden and destructive feelings. "Remove anger from your heart," "From where did you come... and before Whom are you destined to give an accounting?" "Since everyone is equal before *HaShem*, Who when angry cuts down the arrogant... therefore, lower yourself and *HaShem* will uplift you," "With all your words, actions and thoughts and at all times, think in your heart that you are standing before *HaShem*." All this and more is contained in this page-long letter. And at the end, "Every day that you read this, They will answer you from Heaven, whatever you request." May we only be worthy of properly reading and following its ideals!

Initially I tried to read the *Ramban*'s work weekly as advised and I was able to get some direction from it. One day, I had an inspired thought; I could memorize it. I started by memorizing a few sentences each week and within a couple of months achieved my goal. At that point I was able to review the *Igeress* daily whether on a walk, while waiting on line at the market or when holding the phone and being subjected to some undesirable music. It's great for chasing away destructive thoughts as well. Basically, it gives me something positive to think about whenever I want to.

Memorizing it forced me to pay more attention and concentrate on the actual phrasing of the words and the order in which they are all positioned. It has greatly enhanced my working on the lofty goals set forth.

The *Igeress* can also come in handy when a good quote is needed. The other day I bought a *siddur* for my grandson and wanted to write a meaningful inscription. I was at a loss for words, until the *Ramban* rescued me. "Concentrate on your prayers by removing all worldly thoughts... prepare your heart... purify your thoughts... and your prayer will be pure, clear, clean, devout and acceptable..." Amen!

While reciting it, I include my *tefilla* that my heart be rid of the bad *middos* described and that I become worthy of that awesome *bracha*, "... and *HaShem* will uplift you."

Shmiras Haloshon
Tailor Your Talk

Everyone deals with challenges in their lives. Many are searching for a spiritual remedy, a *segulah*, but we needn't go to *kivrei Tzaddikim* and travel for *brachos*; working on our *shmiras haloshon* is our best *segulah*. Consider these facts. We observe the *halochos* of *Shabbos* but once a week, *kashrus* a few times a day. *Shmiras haloshon* is all day long. Thus, being careless about this *mitzva* will cause us to accumulate many *aveiros*. Happily, the opposite is true as well; being careful will bring us much reward as we come close to *HaShem* through proper observation of this precious *mitzva*.

The good news is that today we are very fortunate; there are so many *sefarim*, booklets, articles, *shiurim* and more, each providing us with the *halochos* of *shmiras haloshon* in an easy to comprehend manner. I recently saw a clever, concise abridgement of the *halochos*. Invest just one minute a day, and you can review all the main *halochos* weekly!

Yes, it's all easy enough to study, but keeping the *halochos* is another story. That is harder than ever. Most people today are in touch with many more people than was possible in years past. We read about people all over the globe; we travel, maintain long distance relationships, and have larger and extended families. We meet people in school, on vacation, at *simchos* and at work. Although we can benefit from all these interactions and gain a lot with each relationship, there is always danger lurking. An innocent speaker doesn't realize that a seemingly innocuous remark is actually portraying the subject in a bad light. A truly fine comment is made, but the response is *loshon hora*. Perhaps it's an inquiry or comment about a former classmate, relative, even a store you used to frequent; the conversation develops and leads to *loshon hora*. It seems impossible to converse and avoid it.

We mustn't despair! Peruse this array of ideas, ranging from improved mindset to practical avoidance, on how to conquer our *yetzer hora* and emerge victorious in the fight against *loshon hora*. I wish all, myself included, *hatzlacha* in overcoming this tenacious foe as we strengthen ourselves in **SHMIRAS HALOSHON**!

❦ *S*tart off by *davening*. At the end of every *Shemoneh Esrei* we ask *HaShem* to guard our tongue from speaking evil. Pause a moment and be sure to focus when you say it. There is also a beautiful prayer composed by the *Chofetz Chaim* which says it all. Keep in mind that regrettably, speaking *loshon hora* without doing proper *teshuva* greatly weakens the power of our *tefillos*; it actually damages our spiritual tongue.

❦ *H*ow about using the incident as a mirror? Ask yourself, "Why did *HaShem* cause me to hear/see this? Maybe there is a hint to something I must work on." Check your underlying motivation in speaking; often it is arrogance. Another tactic is to picture the perpetrator as a close friend or even as yourself. How would you view the situation in that case? Remembering your mistakes will come in handy…

❦ *M*otivate yourself to stop and deliberate before responding to comments. "Put brain in motion before putting mouth in gear," is a great motto that can save lots of aggravation. There are many stories of people who held their tongues and found salvation in health and other areas. If you are hurt or insulted, don't respond; take advantage of this propitious moment and *daven*.

🐾 *I*f you have trained yourself to judge favorably, you'll be your very own best lawyer! When our final judgment comes upon us, we will be called upon to judge our own lives, but we won't recognize ourselves. Not only that, but *HaShem* judges us in the way that we judge others. Untamed, our initial reaction could bring us to rash conversation. Train yourself by playing the following game: Try to think of five reasons that make this deed totally acceptable, or at least not so bad. Minimally, such a game will probably defuse and calm down your emotional feelings. If you have a sense of humor, it could distract you, remove negative feelings and even put you in a laughing mood. Conclusion: Make judging favorably a firm habit. ~> **Warning!** ~> When defending someone, be sure to steer clear of unnecessarily vilifying the other side.

🐾 *R*ather than waste precious time discussing people, use your time wisely to gain *mitzvo*s. Share recipes, tips, and encouraging stories. Formulate plans on how to help those in need in your community. Work on finding a mate for singles you know. You'll fill your conversation time productively.

🐾 *A*n important part of keeping the laws is reviewing the *halochos* daily. You may find it difficult to maintain this practice alone, so get a study partner. Some good choices are family members, friends you are in touch with regularly anyway or people that do not yet know much about *Yiddishkeit*. It can even be used as a vehicle to build a relationship with your "in-law" relatives!

🐾 *S*hidduchim are particularly important; therefore, be prepared. Keep in mind that there are limitations even when speaking for a positive purpose: *loshon hora l'toeles*. Seven conditions must be followed and one must still keep in mind to say only the minimum; there is no such thing as a carte blanche situation. Sometimes, there is information that **must** be revealed; "I won't get involved" is not the proper approach.

🐾 *H*ave a topic in your back pocket all the time and be prepared to change the subject if it turns to *loshon hora*. I once saw a funny suggestion: spill your drink or food at a *simcha* if necessary; it's a great way to divert everyone's attention! Of course, this would be a last resort, but we must remember that *shmiras haloshon* is a *halacha* which we must keep with the same level of urgency as any of the *mitzvos*. Since there are thirty-one references to *shmiras haloshon* in the Torah, each word can generate several *aveiros*. Do the math; even a short conversation containing *loshon hora* can be VERY expensive.

✋ *A*nother concept that serves as a deterrent to speaking *loshon hora* is some self-protection. *HaShem* is willing to overlook our *aveiros*, giving us time to do *teshuva*. I heard from Rabbi Mendel Kessin that *HaShem* established a system whereby He is forced (so to speak) to "bring us into court" and check into our behavior when we speak *loshon hora*, since the running of the world is based on *middah k'neged middah*. We are dealt with in the same manner as we deal with others. When we begin to denigrate someone, **we** are scrutinized. Think of how much punishment is brought into the world by our seemingly "idle chit-chat." No wonder we're exhausted, as our *neshomos* are being brought to court countless times throughout the day.

✋ *L*ots of people or groups under discussion? Beware, you may be getting involved in wholesale *loshon hara*, not mitigated by the fact that no names were mentioned.

✋ *O*ut and about? Beware! Lingering in an area where many people in your circle pass by and beginning a conversation, often leads others to join. As the crowd grows, chances are *loshon hora* will be spoken; watch out! You are considered to have started it. It's wonderful to greet others, but public areas aren't the place for lengthy conversations.

✋ *S*ecrets may not be *loshon hora*; revealing them is. Once you have been told a secret, fulfill your obligation and guard it well, even if it seems trivial to you. ~> *Tip!* ~> Before confiding in someone, verify that they are willing. Not everyone is capable of maintaining secrecy; it's unfair to thrust a mental burden on someone without their prior consent.

❧ *H*ow many times have we heard about the horrible repercussions of *loshon hora*? Bitter arguments, people losing jobs, breaking off *shidduchim* or partnerships and worse. Not to mention causing *HaShem* to punish the person you have slandered by not judging favorably. Thinking about possible consequences of our words can give us the strength to refrain.

❧ *O*ptical illusions are entertaining and much of what we perceive as reality is illusion as well. Someone has a gorgeous home; they must be prosperous. Why don't they give... Oops, turns out the home is something their wealthy relatives gave them, but this family can barely keep it up and hasn't a dollar to spare. Another person seems so annoying or even rude... Turns out he is dealing with a severe illness. The list goes on and on. We really never know.

❧ *N*ever forget that *HaShem* is watching us, providing us with our every need. When we intensify our trust in Him, we will be able to withstand the temptation to resort to using *loshon hora* to accomplish anything at all. Reading and sharing the many beautiful stories that substantiate *HaShem*'s great kindness will surely strengthen us. Just keep your eyes and ears open and you'll see them happen, even to you!

Translation of the Tefilla of the Chofetz Chaim

Master of the universe, may it be Your will, merciful and beneficent G-d, that you grant me the merit today, and every day, to guard my mouth and tongue from loshon hora and rechilus (tale-bearing) and from accepting such talk as true. And that I be careful not to speak about an individual, how much more so about all of Israel or a part of the Jewish people, or all the more so to complain about an aspect of the way the Holy One, Blessed be He, runs the world. And may I be careful not to speak any words of falsehood, flattery, mockery, discord, anger, arrogance, hurtfulness, words that pale one's face and any forbidden speech. And let me be worthy only to speak words that are necessary for my body or soul. And may all my deeds and words be for the sake of Heaven.

Pathways to Chessed

We all know that *chessed* is one of the pillars of our world. We are so fortunate to have an abundance of biographies and stories available to us today, depicting various benevolent acts of *Gedolim* and "plain folks." As we try to absorb all we read, we become inspired. We want to do *chessed*; we want to be a part of our community, as givers and not as takers. We want to, but we are just too busy. Too busy to run a *gemach*, visit a homebound person or volunteer at a school or *shul*. How can we become part of the *chessed* infrastructure, when our plates are already as full as they are?

Begin with the realization that the soul is willing, but the flesh is weak. Inside, you **do** desire to do *chessed*. Besides being a *mitzva*, the wonderful feeling that comes with a *chessed* performance is incomparable. Our problem is that we are over-extended, involved in many activities. How can we bring more *chessed* into our lives?

Let's start with this encouraging thought: You probably are already doing a lot of *chessed* and just not realizing it. Possibly you just **think** that you do not perform enough acts of *chessed*, but the reality is different. You may be pleasantly surprised and uplifted as you reframe many of your existing activities, and note that with the proper *kavana*, your actions are truly *chessed*! Additionally, a bit of analysis will reveal that incorporating small acts of *chessed* into your present schedule is not quite as arduous as you had thought.

As you peruse this list, understand and accept that as life goes on and your obligations and responsibilities change, so might your mood and your available time. Activities that just don't fit in now may become a part of your life in the future. Stay calm and do what you can, when you can. Look forward to a time when you will be able to do more. In the meantime, check these suggestions and set your brain spinning out ideas that can ease you into more *chessed* activities.

~> **Remember!** ~> We perform acts of *chessed*, because *chessed* is a *mitzva*. When we carry out *chessed* activities with the aim of benefiting the recipient, then we will find that the more *chessed* we do, the greater our love will grow. Which will help us grow in fulfilling *v'ahavta l'reacha kamocha*.

🐾 Think *chessed*. Among the plethora of tips Rabbi Zelig Pliskin offers in his many books is the following gem: When you want to work on a particular *middah* or issue, decide to think about it every time you do something that you do a few times a day, such as glancing at your watch. In this example, try to associate "time" with *chessed*; whenever you look at a clock, think "*chessed*." Even if initially, all you do is think about it in vague terms, it's a start. As you progress, look for *chessed* opportunities and you'll find. They're all over!

🐾 Analyze every task you undertake as part of your normal daily activities and see if there is an aspect of *chessed* in it. I heard from Rebbetzin Esther Baila Schwartz that because *HaShem* wanted us to merit doing many *mitzvos*, He has made things that we do in any case be a *mitzva*. For example, everyone puts on shoes. When we put them on properly, first the right, then the left, tie the left, then the right, we get a *mitzva*. It's no extra effort! Along these lines, have *kavana* for the *chessed* aspect of whatever you do. Going out for any reason? A friendly smile and short greeting to people you pass on the street can change that person's mindset, day or even their life! Cleaning your home, laundering clothing, preparing a meal? These are all clearly *chassadim* for your family. Reading a book? Before you begin, have in mind that if you can, you will share anything that you read with a friend. Be on the lookout for any sharable sections, be it inspiration, information, even a good laugh, and voila! You can add your reading time to your *chessed* collection. Don't forget to follow through in a subsequent conversation with a friend! Are you going shopping? If you pick up something for a neighbor as well, you can double dip! Perform *chessed* for your family **and** your neighbor. Driving somewhere? Consider planning in advance and offering a ride to your car-less friends. If you didn't plan, even last-minute invitations are often gratefully accepted and very appreciated. These ideas will help you develop yourself as a *chessed* person.

🐾 Don't forget to maximize *chessed* opportunities in the home. With your husband. With your parents. With your family. It's ironic but true that many people treat strangers more kindly than their loved ones. If you find you are guilty of this, work on changing; start now! Whatever extra time this entails, it is worth it. Remember, our parents deserve whatever *chessed* we can do for them. And when you care for your husband like a king, he will rise to the occasion. You'll reap great rewards in treating your children with *chessed* as well.

🐾 Sharing information is a *chessed* that can pay infinite dividends. Did you hear about a great time-saving tip, laundry hint, a way to economize or a fabulous recipe? Tell a friend and sit back as she benefits and shares with **her** friends. Sort of like the multi-level marketing tactics; everyone in the chain gains as the word is spread around!

🐾 Work on showing consideration for others. One way to do so is by keeping quiet and ensuring your family does the same. Especially when you are out late or during the afternoon when many people rest. Truthfully, being noiseless when returning from a late-night *simcha* can be difficult; take care to remind everyone **before** you exit the car or bus that it is *ossur* to steal sleep. Dispose of your trash properly and ensure that your possessions (strollers and bicycles, to name a few) do not block people's way. When driving, obeying traffic laws is a *chessed*! Signaling, waiting for people to cross, not stopping to speak to a friend in the next lane (!) and thereby blocking traffic, always parking legally and of course driving carefully, are all ways of fulfilling *v'ahavta l'reacha kamocha*. Out in public? Remember to speak softly, especially when using a cell phone. Avoid pushing or bumping into others.

🖐 Branch out to little *chassodim* that come up during the day. One of my favorites is to offer people my place in line while shopping. When I have time and notice someone with just a few items or looking anxious, I ask, "Are you in a rush?" Some people politely decline, but most are so grateful; it's worth the extra couple of minutes delay. If you do decide to try this, don't forget that you need to actually go to their place in the line, or ask others behind you if they wish to share in this *chessed*. Use the extra waiting time to mentally pat yourself on the back and prepare for your next *chessed*. Is someone loaded down with packages or a stroller? Try to open the door for them, help them load their car or maneuver their packages, according to your ability. I was once walking with an empty stroller, on my way to purchase some groceries, when I saw a woman ahead of me walking with her young child. As I was enjoying the heartwarming sight of them strolling together, the mother suddenly stopped and picked up her little girl. I quickly caught up with them and offered a ride for the child, which was gratefully accepted.

🖐 Stopping at someone's house? Call first and see if they need anything. Before you depart, see if you can help them with anything on your way to your next stop, or try offering to take their trash as you exit their home! Admittedly, it may be a bit hard to convince them to allow you to do this, but you may occasionally succeed. At the very least you will probably give them a good laugh!

🖐 Offer to take a neighbor's baby for a stroll if you are out on an errand or an exercise walk. You'll help yourself at the same time – weight bearing exercise is more effective and pushing a stroller definitely qualifies!

✋ When attending a *simcha* without waiters, a good way to do a *chessed* and control your *noshing* at the same time is to help clear away the used paper goods left around and refill platters as needed. You can also greet and offer refreshments to other guests not as mobile as you. It's actually a wonderful way to increase your own good time at the *simcha*. Of course, you need to know your hostess; if any of this will make her uncomfortable, skip it.

✋ When you are at a *shiur* or *simcha*, keep your eye open for loners. It is possible that they have lots of friends, but just don't know anyone at this forum. You can introduce yourself or just smile and say hello. As long as you are walking in the same direction, take advantage. It's relatively easy to start a conversation about the event just attended, of course without any *loshon hora*!

✋ Don't let the best be the enemy of the good. Any *chessed* at all is great for exercising our *chessed* muscles and can mean so much for the recipient, even if it is not done in the best possible way. Certainly, it is nice to offer a delicious hot meal to a friend that just had a baby, but a potful of yesterday's soup will also be much appreciated. Bringing someone hand-me-downs or returning items *erev Shabbos*? Granted, that is not the best time, but if it is the only time that works for you, call with an apology and see if you can come by. They may still value your offering. Personally, I like to do *chessed* whenever I can; but I couldn't if I had to do the whole nine yards each time!

✋ If you have spare time in your weekly schedule, do more than incidental *chessed*; engage in an out-and-out *chessed* activity. The choices are endless; visit a nursing facility or hospital, find a family for whom you can run errands, watch someone's baby while they go out, tutor or help a child with homework. There are so many opportunities. Schools are great places to volunteer; they often cannot afford an extra pair of hands that can make such a difference in a child's day. Try offering help on trips, supervising during recess or shopping for special needs. Unfortunately, we hear of so many sick people. They all need help on many levels, and will assuredly welcome most any offer.

✋ We all realize that the elderly need help; we may not realize that children do as well. Whether a young one is struggling with packages, trying to reach a toy or possession that has gotten away or needs to cross the street, keep your eyes open as you pass children and you will find opportunities. The other day I passed a little boy, maybe three years old, struggling to get his bike up a few stairs. When I offered to help, he immediately let go. I knew it would be an even bigger *chessed* to involve him, so I said, "No, I want to **help** you." Together we brought it up the stairs.

✋ On another occasion, I saw a second-grade girl crying. She told me that she didn't want to go into class because she had lost a 50-*shekel* bill on the floor and couldn't find it. I told her that I would look for it. "It's probably sitting on the desk in the office right now," I assured her. "Go to class, I'll look." I knew there was really nothing else she could do at that point. I looked at the floor on the way to the office and didn't see it. The secretary was on the phone, I glanced at her desk; sure enough, there was the missing 50 *shekels*! Took me about five minutes, all told. Time well invested.

✋ Continuing on the topic of children, share your *chessed* activities with them. Challenge them to develop their own opportunities. Give them ideas; school time is loaded with prospects. They can let someone ahead of them at the water fountain, retrieve a pen or pencil that dropped, loan out school supplies. Teach them to keep their eyes peeled for *chessed* opportunities. When they share their accomplishments, you have a wonderful occasion to praise (and reward) them. To bring home the importance of their *chessed* activities even more, keep a notebook with their accomplishments; they will make great bedtime stories!

🐾 Remove *chessed* roadblocks. Don't discriminate or allow negative thoughts. "Why don't they manage themselves?" or "What group does she belong to? Why aren't **her** friends helping her?" and other such directives are straight from your *yetzer hora*. Simply help whoever is in need.

🐾 ~> **Warning!** ~> When initiating any *chessed* project, offer before charging in. It's even advisable to start with a hint, or somehow feel them out and clarify if they will accept. Beware of hurting or insulting people on your *chessed* trail. Sometimes it is a *chessed* to allow people to manage on their own! In any event, if they don't want help for any reason, move on. You will surely find accepting souls elsewhere.

🐾 Don't forget about a very important person in your life who needs *chessed*: you! Find time to do what it takes to keep you in a *chessed-dik* frame of mind. If you are unwinding in order to generate energy to do *chessed*, your relaxation time takes on new meaning; yes, it is a *chessed*! Consider *v'ahavta l'reacha kamocha* from the other side. The nicer you are to yourself, the more you can be nice to others as well.

🐾 Let us follow Rabbi Avigdor Miller's teaching. Keep in mind that loving each Jew is a *mitzva*; so is giving them a *bracha* and wishing them well. He encourages us to bless Jews in our hearts and to say aloud, "I love my people." This is a *mitzva*, a *chessed* that can bring us great rewards.

🐾 Not in the mood for *chessed*? Feeling even hypocritical when being kind? Don't give up. The recipient benefits from your kind deed and is delighted in your help **regardless** of your thoughts. And the *Mesilas Yesharim* teaches that our deeds influence and change us. So paste on a smile and work on improving your thoughts to your best ability. Don't despair! Continue to perform acts of *chessed* whenever you can.

Indulging in this pastime will encourage growth and bring us closer to *HaShem* as we emulate His ways. After all, isn't that what we are created for?

Get More Done, with Chessed

The phone rings. Your friend is on the line and starts with a cheerful greeting. The greeting is followed by the real reason for the call. She wants to know if you can cook a meal for a new mother, visit a shut-in, watch someone's baby; the possibilities are endless. Your first (untrained) reaction may be "NO! I don't have the time! I can barely manage to get through the day, without adding another thing to do. If I add in this project – forget it!"

Logically, that makes sense. Our day contains only a certain number of hours; when we spend time on one project, there will be less left for another. Well, logic has to take a back seat when *chessed* is involved. To my very pleasant surprise, I have seen time and time again that when I agree to do a favor, other things fall into place. I often accomplish more than I do on a day without a boost of *chessed*.

Certainly, part of it can be attributed to a higher energy level. Getting involved in a project of any type can fill us with gusto and zest. In the well-known book, *How to Stop Worrying and Start Living*, Dale Carnegie describes this phenomenon and explains how people can use it for their benefit. He tells of someone coming home from a long day at work, with one desire; to get to sleep. Unexpectedly, the phone rings! A friend is calling to invite our exhausted subject to a party or some social gathering. Magically, exhaustion disappears, energy flows in, our tired employee is transformed and out the door!

We *mitzva*-observers have more than that. We have the extra enthusiasm for doing *chessed*; a *mitzva* which is the cornerstone of our belief system. It's a *mitzva* which keeps the world spinning!

Additionally, I have found that often there's a bonus; our *chessed* may benefit us here and now. We often see "fruits" of our *mitzva;* of course the principle is reserved for *Olam Haba*.

Let's put theory aside. Here are a few real-life examples, first person accounts, truthfully reported!

🐾 Malka lives in the same city as her married daughter, Chaya, who has a few children already. Although Malka still has young ones at home, and needs help herself, most Thursday afternoons she sends her teenager, Miriam, over to Chaya. One week, Malka had company coming and the house needed a lot of attention. She told Miriam, "I think we'll cancel with Chaya this week. We have too much to do!" "I thought the same..." Miriam replied. Malka called Chaya, who graciously said she'd manage. A little later however, she called back and said, "My baby won't stop crying and I cannot get anything done. Can I have just one hour of help?" Malka immediately told Miriam, "If she's calling back, she must be desperate; drop everything and go!" Off she went, leaving Malka to manage with only some younger, less capable assistants. The next morning, Malka smiled at Miriam and said, "This is really interesting. I don't know how, but so much got done!" "Mommy! I also noticed and thought the same thing. How did that happen?" she responded. How indeed?

🐾 Rivka received a call one day from the principal of her daughters' elementary school. "We are planning the sixth-grade mass *bas mitzva* party. Can you help me determine how much material would be needed to make collars, sashes and roses for 70 girls?" Rivka sat with the principal and calculated the amount of fabric needed. Then the principal had another request. "Could you supervise while the girls cut the fabric?" Rivka knew that cutting straight is not so easy; it would be difficult to show and explain. And might not come out as it should. Instead, she impulsively offered to do it. A few days later she received a bolt of 42 meters by a meter and a half; quite a large amount. It hadn't seemed like so much on paper; she suddenly realized she had volunteered for a pretty big job! Undaunted, Rivka began to measure and cut, and actually enjoyed doing it. She worked quickly and efficiently, but it did take time. By Thursday evening she had only completed about half the job. She realized that she would have to finish it on the upcoming long *Motzei Shabbos*. Now, even though the winter *Motzei Shabbos* is long, Rivka seldom finishes cleaning up from *Shabbos*. Her children like to have a *Melave Malka*, get their homework sheets signed and hear stories. Then they need to say *Shema* and go to bed! She can rarely squeeze in anything extra. "I don't think I did anything different on this particular *Motzei Shabbos*. Somehow, the children were more cooperative. They helped out and went to bed nicely. On the whole, I accomplished more than usual, and completed the project!"

Sara, a wonderful girl from a very simple home, became a *kallah*. A well-to-do member of the community was approached to host a shower for her. "I'd be truly delighted," was the reply. A few weeks later, the hostess' daughter became a *kallah*. When Sara's sister became a *kallah* a year or two later, a different person, also with a large home and generous heart, made the *vort*. Their daughter had been in *shidduchim* a couple of years already; amazingly, a few weeks after hosting the *vort*, their daughter became a *kallah*. The chain of *simchos* didn't end there. The hostess of the next event, a shower for Sara's sister, later confided, "Honestly, I didn't do it for any ulterior motive, but right after I made the party, a *shidduch* was suggested for my daughter. And now she just became a *kallah*!"

🐾 For years Rochel chided herself daily for forgetting to take along tissues when out on errands or walks. She generally needed one within minutes of leaving the house, but somehow just couldn't remember to take any. One day, when Rochel was out and about, she noticed a child with a runny nose. "I must take tissues so that I can help all of these young ones!" she decided. That turned around the entire situation. Now she rarely leaves her house without a pack of tissues. Happily, her little *gemach* did not stagnate; it actually expanded. Her Ziploc bag now contains not only tissues, but safety pins, sandwich bags, a small pen, note papers, stickers for cheering up crying babies and more. Although she regularly helps many, guess who is her best customer? Yes, Rochel finally has tissues whenever she needs them.

It is proper to insert a warning at this point. We cannot say yes to every request and cannot compromise our family's needs. Try to project to the best of your ability whether or not this *chessed* will probably fit in with your current workload. In some cases, **not** doing is the *chessed*. If it is something that will not take away from others you are responsible for, but rather will just add a little to your own tasks, try to take it on.

This idea is actually based on a *pasuk* in *Tehillim*, 37:3, which states: "Trust *HaShem* and do good, dwell in the land and be nurtured by your faith." We ourselves are nurtured by our trust in *HaShem* and our fulfilling His will through our acts of "doing good" – *chessed*.

Think about these examples next time you get **the call**. Say yes, if you can and watch the *siyata dishmaya*. And remember to share the story with others!

Conversing with Kavod

Do you find it difficult to make phone calls? Do you postpone calling relatives and friends to keep in touch or share *simchos*? If so, read on, for some "tricks of the trade;" skills and techniques that will help transform your discomfort to pleasure. After all, most of us were not trained in the art of phone conversation.

When children become verbal, often one of their favorite pastimes is speaking on the telephone. Saying "hi" and "I love you!" get lots of excited responses; as their vocabulary increases, so does the fun. As they grow, the telephone can play a big part in their socialization when it is used for speaking with friends and perhaps for getting some studying done. But basically, they call those with whom they feel very comfortable and that's it. Naturally, with this pleasurable activity, there's an immediate gratification that supplies a constant reinforcement to these calls.

As they matured, their parents may have encouraged them to expand their horizons. Perhaps they had to speak with some relatives or friends of the family occasionally. Even that was in all likelihood quite limited, however, to an occasional thank you, *Mazal Tov* wishes and the like. Within a couple of minutes it was all over. Clearly, even during that developing epoch, conversations were still almost entirely a simple and pleasurable activity, and continued thus through young adulthood. They spoke by their own free choice only with those whose conversations they enjoyed.

As they move out of their parents' home, all that changes. In a normal situation, now there are parents and siblings with whom to stay in touch. After a marriage, there is a new set of parents and family who need regular calls. At about the same time, they may realize that their dear aunts and uncles, grandparents and cousins, many of whom had done at least a few nice things for them over the years, would appreciate hearing from them as well. These relatives have aged and may not be as busy as they were in years past. At such a stage, calls can be the highlight of their day.

Chances are that some of those in this group will be difficult customers. Ornery, critical and otherwise difficult people can challenge our willingness and ability to engage in this *chessed* activity. Furthermore, as we come to understand that even these problematical people don't need just talking to, but rather *kavod-dik* talking to, it may seem like mission impossible.

One resolution to this problem is to limit ourselves to the easy relationships. As for the tough calls, we might tend to decide to cut down on those, in frequency, duration or both. At first glance, this seems like a good way out. You find it very hard to listen to all types of *mussar*, almost certainly rather repetitive. It can be a strain to speak without arguing and to be careful to avoid particular topics. If you feel this way, the easier calls may be a good starting point, but don't eliminate the challenging individuals from your radar screen! Consider adding them on one at a time, as you refine your skills. Refusing to take on the tough calls **is** a solution; but it's not taking the high road. It's merely an easy-way-out solution. It should only be exercised as a last choice.

When we implement this option, we generate three negative consequences. One is hurting those we love. It's inevitable. They might be longing for such elusive phone calls and feel hurt, although they may not admit it. The second is losing out on performing a very special *mitzva*. You are in a unique position to bring happiness and *nachas* to your loved one. Most probably, for the same reasons you do not enjoy calling them, no one else does either.

Thirdly, you will miss out on the many benefits that come with these relationships. Free advice is bound to come your way. Some of it may be way off the mark, but other insights might prove useful; after all, it is probably coming from someone who knows your foibles well and/or may be speaking with a voice of experience. Character development can come about as you realize that it is actually worth reckoning with some of their counsel which you originally thought to reject. You'll become a more judicious thinker as you decide. Alternatively, you will learn a new skill; how to deflect and ignore hurtful, inapplicable remarks. Just the fact that you work on yourself to continue the bond can boost you to make great strides in character improvement. Think of it this way: People spend a small fortune on personal trainers; you can have one – even several – at no charge!

On a practical level, how can we go about maintaining these relationships in a beneficial way? The suggestions below will make **any** type of phone call easier and can serve as "starters" for you to generate your unique solutions. Of course, these tips apply equally to visits.

🐾 Prepare yourself mentally beforehand. You may find it worthwhile to keep a written list of do's-and-don'ts that you can review. If you do keep such a list, don't forget that you will also need to keep updating it! See sample list below.

🐾 Ensure that your intended conversationalist has time to talk. Could be they have some pressing need and would rather enjoy your call later. If applicable, set a time.

🐾 In anticipation of your next call/visit, jot down brief notes concerning anything of interest that occurs. Try to do this on a regular basis or you'll probably forget all about it; *Motzei Shabbos* may be a good time. What seems run of the mill to you can be very interesting to others. Keep your ears open and your eyes peeled for incidents or anecdotes that might appeal to them. ~> **Bonus!** ~> Record these in a notebook, you'll have a wonderful diary to enjoy for years to come! Just remember to be sensitive to each one's situation. Keep in mind which topics have gone over well in the past and which have resulted in unpleasantness. If you plan to call a few different people, you may want to indicate on your list which news is good for whom.

❧ Speaking of news, unless you are positive that it will be appreciated, keep away from all kinds of unpleasant updates. You do not have to be the harbinger of bad tidings of any sort. Again, weigh your decision with all your experiences in past conversations with this relative or others of similar backgrounds. When in doubt, leave it out. If you are asked, "Why didn't you tell me about Uncle Moshe's operation…" or what-have-you, try one of these: "I just heard about it myself… thought you knew… didn't have a chance to tell you… didn't want to upset you… sorry, I'll try to let you know of such things next time." Do what you can to avoid arguments and make a note for the future.

❧ If you **do** have to inform someone of some unpleasant information, try to have such a conversation early in the day. Any recipient of disquieting news is likely to mull it over for a long time, more so regarding those living alone or with few distractions. When relayed in the evening, it could even affect their ability to fall asleep calmly. Additionally, divulge such news early in the conversation and quickly move on to more pleasant topics. Hopefully, they will have **some** activities and diversions during the day and will be relaxed by the time bedtime rolls around. Of course, it is still a good idea to ask before beginning your topic, "Is this a good time for discussing a dilemma?"

❧ Try to insert a few compliments, even if you have to refer back to ancient history. "The other day, I was talking to my friend and he mentioned Waco. I was so glad that you had reviewed the map with me in fifth grade; I actually remembered that it was in Texas!" or "My friend needed to know how to remove spit up stains and I remembered how you used to put the baby's shirts in the sun for extra whitening." Think of any little tips you may have learned, seen or somehow absorbed from this person; try to thank them occasionally. This can be a great source of happiness to them.

🐾 Share a thought on the *Parsha*, a story you read, an idea from a *shiur*, even a good joke or some interesting news you heard.

🐾 Solicit advice. People love to give their opinions and it will give you more fuel for future conversations. And you could procure some good solutions. A friend told her mother that her little one kept waking up at night. Her mother advised her to talk to the toddler right before bedtime and explain that she is disturbing Mommy's sleep. My friend didn't think her young child would grasp this idea and/or retain it, but out of respect for her Mom, she tried it. It worked!

🐾 Avoid arguing at all costs. It is a lack of *derech eretz* and in all likelihood will not accomplish a thing. Practice saying "Umm-hmm" and "What do you say?" and be prepared to say them! Here are some more phrases that may help you in case you find yourself on thin ice: "In most cases, what you say is true." In this case however, not. So you are agreeing in general, but not saying that you agree in this case, which you may feel strongly about. "I would have to think about that before responding." "I never considered it in that light before." "You have a point." How effective can this approach be? A mature man, already with a family of his own, would call his mother on a daily basis. Although they had very different views on basic *hashkofos* and the mother repeatedly challenged her son, he would consistently avoid any arguing. Over the years, she came to respect the value of his approach to *Yiddishkeit*.

🐾 Don't forget to listen. Many of us are in the bad habit of interrupting or not really paying attention. Or perhaps worse, we interject a better, albeit related, story when the speaker was just getting into his/her presentation. We're forgetting! Most people, especially in this group of difficult customers, love to talk.

Letting them, with occasional "active listening" responses, can go a long way.

🐾 When a real response **is** called for, try questioning rather than offering your opinion. "How did you feel when that happened?" can be much more valuable than, "That must have been awful for you." There are many good books on this topic.

🐾 Considering sharing private information? Don't do so hastily. Not everyone can/wants to keep a secret; see **Shimras Haloshon**.

🐾 If you are short on time and just cannot spend so much of it on the phone, try to prepare a task that doesn't require much concentration and is easy to do while talking; mending, polishing silver, peeling vegetables and folding laundry are good choices. You might be more relaxed and patient and even enjoy the call more, since you know you are getting a boring task out of the way at the same time. I've experienced such calls late at night, when I was so tired and just wanted to go to bed. But I could not postpone the conversation. The call energized me; equipped with a cordless, I cleared the counters, then swept and washed the floor. Alternatively, begin your conversation with something like, "I wanted to say hello, even though I only have a few minutes." End the conversation by apologizing and plan for a bigger time slot next time.

Sample do and don't list:

🐾 **Do** remember to ask about close relatives by name, upcoming *simchos*, projects or events. Easy, with a notebook!

🐾 **Do** refer to anything they mentioned in a previous conversation. Did they ask you for a recipe? Mention a get together, *shiur*, show or a simcha? Ask how it went.

🐾 **Do** share inspiring thoughts that you heard or read.

🐾 **Do** offer to learn *shmiras haloshon* or some similar topic together. A short paragraph is ample; you'll progress a bit each time and will have a real feeling of accomplishment from the conversation, even if the rest was uneventful.

🐾 **Don't** mention anyone with whom they are annoyed or have grievances.

🐾 **Don't** forget who is on the other end of the phone. Is it someone with a special situation? Childless, divorced or widowed? Had to deal with unemployment, illness or other severe issues? If these or any other problems apply, remind yourself before the call of their special situation. As you meander in your conversation, beware! A simple, "My married daughter came for vacation with my new grandchild!" might be better off not mentioned. It could arouse painful feelings.

🐾 **Don't** feel obligated to respond to each comment or query. Be ready to say "I don't know" when experience has shown that the question is referring to a topic that is best avoided. When you want to remain silent, it may be best to change the topic. And a sense of humor can glide you over many a rough spot.

🐾 **Don't** lower your guard any time you are in a room with a phone in use. ~> ***Beware!*** ~> Although you may not hear the person on the other end and may not even be near the phone, they may be able to hear your every word. I have overheard comments on many such occasions; some were not so complimentary.

🐾 **Don't** hang up first unless you absolutely must. Wait for them to end the conversation and hang up; then it's your turn. You won't risk giving them the impression that you are rushing to end the call. Of course, some times you may need to get off ASAP. As my mother-in-law, *a"h,* would say, "Know *vie ahn* and *vie aus*;" when to apply each rule.

As in any worthwhile undertaking, Conversing with *Kavod* is an effort, but you will find that the dividends are priceless. *B'hatzlacha* in this big *mitzva*!

Use Your Phone
For Fun and (Spiritual) Profit

Are you new to your community? Or do you feel like a newcomer? Do you have the feeling that no one notices you, cares about you or has anything more to say to you than a polite, "Hi, how are you?" and often, they have moved on before you can even reply!?

If you are nodding your head, you are not alone. Many people find that everyone is so busy; no one has time for a friendly chat. Truthfully, for many with jobs and/or young children in the house, there is simply no time to socialize. But not everyone is in this category. For those that have a quieter home, the silence can be painfully deafening.

Getting out, going to *shiurim*, visiting sick people, working with other volunteers; all of these are great, albeit obvious, solutions to this problem. But for those of us that are not able to get out much, which happens for a variety of reasons, we are left with our four walls for a good part of the day. Of course, we can listen to music or *shiurim*, and that can be most helpful, but sometimes we crave interaction.

Enter the much-maligned telephone. Responsible for being a conduit to endless *loshon hora*? Pleads the telephone, "guilty as charged." But it doesn't have to be that way. Fires can burn down houses and cause much damage, and yet we do not refrain from cooking. So too, telephones **can** lead to *loshon hora*; but they can **also** work wonders. It's up to us to use them properly.

Telephones can open worlds of opportunity. You can make calls! Yes – you! You can start with relatives and friends that you do not run into often. Give them a call. Did someone celebrate a *simcha* in their family? Call and wish *Mazal Tov*. We often receive invitations from relatives and friends with whom we are out of touch. Some say they are hunting for a gift; I think not. Rather, they would be delighted to get your *Mazal Tov* wishes and hear the latest news; only the kosher type of course! As an added bonus, keeping in touch with faraway friends enables us to get or even offer *chizuk,* as we can speak about challenges confronting us. It is easier to pour your heart out to someone that you will probably never see than your ever-present closer friends. Both sides can get a new viewpoint on their struggles and hang up enriched.

How about older relatives? Most of them would love to get a "Good *Shabbos"* call. If you cannot do it every week, consider making a *Rosh Chodesh* list and call once a month. Less time than that? Let the minimum be *Erev Rosh Hashana* and *Erev Pesach*. Of course, *"erev"* doesn't mean literally the day before. *Rosh Chodesh Elul* and the day after *Purim* are good times to begin, especially if you have a decent size list. As it gets closer to *Yom Tov*, there is simply no time for calls. Beginning early also helps spread the *mitzva*; those you call can pass it on and call **their** friends, relatives, former classmates and neighbors.

Maybe you (or your family or friends) know some invalids. If you have no time for visits, how about if you call just to see how they feel. They would love to know that someone cares. When a former neighbor of mine became an *almana,* I tried to call her occasionally. She couldn't stop thanking me for thinking of her. Unfortunately, she became ill shortly after her husband's passing and was *niftar*. At the *shiva,* her daughters told me how much their mother appreciated my calls. I felt so uncomfortable; truthfully, I had only called a couple of times. I was glad that I had at least done that, since it seemed that each call meant a lot.

Is it hard for you to make a call? Firstly, make it easier by getting a comfortable phone. If you are in the habit of holding it with your shoulder pressed up against your ear, get a hands-free device. You can use the speaker function if your phone has one; just remember to issue a warning, so they know that others may hear the conversation! Take advantage of the phonebook capability found on most phones today – makes dialing a snap. Now you can talk and move around freely, tidying the house or preparing meals as you spread some happiness. You'll have a real feeling of accomplishment when you complete your phone calls!

Need a topic? As you go through your day, keep your eyes and ears open for sights and anecdotes to brighten other people's lives. Do you have information about a sale, great book to recommend, recipe, *mitzva* opportunity? Share it!

And how about learning? Personally, I saw that over the years, despite my excellent intentions, I just wasn't studying *shmiras haloshon* on a daily basis. I thought I would learn with my children at the dinner table or with my husband late in the evening or by myself when I could catch a minute. Nothing worked. I even had a telephone partner, but somehow, we just weren't regular. Either I called her before she had a chance to *daven* or we were sidetracked into a big conversation concerning our children and their challenges. Days and months passed and I just wasn't reviewing the *halachos*.

Providentially, an idea popped into my head one day. I would acquire a few *chavrusas*. Between them all, I was bound to learn regularly. The first person I contacted was a friend with whom I was somewhat out of touch. I knew that she was a growing type of person and probably even had a *chavrusa* already, but decided to try. To my relief, she was very receptive. We started right away and although it was often only three or four times a week, I saw I was heading in the right direction. Next, I thought I would solicit my mother. After all, we were on the phone anyway on a daily basis; why not improve the quality of our phone time? At first she demurred, but when I pointed out that it would be a *zechus* for her granddaughter to find a *shidduch*, that convinced her. Another hit; and we have been quite regular. And yes, a few months later my niece became a *kallah* and we both attended her *chasuna*!

At about this time, I received an unexpected phone call that I recognized as *hashgachas HaShem*. A different former neighbor of mine called and asked if I was studying the *sefer Chofetz Chaim*. We hadn't been in very close touch since my move, but I was delighted to hear from her. I told her that I wasn't, since up until that point I had been studying *Guard Your Tongue*, by Rabbi Zelig Pliskin. We began right away, following the calendar of the *Chofetz Chaim* Heritage Foundation. Although we are not always learning the correct day's lesson, we have been going strong since we started, barely missing a day; on *Shabbos* we try to learn on our own.

Well, learning on the phone was getting addictive for me. I thought about the *almana* I called on a daily basis. We enjoyed chatting with each other, but I wanted to add this new dimension. I asked her if she would like me to read to her from *Gateway to Happiness*, a wonderful *sefer*, also by Rabbi Zelig Pliskin. This book is full of great methods that can be used to motivate oneself to a positive attitude and outlook. My friend was eager to learn, right from the start. We now begin each conversation with some light talk; after a few minutes, she will usually ask, "What are you reading to me today?" I know I wouldn't have found time to study these valuable insights if not for her. I found another partner with whom to study the *Shemoneh Esrei sefer* by Rabbi Avrohom Chaim Feuer, and still another with whom I am studying *Modesty*, by Rabbi Pesach Eliyahu Falk.

Sometime later I was on the phone with a good friend of mine; we used to be neighbors, but now live thousands of miles apart. We are both busy with our families and don't find much time to talk; through the years we just get on the phone when we have some issues to discuss. "What's going on?" she demanded.

"You know, when I see your old cronies, your name comes up. Lately, it seems that you are learning with everyone but me!" I reminded her that I had offered to learn with her, but she had pushed me off. "Well, let's start now." Said and done! We began to plow our way through Rabbi Shimshon Pinkus' *sefer*, *Nefesh Chaya*, all about the role of a Jewish woman. As an extra bonus, I get to bone up on my Hebrew while we study.

I realize that this may sound like a grueling schedule, but it's not. It's not quite as busy as it sounds; the learning itself is about three minutes or less per session. And the learning turns the call into a truly meaningful event! I also discovered that although looking inside the book was helpful for better concentration, when the other person was reading, we managed with just one book as well. Since our study sessions were so short, I was able to focus on the words while listening. And it was clear to me that when I was reading to my partner, she was able to do the same.

If you really get ambitious, contact the Partners-in-Torah program or some other organizations that will set you up with a study partner. Not on a teaching level? Sign up for a tutor! They will even pay for the phone call!

Not in the mood for talking much? There are wonderful shiurim to listen to, at no charge. In the USA, call The Chofetz Chaim Heritage Foundation at 1-845-356-6665, or Kol Haloshon at 1-718-906-6400. In *Eretz Yisroel*, the numbers are 03- 929-0707 and 03-617-1111, respectively. Check out all the features and variety of topics and speakers; there's a tremendous selection.

Another great treasure that can be mined through the telephone is working on *shidduchim*. NO, no, don't hang up on me! I realize that it is a BIG job, but it is such an important one and works so well with a phone, that it cannot be overlooked. As you speak to different people, try asking them who they know who needs a *shidduch*. Even if you feel that you cannot be a real *shadchan*, you can pass the names on to someone more bold; just keep in mind, you never know whom *HaShem* has in mind as a messenger.

We have all heard way-out stories of people who were put together by the most unlikely of *shadchanim*. One of my favorite anecdotes features a bus driver who paid attention to his commuters. He noticed among his regular passengers a young religious lady and at a different time, a young religious man. Of course, they each ignored his overtures, but he persevered and actually persuaded them to meet! And they took it from there, ending up under the c*huppa*!

Or how about this gem? A little girl wanted to get a new dress, but her mother informed her that she would have to wait for her older cousin to get married. Our junior *shadchan* made an announcement in her class next day: "My cousin needs to get married! Does anyone have a brother or cousin for her?" You guessed it. She earned her new dress, fair and square. So it may be worth a try. Even if you are not successful, you will still have done a big *mitzva*, because most people are glad to know that someone is thinking of them or their loved ones.

Remember: As you assist others, you will be the first beneficiary of your largess. Meaning, when you help others you help yourself first! You'll open windows of new and improved relationships and be lonely no more. *B'hatzlacha!*

Ascribe Positive Motives

Judging favorably is a *mitzva* in the Torah, not simply a nice thing to do. Is it easy? Not for most people, especially since most of us have not been properly trained. We need to work on ourselves to change how we think. It's clearly worth the effort, since there are so many side benefits to this *mitzva*:

- Training ourselves to think positively will serve us in good stead for dealing with all kinds of situations.
- Avoiding *loshon hara* – we know how very important that is!
- Gaining a merit to be judged favorably by *HaShem*; who doesn't need that?
- And even actually contributing to a positive judgment in *Shomayim* concerning the topic at hand for the subject!

All this and more are among the wonderful fruits of our labor.

But we can do even more with this attitude. Let's develop the concept a bit. Many childrearing and relationship-improving books are full of one of the best motivators yet to be popularized: It's the catch-them-doing-something-good-and-comment method. Interacting with our friends and loved ones in such a manner is a goal towards which most of us can strive. Although mastering this skill is not so simply accomplished, I would like to suggest something that is an enhanced form of judging favorably: Develop and embellish the bit of good observed in others. That is, search out and find even a one percent positive factor in the undesirable action and expand upon that one percent. Rabbi Chaim Shmuelevitz, *zt"l*, states that we do the things we do for a variety of motivations, some of which we ourselves are simply not aware. If we embrace a practice of searching out the **good** component in disturbing situations and building upon this element, we can encourage others and especially our loved ones to greater successes.

Actually, recent research has shown that feedback, even 360 degree feedback, is most effective when focusing on the positive. Telling people what they do wrong and what they need to improve on simply does not work effectively. Telling people their strengths give them what they need to build and do even better.

The first time I thought seriously about this topic was when I read an amazing story about a man who has truly mastered this skill, as evidenced in the following:

> Shlomo was in a hospital when he heard a lot of shouting in the hallway. He left his room to investigate and encountered a bare-headed man, who broke off what he was saying when our hero, Shlomo, appeared. "Here is a Rabbi!" he declared. "Let him tell us what is correct."
>
> "I am not a Rabbi," corrected Shlomo, "but I do follow the dictates of Rabbis. Perhaps I can help."
>
> Said the Jew, "My mother is here in the hospital, but I shall not visit her. Nor shall I say *Kaddish* for her when the time comes. While I have been out of the country all these years, my conniving sister persuaded our mother to put her apartment in my sister's name. This is outright robbery!"

The sister tearfully explained, "My brother has nothing to do with us in any way. He has left our traditions and does not even call us. I have waited on my mother and cared for her all these years. She insisted on giving me her apartment. Now she is so ill, yet listen to how he talks!"

To me, the case was clear. The brother was a bum and needed to get lost. Quick. Hopeless case, selfish, inconsiderate and ungracious; you name it. But our star did not see it as I did.

Shlomo walked over to the man, put out his hand and gazed at him in sympathy. "I understand you. You came all the way over here to see your mother. You love your mother and you miss your home where you grew up. Unfortunately, your *yetzer hara* got the better of you and you have been away all these years. Really, you are a good person." Shlomo said a few more things along this vein and our nasty ogre broke down in tears. He also went in to visit his mother. Later, he asked Shlomo to keep in touch with him. Amazingly, he went on to become a *ba'al teshuva*.

In another story…

A fourth grade *Rebbi*, new to the school, was surprised to see his student, Chaim, just stand up and start to walk out. The school year had just begun and the *Rebbi* naturally wanted to maintain discipline in the class. "Where are you going?" asked the *Rebbi*.

Replied Chaim, very confidently, "I think I left something outside during recess. I want to check."

"Oh no," said the *Rebbi*. "Sit down. You will have to wait until after class for that."

Chaim sat down, quite annoyed. His astonishment at not getting his way was obvious and very puzzling to the *Rebbi*.

The next day, Chaim came into class and threw a note on the *Rebbi*'s desk as he went to his seat. As the boys began to *daven*, the *Rebbi* went out of the classroom to read the note, clueless as to what it was about. The *Rebbi* had a big shock upon reading it. "Dear *Rebbi* – if you value your job, leave me alone. I have connections. My father is on the board, the principal is my cousin, every *Rebbi* I have had knows I do what I want and they don't bother me." The *Rebbi* was scandalized – but had to think fast. He closed his eyes, begged *HaShem* for help and re-entered the room.

"Chaim, thank you so much for your note. Please come with me, I want to help you out. Class, you can have an early recess."

Chaim, surprised at this request, rose. The *Rebbi* put his arm around Chaim's shoulder and spoke without a pause, while walking Chaim to the teachers' room. "Chaim, I just love getting notes from my *talmidim*. Truthfully, I couldn't understand exactly what you meant to say, but I understand that you don't feel so well. Let me make you a nice sweet cup of tea and we'll talk."

Chaim, overwhelmed, began to drink the tea.

"As I was telling you, Chaim, I really love to get notes. But yours was unclear. Could you read it to me?"

It seems that although Chaim was extremely brazen, even he had some shame. "No! No, I can't! *Rebbi*, please, give me back the note," Chaim said and tried to grab it away.

"Chaim, what do you mean? I love getting notes. I keep all my notes. But, if you are not ready to read it now, here is what we can do. Go to the office and get an envelope. We will seal the letter inside and I'll keep it with my other notes. When you want to go over it with me, you can."

Chaim ran to the office and came back with an

envelope. The *Rebbi* put the note in and sealed it. "Chaim, are you feeling a little better? Let's go back; there are still a few minutes of recess left." They walked back together, as friends who understood each other. Chaim never did get around to reading *Rebbi* that note, and he had a great year. Turns out it was the first time that he was treated like and behaved as just another child. The *Rebbi* accomplished this by ignoring the inappropriate behavior and treating Chaim like a good boy; enlarging larger than life, Chaim's good deed. After all, Chaim wrote the *Rebbi* a note!

I decided to try this technique in our home and waited for my opportunity. It came a few days before *Pesach*, when I was trying to use up our freezer-burnt bread. I microwaved it with some cheese and offered it to one of my adolescents, who said, "If no one else wants it, I'll have it." Meanwhile, some of the younger ones were around the table as well and I didn't really notice who was eating what. I just kept making more and more. Apparently, my teenager was missing it all as the little ones grabbed fast. As I was serving a third or fourth batch, my teenager said, "I'll make sure to get some this time," and he sprinkled it all with hot peppers. As he did, my six-year-old burst into tears.

I wanted to scream at the older one, reprimand him for being selfish and do all the things a good, protective mother does, but luckily, I remembered to Ascribe Positive Motives.

I went over to the six-year-old and said, "Now, now, your brother didn't mean to take anything away from you. He thought you didn't want any. He meant to share; he even said in the beginning that anyone can have." I felt like I was exaggerating; I didn't exactly believe what I was saying, but... Miraculously, the big brother picked up a piece of bread and attempted to wipe off the hot peppers. My six-year-old calmed down, leaving me amazed. I almost hadn't judged my teen favorably. Had I reacted with a knee-jerk reaction and yelled at him, I am certain that he would have stormed angrily out of the room and rightfully so!

The common thread in each of these incidents is that the offense was totally ignored – not even a comment was given to it – and a positive motive was revealed and magnified.

So here is a plan of action: On the way to a meeting or while waiting for whomever to come home, prepare mentally to **think before reacting to the next stimulus**. Review in your mind your desire to find a positive aspect to the next occurrence of challenging behavior. Remember to magnify and reflect back as in a magic mirror, the goodness of the deed or spoken words, although it did not come across in that way. Expose and expand the small point of virtue, develop and embellish it as you respond. The person may feel, "I didn't realize that I was thinking in that way," and they will hopefully rise to the occasion. Just remember to Ascribe Positive Motives! You will be truly amazed both at the initial reaction and the fruits of your well thought out words.

Make Change Part Of Your Routine

Life is a habit, my Great-Aunt Rose, *a"h*, used to tell me. And indeed, it is. We could hardly get anything done if we had to give great thought to the many seemingly insignificant things that we do each day. We tend to rise at a fixed time, schedule meals, shop and perform mundane household tasks; one week is like the next. Even keeping in touch with family and friends can tend to take on a certain routine, which is comforting and effectual. It gives us a chance to think about other things as we eat, clean up and even do errands all on autopilot.

Occasionally, we need a change from all of that. Especially if you are raising children; as much as they need routine for their security, they need to change that routine sporadically as well. They can gain in their own feelings of security as they learn that things can be done in different ways and still work out satisfactorily.

Take bedtime, for example. A friend of mine told me what she was going through. Every night she spent ninety minutes putting three children, ages three through six, to bed. Story time was becoming a disaster, as everyone jumped around and interrupted with lots of questions. And an old house rule "Get into pajamas before you pick a book" held her in a deadlock with one child who regularly refused and could never select that evening's story.

Enter CHANGE. "Tonight, I'm going to put each of you to bed separately, with your own reading time." She began with the youngest; read her a story for five minutes and put her to bed. The next child came running, thrilled to have this new private time. "See Mommy, you only had to call me once!" she proudly proclaimed. The oldest, our pajama procrastinator, hesitantly approached Mommy. "Can I pick a book?" he asked, still in his clothes. "Sure! We have new rules, starting tonight."

Going-to-bed-time dropped dramatically. By over thirty minutes! And amidst content children.

She was delighted, but realistic in her expectations. Sure enough, her good fortune only lasted several months. At that point, it was time for change again. She saw that, as with any system of dealing with people, nothing works all the time. Monotony sets in and the natives get restless. It is clear that we have to change and change again, which is beneficial, because change stimulates us and encourages growth. This woman's children matured and she too, grew as a mother with each innovation.

Interestingly, this has been shown to apply in the workforce as well. I read of a factory, where improved lighting was recommended to enhance productivity. It worked; only for a few months. Then things slowed down. So they changed the lighting again, this time by decreasing it. And productivity went up again.

So examine your present lifestyle; run a reality check for dullness and get creative. With your husband and all your loved ones, on the job or in any aspect of your life. Do some soul-searching, consult with a mentor. Try some of these big and little changes to give everyone a new perspective and a bit of fun.

- Rearrange furniture, pictures or knick-knacks.
- Change your route to school or work.
- Try a new parking area; walk on the other side of the street; use a different entrance.

🐾 Switch from tablecloth to placemats; disposables to dishes; vary the menu or recipe. You can serve pancakes or cereal for supper, *cholent* for breakfast!

🐾 Rearrange your drawers, closets, storage space or bookshelf.

🐾 Reschedule time spent with your children. For example, play a game instead of reading a story; alternate its place in the bedtime routine.

🐾 Change the way you manage your time. Do you write and use a schedule to get through the day or busy times? Change the way you organize it, for example be more or less detailed. Or try to work spontaneously! Never schedule your time? Try it!

Variety invigorates us. It inspires us and adds to our zest of living. When you feel a bit flat, notice your days getting monotonous or find yourself entrenched in a problematic situation, do some investigating and experimenting. See if a change in routine won't help enhance your situation and brighten your day.

How to be a Loveable Child

Articles, books and classes flourish nowadays, all awaiting our attention. They are there to facilitate the child rearing process. We are fortunate to have all of these resources; parents should take advantage, enabling themselves to do the best they can in raising their children. As we are improving our parenting skills however, many of us have to work on our "childrening" skills as well.

A new phenomenon has come into play over recent years. Some children, now grown, feel that they were not raised properly. Young adults, some new parents themselves, have very high expectations of what their parents "owe" them; yet seem to think they "owe" their parents nothing. Especially as they read the very materials designed to help parents, they may think, "If only my parents had raised me better. Since they made so many mistakes, they are not even true parents. Therefore, they are not deserving of any respect." Thankfully, many children do not feel this way, but some do. Despite their families' best efforts, these children look back with confusion, dissatisfaction or a lack of something in the relationship. Perhaps at such a stage, it is possible to provide information directly to such children about how to relate to parents.

How can grown-up children rectify the situation from their side? After all, once they have matured, their parents are no longer raising them, yet these children are obligated to treat their parents respectfully. What is the proper way for them to relate to their parents, despite the fact that for whatever reason, respect for their parents is not ingrained in them?

They can start with accepting their Torah-defined role: an individual with free will. No matter what our parents, *Rebbis,* teachers, friends and relatives did or didn't do, we need to "choose life." Choosing life means performing *mitzvos,* which includes respecting parents and being grateful for anything their parents did for them.

Are there no respectful feelings? Adopt an "as if" attitude. The *Mesilas Yesharim* teaches us that our external behavior has a great influence on our thoughts. We need to act in a respectful way, even if no feelings of respect exist. It can be very difficult, granted; changing our behavior always is. And you may not get a warm response initially. Perhaps your parents won't accept your new behavior graciously or they will keep behaving in ways you find challenging. The main point is to always behave respectfully. In some situations, it may help to create a healthy distance. Consider relating to your parents as if they were your aunt and uncle or grandparents.

Sounds like a vague charge? Here are some specifics, all based on *halacha*:

🐾 *Daven* for your parents' welfare.

🐾 Hold your parents in high esteem, as if they were dignitaries. Think: These people are Nobel Prize winners!

🐾 Address them respectfully at all times; politely at least, loving and warm if you can. Always do your utmost to use a pleasant tone of voice.

🐾 Strive to enhance their stature in front of others. That is, as you speak to friends or relatives and your parents are mentioned, think of something complimentary to say about them; avoid any negative comments at all costs.

🐾 Develop in yourself feelings of awe and veneration

toward your parents. This especially will do wonders for your *avoda*s *HaShem*, since respecting parents serves as a stepping stone to respecting *HaShem*. Feel free to use your imagination to make the feelings more real. Some useful metaphors can be thunder and lightning, Cossacks, kings from days of yore. Or employ the feelings experienced during *Neila* and the like.

🐾 Take care not to offend. This is easier when you master the skill of thinking before you speak. Consider how you would feel if such a remark were made to/about you or your spouse or children. When in doubt, leave it out.

🐾 Eliminate interruptions, contradictions, arguments and corrections, which are all strictly forbidden. If your parent is mistaken about something that is **truly** important, first verify that you heard correctly. Do so cautiously; do not repeat what you think you heard if it will sound foolish or comical. When you must correct, try saying, "Is it possible that…" or "I think I learned/heard that…" Phrase it carefully; it is more respectful if your parent does not even realize any kind of error was made. ~> ***Beware!*** ~> Actually, even saying "I agree" to a parent is not permitted, since it is as if you are setting yourself up as a judge.

🐾 Do not attempt to educate or discipline your parents.

🐾 Develop in yourself a sincere desire to please. Try to preempt parental requests. When possible, offer your help in a specific way. It can be small, like taking out the trash. It can be big, like helping them clean for *Pesach* or taking them, your younger siblings or elderly grandparents out for a few hours.

🐾 Rise when they enter the room, escort them as they leave, do not enter a room before them and request permission to leave their presence. Extra credit: Accompany them when possible, especially when one of your parents is out alone. For example, join your father when he goes to shul, your mother when she goes to a shiur or shopping. Of course, it is not always possible or even desirable; just keep your antennas up!

🐾 Be ready to apologize when you are remiss and repent to *HaShem* privately, as with any wrongdoing.

🐾 Take a different perspective by putting yourself in their shoes. Just as you are struggling while you raise your children, so did your parents. Admittedly, your style may be totally different and you may feel secure in the knowledge that you are not committing the grievous errors of your parents. Guess what? In all probability, your parents may have thought the same; possibly they felt abused or mistreated by **their** parents and thought **they** were doing a fantastic job with you. In the future, you may find your maturing children feeling disappointed or worse toward you, just as you feel toward your parents. Be bold; break the chain while you can. Respect them properly and daven that your children will do the same for you.

Naturally, this is not a one-day or even one-month program. It will take years. As long as you are progressing, you will come to experience great satisfaction. Side benefits abound:

🐾 Self-respect is a natural byproduct of showing respect to others.

🐾 Your other relationships may flourish as you show respect and behave in a humble manner with everyone.

🐾 Your *avoda*s *HaShem* will become more meaningful.

Contemplate this sterling example of honoring parents. A young man traveling internationally was asked by a friend to buy duty-free cigarettes. He refused, explaining, "My parents paid for my ticket; they would be very upset if I would do such a thing." I assume they had never discussed such a purchase; he simply knew how they felt about smoking and honored their wishes, elevating their prestige as he did so. Hopefully, his friend absorbed the full impact of the response.

Just reading this and considering this path means you are a special person. Make the most of yourself and your life, in this world and the next. Become a loveable child. And while you are at it, a loveable child-in-law as well.

Train Your Brain

A golden-aged Bubby was once asked, "There are so many appliances, gadgets and machines that have been invented during your lifetime. Which is the best? A real must-have! The food processor? Dishwasher? Vacuum cleaner?"

Answered the Bubby with a smile, "Actually, it's the kitchen faucet."

Life is full of challenges. Exasperating, frightening, these minor and major trials seem to crop up all the time, making us feel that we always have something to deal with. Although we try to remind ourselves that everything is for the best, how can we actualize that theory and keep ourselves calm and functioning? Today we are avalanched with "appliances"; so much information, ideas and guidance. There are countless books, articles and audios full of great ideas on how to cope, raise children, have good relationships and so much more. We can gain a lot from them, since we need constant reminders to help us throughout our day. We should make use of them, just as we make use of a variety of kitchen appliances.

But which is the kitchen faucet? The basic appliance?

Actually, there are two basic appliances. The *Gemara* says that it is our *tefillos* that make things happen. Through *davening* we can merit many amazing things; it's a component of our *hishtadlus*. That's **part one.**

When *HaShem* presents us with challenges, we need to *daven*, but we also need to respond, using the talents and skills that He has given us. *HaShem* gave us each a very basic and powerful appliance to access these abilities.

That brings us to **part two**: our brain.

Rabbi Avigdor Miller on his many tapes, Rabbi Zelig Pliskin in his many books and many other sources enlighten us about a fascinating, but often overlooked process. We choose what to think. We don't have to allow our minds to wander on useless and destructive thoughts; we aren't even allowed to. Besides being *ossur*, non-constructive thoughts are among the worst forms of *bal tashchis* that there can be!

So how do we work on training our brain so that we can use it to solve our problems, deal with life and earn us a good portion in *Olam Haba*? How can we maximize the benefit of our wonderful, potential-packed appliance?

Here are some practical ideas, gleaned from many sources.

Start by teaching yourself to direct your thoughts. During the day, does your mind wander to useless, post-mortem type of thinking? Do you find yourself mulling over conversations or situations that are beyond your ability to improve? Stop yourself and think about something else. Remember! Negative thoughts are simply traps of the *yetzer hora*! Since you cannot concentrate on two different thoughts at the same time, pick another topic! Rabbi Avigdor Miller recommends thinking about *Olam Haba*, picturing our *avos* and the events that are depicted in the Torah. You can create and review a *hakaros hatov* list as you think about all that *HaShem* has done for you.

Memorizing is another way to gain thought control and it can be fun. Wait! Don't say you cannot, unless you have **really** tried. The fact that you do not know *tefillos* by heart, even though you have recited them thousands of times, is not proof. Rabbi Aryeh Kaplan points out that our brain is set to "disallow" when it comes to memorizing. For good reason. We could not function if we had everything we read, heard or saw in the forefront of our brain, clogging it up. So *HaShem* made us forget lots of things. But, says Rabbi Kaplan, when you start to memorize things, you are letting your brain know that this is information you do **not** want to forget. He writes of his own experience in memorizing *mishnayos*. The first few took about twenty reads. As he continued memorizing, fewer reads and less effort were required, until he was able to memorize a *mishna* after just a few reads. Admittedly, he was a genius, so the rest of us will need to put in a bit more effort, but the idea still stands. You **can** put your brain into "memorize mode."

Start with something small such as the *tefilla* of the *Chofetz Chaim* for guarding one's speech. You will need to block off everything other than the few words you are memorizing. This can be accomplished by using two index cards, or taking one card and cutting out a window which will display only a few words. Keep moving the card(s) as you work. After reading a phrase several times, cover it; reveal one word at a time only **after** you recite it. In this way you can immediately check yourself. Repeat until you have mastered it and move on. Do as little as a line a day.

For text that you understand, you will find the flow logical, making it easier to remember everything in order. If you have difficulties connecting seemingly unrelated thoughts, make your own connection. For example, in memorizing the *tefilla* of the *Shlah Hakadosh*, for success with children, I couldn't connect "Your great name" (*hagadol*) to the next words "*v'al kiyum.*" I recognized that 100 was a great (*gadol*) number; it was also the *gematriah* of both '*al*' and of the '*kuf*' in *kiyum*. So it followed "...*hagadol. V'Al kiyum...*" Thus, I was able to keep these two thoughts connected. Really, any little idea will help you remember, it needn't make so much sense. You just need to construct an association! Whichever *tefilla* you choose to commit to memory, if you spend as little as ten minutes a day working on it, you will probably know it by heart within a reasonable amount of time. With that accomplished, you can recite it daily or even a few times a day. Perfect for keeping yourself busy while waiting for someone or distracting yourself while at the dentist. And you'll be accomplishing so much with your *davening*, all at the same time!

If you aren't in the frame of mind for memorization, try to review a *shiur* you attended. See if you can remember the points that interested you or some of the *halochos* you learned or stories that were given over; this can be particularly effective right after a *shiur*. This will help you review what you learned, while you force yourself to think about what you have consciously chosen to think about. It will also allow you to share it with others! Another option is to sing in your head; you do not need an iPod! Continuing to develop the habit of focusing your thinking will make it easier to squeeze more out of your brain.

Are you feeling nervous and apprehensive, concerned about the outcome of some upcoming activity? Instead of wallowing in worry, try to focus on developing a plan of action. Mentally organize details that need tending to, whether it is shopping, playing with a child or planning a party or some such event. You can do this by using your brain to actually picture these activities in your mind and how they might develop, especially if it is something that is usually challenging for you. Prepare yourself by recalling past successes and failures and how they came to be. Strategize to do your best to triumph.

Once you have taken the reins on your thoughts, you are ready to develop your imagination to enable you to cope with challenges. Are you upset because someone hurt your feelings? Imagine that they called you and apologized; begged your forgiveness and sent a dozen roses. Take a few minutes to create this scene in your head. Picture their tears, feel their hugs, smell the roses. Would you still be angry if they did all that? Probably not. So make believe they did. After all, your antagonist probably didn't mean it, didn't realize anything had even happened or was in a bad mood. If aware, the offender is likely to be full of regret but too embarrassed to apologize.

Remind yourself that each person is just *HaShem*'s messenger to give us what we deserve. Certainly, if it is a major offense and needs dealing with, you may have to take action, hopefully with the guidance of a wise person, typically a *Rav* or *Rebbetzin*. But most of our annoyances are minor and best forgotten as quickly as possible. Try thinking: "Thank you for giving me the opportunity to control myself" or "Thank you for cleansing me from some *aveira* I committed." Bear in mind that in the bedtime *Shema*, we ask *HaShem* to erase our sins, but not with big *yesurim*. If this suffering can be put in the small *yesurim* section, we must be grateful.

Take it a step further. Imagine yourself having an entire detailed conversation with this person and you may see the incident from their point of view. Or try, in your mind, discussing it in detail with someone you respect. Select a speaker, teacher, author; it can even be someone no longer in this world. Anyone will do, as long as you know and respect their style and way of thinking. Think about how they might respond as you present your problem. Hear **their** advice as you go over different possible reactions and you will amaze yourself at the insights you yourself can provide, while playing the role of mentor. This is not a one-minute thought process, but can actually take half an hour or more, if you really throw yourself into it. You can also try to picture the beautiful jewel *HaShem* is adding to your *Olam Haba* as a reward for your practicing good *middos*. Picture *HaShem* loving you with the strength of the sun at midday, as we learn is the case for those who control their speech. Use this *ais ratzon,* this special time, to *daven* for someone in need.

Or try this mental dialogue as another way to stay calm in a difficult situation. Even more than calm; delighted! Picture receiving the following call. "Hi. This is R' Avrohom, Esther's uncle. I heard you have been hosting/studying/working with Esther, and I know she is not the easiest person around. I wanted to let you know that I will be sending you a hundred dollars a week, just to say thank you. And if she says or does anything particularly challenging, just keep track of it. I'll give you an additional fifty dollars for each annoyance. Thanks so much." As an adjunct, picture yourself deep in debt prior to the call.

Increase the amounts if it helps you. Now, how would you feel whenever Esther comes around? Usually we forget to think about it this way, but isn't the *mitzva* of getting along and helping a difficult person worth more than any stipend?

If you feel you simply must "have it out" with someone, mentally review your planned conversation first. Just be sure to fill in both sides! You can even try to switch roles and see what you come up with. This can generate many ideas and help you understand the other person's viewpoint. If you are successful, great.

If not, try another approach: Avoid judging, judge favorably or at the very least, reserve negative judgment. Don't continue to waste your valuable thinking time mulling over why the other person did what he did or what he should have done. Determine what **your** options and needs are, and develop a strategy to fulfill your goal. Don't let yourself get sidetracked; if you find yourself suddenly thinking about a new topic, refocus. Initially, it may help to write down your options, possibilities and ideas. As you start spending your "thinking free-time" in this manner, you will be training yourself to direct your thoughts, instead of allowing your thoughts to direct you. When someone hurts you, you will be able to remind yourself that it is time to direct your thoughts in a beneficial way and use your newly developed and practiced technique.

At this point, decide if you should approach the perpetrator of the misdeed. You may want to for a variety of reasons: To give *mussar*, to prevent further problems, to assure them that you are no longer upset or some other purpose. You are now fully prepared. Your chances of handling it in a *middos-dik* way are high, due to having given each angle much consideration.

Realize that there are three parts to every response we have to anything. First, there is the stimulus; the event that triggers us. It seems to be followed by a response, our reaction. Actually, in between, comes the hidden part; our interpretation. And that is what we can work on changing, to prevent ourselves from responding poorly. Remind yourself constantly that you are here for a purpose, and life is too short to be little.

Are you interested in improving in a particular area? Would you like to think before speaking, keep anger out of your life, become less critical? Rabbi Yisroel Salanter, known as the father of the *mussar* movement, would repeat verses related to his goal over and over again. Rebbitzen Esther Greenberg recommends that we choose a phrase and drill it into our brain by repeating it a hundred times a day. It's easier to do than it sounds – and is unbelievably effective!

Lastly, we can use our brain to have the proper *kavana* for everything we do. Rabbi Avigdor Miller points out that as a woman performs any mundane job for her family, ranging from cleaning messes to serving food, she is an extension of *HaShem*'s desire, but only under one condition. She must have *kavana*. She must **intend** to fulfill *HaShem*'s will. When she does, she receives full credit for all the Torah learning of her husband and sons. She is earning a golden throne, equal to that of any *Tzaddik*. But she must have the *kavana*.

So we can accomplish a lot. Yes, *HaShem* desires our *tefillos*. But He also wants us to use our latent capabilities and grow in the process. We must exert ourselves. By using our brain to determine the proper response to every stimulus, we can keep ourselves in a pleasant mood and thereby avoid many unpleasant and inappropriate reactions. When we choose to think happiness-producing thoughts and train ourselves to reframe and grow from each (perceived) annoyance, we can come closer to filling our potential. And when we do every deed for the sake of *HaShem*, we earn a beautiful place in Olam Haba. When we properly analyze life, we will find that our frustrations and difficulties are not what they first appeared to be. They are actually our golden opportunities.

Da'as Torah
It's for Me and You!

Newspapers and magazines are teeming with spicy issues to contemplate:

❧ Is it really a breach of *Halacha* to smoke? Or is it just forbidden to start, or to smoke in public? What are a person's responsibilities vis-à-vis his own health and that of his loved ones? And everyone else in his smoky airspace?

❧ Today, with so many alternatives and styles available, hair covering has become a hot topic. Should a married woman cover her hair with a hat or scarf, or is a wig more appropriate? What are the limitations on wigs? How natural is too natural?

❧ What about paying tuition? Can a family plead poverty while taking vacations, buying a home, supporting a son or son-in-law? If they receive assistance, is that a debt that needs to be repaid?

❧ How about *Shabbos* expenses? How can we determine the proper amount to spend on all the extras? And what about the preparations? Should a woman take upon herself to be ready by *chatzos* or just worry about the time on the calendar? If she lights right at *shkia*, is that wrong? If she is ready early, how should the afternoon be properly spent?

❧ Our children live such different lives than any generation in history. Are they overindulged? Should they help more, manage with less? Where do we draw the line before we drown in their endless needs?

✋ Should we establish or join groups dedicated to encouraging all people to perform a particular *mitzva* in a way that would normally be done by only those on a very high level?

We need not, and should not, make such decisions alone. We need and have *Da'as Torah* to guide us.

Da'as Torah is an expression we have used and heard stories about, but for many of us, it does not play a big part in our lives. Decisions are made based on experiences, anecdotal input, advice columns. Unintentionally, we can cause irreparable damage to ourselves, families and communities.

It isn't necessary to blunder about in life. We are so fortunate to live in a day and age when it is possible to reach almost any *Rav* of our choice – in America, *Eretz Yisroel*, Europe – with a mere phone call. True, it may take a few attempts, but I have found many times, even when calling top *Rabbonim*, that I get through relatively quickly. So the *hadracha* **is** there for us, just for the asking.

And what valuable *hadracha* there is to tap into! Speaking to a true *Da'as Torah* is often mind altering. For one, it is totally correct and in line with *halacha* and *hashkafa*. That is especially important in our times, when we are bombarded with articles by every *daya zugger* (person with an opinion) – usually written without being checked by a competent *Rav*, let alone one with *Da'as Torah*. In the same vein, we accept as fact our opinions and those of our circle of relatives, friends and acquaintances. All of these sources present seemingly valid lines of thought. But are they all in line with *Da'as Torah*? They may not be. Additionally, the cleverness, innovativeness and foresightedness of *talmidei chochomim* are legendary. Our literature is replete with examples.

Let's start to get a sense of what defines *Da'as Torah*. Rabbi Dr. Abraham J. Twerski, noted psychiatrist, author and lecturer, answers questions submitted by readers of *Hamodia*. Generally, he admirably handles the query presented, but sometimes he recommends that the questioner seek *Da'as Torah*. One letter writer questioned, "But aren't **you** *Da'as Torah*? You are a *Rav* and have advised people for years; aren't you qualified?" Very humbly, Rabbi Twerski explained, "No. I am not *Da'as Torah*. I have read and studied from many secular books and lectures; so despite my Torah studies, I am no longer pure *Da'as Torah*. Everything I have seen has influenced me, however slightly, so that my mindset is no longer pure Torah. *Da'as Torah* is unsullied, undiluted by outside influences." Another *Gadol* commented concerning his brother, "He is a bigger *Da'as Torah* than I – he has never even read the back of a cornflakes box!"

We see that *Rabbonim* who take the yoke of leadership upon themselves are *zochim* to a special *siyata dishmaya* as well. The *Chazon Ish* was once asked a question, but was not able to answer it. He asked his petitioner, "Is this *l'meisa*? Are you asking for an actual situation or is it theoretical? I am asking because if there is no practical application, I do not have *HaShem*'s help, which I need in order to answer."

The story is told of Rav Moshe Feinstein, *zt"l*, who was approached by a tearful woman. She explained that after World War II, she had received a *heter* from a well-recognized *Rav* to remarry and not remain an *aguna*. And now, years later, her first husband appeared, alive and well! What should she do? Rav Moshe questioned her thoroughly but couldn't find any inconsistencies in her story. Suddenly he declared, "You are lying. You did not receive a *heter* from that *Rav*!" Frightened by his outburst, she confessed; she had not really received a *heter*, but just claimed she had so that she could remarry. Everyone asked Rav Moshe, "How did you figure it out?" He replied, "During that terrible time after the war, I was *zoche* to free many *aguna*s. Not once was I proven wrong. The *Rav* she claimed to receive her *heter* from was a giant in Torah, much more than I. If I was *zoche* to such *siyata dishmaya*, he was *zoche* to at least as much. I knew *HaShem* could not have allowed him to err."

"All of man's ways are pure in his eyes (*Mishlei* 16:2)." In determining a plan of action, one **may** have a source to base his opinion on, but he may be unwittingly fooling himself. One has to know when to use which source and how to apply a previous *p'sak*. Only an authentic *talmid chochom*, familiar with a great deal of responsa, can make that decision.

In another story with the *Chazon Ish*, a man came to ask a question but couldn't accept the answer he received. He respectfully challenged the *Chazon Ish*, "Doesn't it say the opposite in this-and-this *sefer*?" "It does," acknowledged the *Chazon Ish*, "but in other sources, it says what I've told you."

Replied the questioner again, "But in this other *sefer*, I understood it to say the opposite as well."

"Listen," explained the *Chazon Ish*. "For every source you can bring me, I will bring you more sources from other *sefarim* to show you that what I say is correct. But if you want to know **my** *Da'as Torah* opinion, there is no need to argue about what it says where. I am familiar with it all and stay by what I have advised."

We learn, we grow and we develop in our knowledge of *Yiddishkeit* but often do not realize how much more there is to know, so we think we know it all. Rebbetzin Berman, *a"h*, was teaching her seminary students and mentioned that the learning of Torah today is so far below the level that existed in pre-war Europe. Some of her students voiced a contrary opinion. "Look at all the *yeshiva*s we have today. So many men are learning!" The Rebbetzin's response was to burst into tears. She saw that the girls had no idea of how great the intensity of learning was years ago.

There is yet another aspect to getting *hadracha*, guidance from true *Da'as Torah*. Aside from being learned, brilliant, full of pure Torah and recipients of *siyata dishmaya*, they are also able to be "*roeh es hanolad*," perceive the ramifications of an action. We may configure a solution to our problem, but due to our narrow-minded understanding, it may not withstand the test of time. We are not capable of seeing the total extent of the issue, nor the results of our resolution.

Using our myopic vision, we may become victims of the Law of Unintended Consequences. As an example, Rabbi

Matisyahu Solomon commented that although all types of *yeshivas* have been created, each solving a particular problem, they each resulted in creating all kinds of new problems. We need *Da'as Torah* with their ability to see the width and breadth of an issue.

A woman took upon herself to always wear stockings as a *zechus* for her father's *refuah shleima*. He recovered, but she found it very challenging to keep her end of the bargain. She came to Rav Shach with her dilemma. He did not respond as many would guess he would. He simply called in two *Rabbonim* and performed *hataras nedarim*, absolving her of her oath. The end result? She was so impressed, that she increased her observance and was *zoche* to sons who became *talmidei chochomim*.

On a more global level, in *Voice of Truth*, a book about the life and insights of Rav Sholom Shwadron, *zt"l*, we find the following sterling illustration. When the state of Israel was being formed, the secular government offered the religious groups a seemingly wonderful arrangement. "Join us and you will retain autonomy in all religious matters," offered the politicians. Rav Sholom, himself *Da'as Torah*, was overjoyed. But he asked **his** *Rav*, the *Brisker Rav*, who thought otherwise. "Once you join them, they will do what they want and you will be powerless to stop them." Rav Sholom exited the home of the *Brisker Rav*, as joyful as he had entered, thrilled to have obtained *Da'as Torah* on what to do. Unfortunately, history proved the accuracy of the *Brisker Rav*'s guidance. To this day, the secular government has taken every opportunity to impose their views onto the daily life of religious communities in *Eretz Yisroel*.

In our time as well, we have seen very clearly how accurate the *Gedolim* were when they foresaw the problems and evils of internet and expanded cell phone use, including texting. Many deemed these technological tools to be innocent and thought the *Rabbonim* were naïve; were those *daya zuggers* ever proven wrong!

Clearly, it is more proper and more beneficial to you, to select a *Rav* with whom you can establish a relationship. This *Rav* might not be the *Da'as Torah* referred to here, but will be able to answer most questions. However, just as we would consult a specialist rather than our local doctor only for serious specific matters, similarly we will avail ourselves of a higher level of *Da'as Torah* for guidance in complicated issues and situations involving the community. By bringing all of your questions to the same *Rav*, you will get the maximum benefit of his insight, as he will have a more complete understanding of your entire situation. When you ask a *halachic* question, you might unintentionally omit relevant points and it will not be apparent. A *Rav* who knows you and your family for years will be able to guide you with tailor-made responses. And he will tell you when you need to consult a *Rav* of higher stature, *Da'as Torah*.

Bottom line, let's quote the *Gemara* (*Sanhedrin* 89): "If they tell you your right is left and your left is right, believe them." Guidance from our *Gedolim* is the only path for us to follow. And after all, if we are having a problem at the time of our final judgment, what better excuse can we offer but, "Sorry; I only did what the *Rav* advised." It's sure to exonerate us from any mistake.

P.S. Yes, dear reader, I did ask a *Rav* to review this.

For the Home

Organize Now!

That's a piece of advice that no one will argue with. *Gedolim, mechanchim* and *l'havdil*, secular authorities, all agree that to accomplish things in life, being organized is the way to go.

True, some of us have a natural predilection toward this skill, while others seem to lack it. Experts assure us, however, that this is an acquirable skill. For some reason we do not use our talents in all areas. Perhaps it is due to shortsighted laziness; but let's leave the "why" for the armchair psychologists. We need to focus on the practical aspects and see where we get. Keep in mind that although it takes time and energy to launch an organized system in any area, in the long run you will recoup this investment, in all likelihood several times over.

Encourage yourself by realizing that although there is room for improvement, the foundation does exist. You are definitely using organizational skills in some aspect of your life. Analyze and see where! Perhaps you use a shopping list; maybe you mark appointments on a calendar or have a storage system in your closet. At the very least, you have organized your kitchen into *milchig* and *fleishig*! So, praise yourself for that and realize that little by little you **can** take on more. You decide, set the pace and select what will work for you. Experiment. Modify. Develop techniques that enable you to accomplish more.

🐾 The market is flooded with books. Try to take out one organizational book from the library once a week, month, quarter or even year; whatever you can tolerate. Every little bit helps! If you can't get yourself to read it from cover to cover to glean ideas, at least skim through it. Check the table of contents and the index. Experiment with any idea that sounds plausible. Ideally, make an "Organize Now!" notebook, where you can collect ideas; some for immediate use and others for future incorporation. This collection will be an invaluable resource and reminder. Our memories aren't the best; sometimes we start things and do not complete them. A record of things that interest you will serve as a re-inspiration and give you a chance to begin anew. If you find a book that really speaks to you, buy it. Keep it in a handy place, where you can just open it and read a paragraph now and then. Keep a bookmark inside or flip through randomly. Even with minimal effort, you have a lot to gain. Through trial and error, you'll discover techniques that work for you.

🐾 Some people work well with lists and charts. If you haven't in the past, don't resign yourself to failure. Lower your expectations and delight in small accomplishments. For example, even when you forget your shopping list at home, or misplace your to-do notes, you might still remember some of it, since you spent time writing it. Other times, finding an old list can serve as a reminder and give one the impetus to get things done!

🐾 When working on a task, aim to complete it. In general, more can be accomplished when a well-defined goal is set. Keeping that in mind, you may want to break a big task into small parts or mini-tasks when possible.

🐾 I find that when I think I am done with a particular chore, if I remind myself to look around as I exit the area, there is often an item or two that somehow didn't catch my eye initially. That extra ensuring glance allows me to complete the task more properly. Even if there is no longer enough time to process the items and truly finish, at least they can be properly stored as they await the next occasion. That glance can actually be a very good habit to develop. Use it whenever you leave an area, even the bathroom. Check to see if any item can be returned to its rightful location, especially if you are heading in that direction. Little by little, you'll reduce clutter.

🐾 "A place for everything and everything in its place" is a lofty goal. A notebook listing the contents – at least in general – of storage areas can save lots of searching time. If you have never done such a thing, do not fear. Simply decide where to store the information; a computer can simplify the task, but a notebook can work as well. Just be very strict about where you keep it, or consider making copies! Over the next couple of weeks, whenever you have a few minutes, investigate and delineate in your notebook the contents of a closet or storage area. Record the information and note the ease with which you find your stored treasures when needed.

🐾 Systematize your errands. Designate one shelf or closet for errand items or items to be returned; keep everything there. If you have an unexpected visit from a friend who lives in a different area, you know just where to retrieve her neighbor's jacket that was left at your house. She probably won't mind taking it to her house, where the neighbor can easily reclaim it. Simultaneously, keep your eye open for any willing recruit.

🐾 De-junk. When it's garbage, file it in the circular file. If you cannot bear to part with it, try to find it a home. I have found customers for old magazines and newspapers, used clothing (even girls' tights, not all in the best condition) and other odds and ends. Simply ask around or post a notice in your local advertising paper. Remember: One person's trash is another's treasure! If you must hold on to the items, but won't use them for a while (toys for grandchildren, for example) box them, mark the contents and store it. Make sure it is clean, so you do not have to check it before Pesach. And don't forget to list the contents and location in your notebook!

🐾 If you are really getting into this, keep track of the contents of your freezer. Tape a sheet of paper to the freezer door, or assign it a page in your notebook. What a life saver! It may seem overwhelming and time consuming, so it isn't for the faint of heart, but it will save you lots of time and even money in the long run.

🐾 Experiment with new locations for items that are not easily accessible or whose location just doesn't feel right. We stored our pots in a spacious cabinet for years. However, no matter how methodically we arranged the cabinet, it wasn't long before all was in disarray. I dreaded finding the exact pot and its matching lid, but thought this was an unsolvable reality I just had to live with it. One day, we transferred the pots to a large drawer and voila! Easy as pie to find exactly what I need. Other such transfers have helped as well. One caveat, however: You may not always zero in on the right place with your first try. Just keep experimenting until you are successful!

🐾 Being organized – at least somewhat – allows you to think about tasks in a more positive way. It also allows your other family members to help more easily. Cries of "I can't clean up, I don't know where anything goes!" will be minimized. Your calls for help will also sound much friendlier.

🐾 When an important or quick task presents itself, just do it right away. Often, we procrastinate for no good reason. When it's done, it's done. Not only will your house be less cluttered, so will your mind.

🐾 Keep a calendar in a prominent area and do your best to record appointments, *simchos*, birthdays, sales, tests and project due dates; in short, anything you do not want to forget. Designate a place nearby for invitations as well; it's best to hold onto them right until the event. Don't forget to consult daily!

🐾 Do members of your household leave around their possessions? By all means, try to get them to stop; but don't make it your problem. Set up a cabinet or drawer in a central area; somewhere very convenient, yet out of sight. A boxed shoe storage system is well suited for this, or create partitions of some type on your own. Label an area for each person. As you come across these neglected possessions, simply place them into the proper slot. Make sure to remind everyone to check and empty their slot regularly.

🐾 Speaking of shoe storage, an over-the-door shoe holder system is fantastic for organized storage of all kinds of small items, in the toy room, office or bathroom.

🐾 Realize that frequently-used areas may not stay organized. Especially if you share living quarters, "the more, the merrier" also means the messier! It is just to be expected and dealt with. Do not despair, simply allocate some time on a regular basis – weekly or monthly – to get things back into shape.

Hopefully, as your family sees less clutter and more orderliness, they will jump on the bandwagon and begin to keep things in their proper place as well. Just be patient and continue modeling; restrain yourself from forcing cooperation or becoming unpleasant. As with other issues, even if they do not collaborate as much as you would like them to, they will most likely appreciate the benefits and use the techniques they have seen when they establish their own homes.

Of course, balance is the key to stability and providing an optimum environment. Organization is only one of the foundations of a happy home. While orderliness is valuable, you can achieve your real goal with or without a mess!

Try a Point Chart... Get Results!

We all find ourselves very busy with the varied demands of running a home. It's funny to imagine this, but in the good old days, a new baby meant two extra helping hands after a few short years. Today, it seems that with each additional child, we either need more outside help or just work harder! We can't turn back the clock, but why not try to motivate our children to take a greater part in running a home?

A proven way to encourage cooperation among children of all ages is a point chart. As with any project, there is an investment of time required. Yes, you must take a few minutes every night, per child, to update the chart. But, hey! That is a great way to spend quality time with your child, review their day and end on a positive note.

I try to accept all their claims with a smile and not quibble as to whether they truly performed the deed as asserted. It's actually an excellent time to **Ascribe Positive Motives**. And after all, points do not cost much, so it doesn't seem worth getting into arguments. Occasional reminders during the day will help them decide to cooperate – and to recall what they did during the evening accounting session!

You may want to review the day with each child privately,

to avoid jealousy and tears. Siblings can tend to remember all kinds of events which would result in lost points; it's better if they do not listen in to each other's ratings.

Points can be redeemed for treats, toys, trips, games with a parent or special projects. Some low-cost favorites are:

🐾 Enjoying a late night while everyone else goes to bed on time

🐾 Mini-vacation; allow a half or whole day off from school, or from usual chores

🐾 Playing a game, working on a puzzle, project or craft just with a parent or whomever your child selects

🐾 Setting up a photo album or scrap book

🐾 Picking the dessert or menu for an upcoming evening, special event or *Shabbos*

🐾 Baking together; the child selects the recipe

🐾 Going out with a parent, even if only for an unimportant errand or shopping trip

🐾 Earning the privilege of switching beds, bedrooms, furniture and/or drawers in accordance with your home setup.

Take advantage of the fact that the perceived value of prizes and awards largely depends on the presentation. Children can thrill in preparing treats; French fries or popcorn are perfect choices if you do not usually offer them. Just remember to add some enthusiasm to your pitch to make it sound special and appealing.

Try an auction occasionally. When I ran one, my children loved it and the points just flew! Select toys, treats and projects. Feel free to include various trinkets you have around the house that are ignored and not needed. An old ownerless knick-knack is boring; presented as a prize that they can own may make them jump!

Compose valuable and amusing coupons. Try "good for leaving your room a mess" or "use to get a ride to the store/park/friend of your choice within a fifteen-minute drive" or "good for permission to bake cookies and not clean up" and so forth. Offer them all for sale at the auction.

I surreptitiously controlled the bidding a bit to ensure that the youngest ones didn't spend hundreds of points on the first items and be left prematurely with an empty gas tank! The children bought a few prizes and everyone had fun.

If you have a small family, recruit your friend or neighbor to run a point program with their children. Join forces for the auction – it will be a double delight!

Although this is geared toward younger children, it can motivate older ones as well; of course you must use a more sophisticated approach. You may want to focus on just one or two areas; for example, getting up and going to bed at specific times. You may also be more successful offering a large specific reward. If you have trouble finding one that appeals to them, don't forget about good old money.

Yes, we do not like to have to pay our children and want them to be altruistic, it's true. But are we? How many kinds of activities do we perform regularly for free? Most adults do not do many. Why expect more from children? Granted, they should not have to be paid for everything, and it's a wonderful idea to talk with them about this concept. Encourage selfless behavior, but be realistic. If your child is not yet on that level, rest assured. That's normal! If you are concerned about how the money will be spent, set clear guidelines when initiating the project.

See this sample chart that has worked for us. Create your own, or fine tune it to suit your needs. An * indicates that points are assigned according to the specific job. Points earned during the bedtime process will probably be easier to credit in the morning or the following evening.

Enjoy the results and share *nachas* with your proud child!

POINT CHART

Listened the first time 5
Went to sleep nicely previous night 10
Went to sleep on time previous night 10
Said *hamapil* previous night 10
Waited in bed quietly until fell asleep previous night ... 8
Made bed in morning 2
Wished others "have a nice day" 4
Left promptly for school 5
Brushed teeth, per minute 2
Shared .... *
Performed jobs .... *
Gave in graciously .... *
Recited *Tehillim* .... *
Threw out indoor trash 1
Threw out outdoor trash 2
Drank a cup of water 1
Homework done and put away 5
Recited *brachos* clearly 3
Answered amein promptly 2
Ate nicely and neatly 4
Set/cleared the table 4
Cooperated during bath time 8
Put on pajamas quickly 2
Put clothing into hamper 2
Turned off light/heater/air conditioner when done 1

* Set points according to specific performance.

Try a Point Chart... Get Results!

It's Clean up Time!

Most of us were trained as young children to know this basic rule of life: Keep your surroundings clean. Even if we were not so cooperative during childhood, we surely see the need as we run our own homes. It's hard for a family to function when there is garbage all over the house. Practically speaking, it's dangerous; you really can slip on banana peels and trip on toys. Messes are also inconvenient. It's not fun when you cannot find your glasses, shoes or a package you left around and now must spend hours trying to locate or replace. Lastly, once in a while, you may want to open your front door – wide! Can you do that if your home is in a state of mayhem?

So we are all agreed, at least in theory, that getting garbage into the garbage can as soon as possible is a right, fine idea. But let's be practical. With lots of children in the house, not accustomed to picking up after themselves, how can we make it happen?

It is possible, with some planning, to get more cooperation; even a small amount can bring about a change. Start by speaking to your children, individually or as a group. Since they may not be aware of the problem, explain it to them. End your plea with a solicitation of their input; they may surprise you with some good ideas. Write down each suggestion, including your own. Review it together and try to be encouraging as you evaluate and eliminate any ideas that you are certain will not work. But don't be hasty to discard ideas! What may seem unrealistic to you could be invigorating and appealing to them.

Here is one idea that works in our home: I give a specific assignment as a function of their age. For example, "Before leaving for school – going to bed, eating a snack, running out to play – please pick up and put away one/two/three times your age." Be prepared to offer a reward, especially when beginning your campaign, to encourage those who perform. As they get used to it, you should raise the performance level until you reach some level of comfort for you all. See **Family Time, Family Fun!** and **Children – Keep Them out of Trouble!** for motivational ideas.

Be sure to remember to thank them for what they have done. A good technique is to describe what you see: "Sara put four cups in the trash!" "Yossi found a tissue under the couch!" In this way you can praise and thank them for what they have actually **done**, even though the task is far from complete. And they can accept your praise and not wonder whether you are exaggerating. When they clean enough to make a real difference, you can add, "Won't [fill in name of loved one] be so proud when she sees/hears!"

While we have the energy flowing, let's look out our windows. No matter where you live, it's important to dispose of garbage properly. Is it a neighborhood where people with all kinds of affiliations live? If so, we need to be extra careful to keep clean; as representatives of *HaShem*, we are certainly scrutinized more closely. Living in a *frum* neighborhood? Your immediate neighbors may not care, but when visitors come, they will be appalled if they are greeted with a mess. Living in *Eretz Yisroel*? Just as we wouldn't want anyone to throw peels on **our** floors in our homes, nor empty cartons and wrappers, we need to explain to our children that the beautiful land of *Eretz Yisroel* is our **real** home. So, no matter what, we need to keep our environment clean and neat.

Therefore, as we train our family to get into the cleaning habit, let's make an effort to keep our neighborhoods presentable. We can and must teach our children to properly dispose of any garbage. No receptacle around? Hold onto it until a bin is spotted. If we actually spell out clearly what we expect from our children, we can begin to solve a big part of the problem.

Realistically speaking, not everyone will be working on this. This apathy may shock or annoy those of us more concerned with cleanliness. But instead of pointing fingers, we can take it a step further. We can instruct our children to show *hakaros hatov* and do a *chessed* for the community they live in, by picking up one, two or three times their age whenever they go out, or at least once a day. We can explain to our children that cleaning up is a sort of tax we should pay for using the wonderful parks and general outdoors provided to us by the local municipality; they are there for everyone's pleasure. Use this opportunity to model judging favorably and persisting in doing right. Explain to your children that despite others' neglect in this area, we can still do our part. They may have a reason for behaving as they do, we don't know.

And perhaps we can motivate others as well. We can encourage a contest through our schools or among our apartment buildings. What a difference it could make. What a *Kiddush HaShem* it would engender if *frum* neighborhoods were free of litter!

And what beautiful *middos* we will be instilling in our children!

Shabbos
Lighting Right on Time

A dear and venerable friend enthusiastically described to me the new atmosphere in her home *Erev Shabbos*. "The children all have their jobs to do and our goal is to be ready an hour before the *z'man*; candle-lighting time printed on the calendar. I tell the children, 'Let's be ready for **our** *Shabbos*.' They know we are doing something special. Of course, I do my part and avoid last minute embellishments; I do not add to the menu Friday afternoon! When everything is ready, each child is awarded a preprinted card, color coded according to how early they were bathed and dressed. The cards are kept until *Pesach*, at which time they each earn a substantial prize, based on the number and color of the cards. Meanwhile, they all sit down to say *Shir HaShirim* or *Tehillim*. As the siren goes off, I am finishing the *bracha*. It is so peaceful and the children are so happy and proud of themselves." I hung up the phone wondering, how does she do it? Can I get my family to perform the same way?

Some time later, while I was still contemplating this elusive goal, a distressed friend told me about a conversation she recently overheard. A woman speaking with her friend admitted that she was having a lot of trouble lighting *Shabbos licht* on time. Of course, she always managed to light before *shkia,* but the *z'man* was beyond her ability. This first part surprised me, but I was more shocked to hear her friend's response: "Relax; most people don't do much better."

Now that was devastating. Many homes sport state-of-the-art kitchens, timers, microwaves, food processors and an endless variety of gadgets to ease food preparation. With all the modern conveniences how can it be that we are not able to *bentch licht* on time? Further incriminating is a fact that everyone is aware of: Somehow we are ready for *Shabbos* more than two hours earlier in the winter than in the summer. The time difference just doesn't seem to work in our favor. The longer the *Erev Shabbos* is, the more things we think of doing, or the later we get started, or, or... The result is a last-minute rush and sadly, cheating ourselves of those extra precious minutes of *Shabbos*. Depriving ourselves of additional time with our *Neshama Yesaira*. Of course, there are other aspects of honoring *Shabbos*, including a clean home, special foods and a cheerful atmosphere; but isn't the value of all of these enhanced when we light on time?

How did this constant last-minute situation come about? How did we get so busy and distracted from our true goal?

It could be we need to re-inspire ourselves. Re-prioritize, refocus. How? Try some of these ideas:

🐾 Listen to some *shiurim* or read stories about the *mesiras nefesh* for *Shabbos* that *Yidden* have had throughout the ages.

🐾 Hear about people who had very little and were desperate to earn money, but wouldn't transact any business after midday *erev Shabbos*.

🐾 Remind ourselves of those righteous people that would get ready early and recite *tehillim*.

🐾 Consider the *Gadol hador* in Bnei Brak, who refused to use a fan during the week because he didn't use electricity on *Shabbos* and wouldn't make himself more comfortable during the week than on *Shabbos*! The heat and humidity would be intolerable for most of us to contemplate.

🐾 Speak to friends and investigate: Who is *bentching licht* early or on time? Pick their brains! Find out what their real approach is to preparing for *Shabbos*. Get their mindset and hear their inspirational thoughts. Try to indoctrinate yourself and incorporate their ideas into your own persona.

👋 We usually define *shmiras Shabbos* as keeping the *Shabbos,* but the *shmira* – the protection – extends to all of our lives. That is, when we watch over *Shabbos*, *Shabbos* watches over us. The *pasuk* (Exodus 31:16) says, "…for your generations." It is for our children and the future of all the Jewish people. A very good return on our investment.

Hopefully those examples will create a greater desire within us to be ready on time. This story sums up the concept. A businessman was traveling through Europe and came to visit the *Chofetz Chaim*, hoping to get a *bracha* from the famous *Tzaddik*. In the course of the conversation, the businessman revealed that his factory was not closed on *Shabbos*. When the *Chofetz Chaim* asked him how this could be, the visitor responded, "My business simply cannot be successful unless it operates on *Shabbos*. However, I will say this. If after I explain how the business operates, the *Chofetz Chaim* can tell me how to close on *Shabbos* and still be profitable, I am willing to follow the suggestion."

The *Chofetz Chaim* shook his head. "No. I will explain to you how important *Shabbos* is and you will figure out how to keep *Shabbos* and be profitable."

Needless to say, we cannot equate lighting at the last minute to *chillul Shabbos*. As long as *Shabbos* is brought into the home before *shkia*, the minimum requirement is fulfilled. But we would be remiss to do the minimum in this area, when we seek much more than the minimum in so many areas of our lives. As the *Chofetz Chaim* explains, if we can acquire the proper mindset, the rest will fall into place.

To appreciate how vital it is to be ready on time, consider this idea: If you had an appointment with an important *Rav* or the president of an important business or tickets to an outstanding concert or event, wouldn't you come early? Or try this: Imagine expecting important guests. You have spent the past few days cooking, baking and cleaning. Everything is ready – but you. The guests arrive, your child or perhaps a housekeeper lets the guests in and seats them in the beautiful and comfortable living room, and there they sit and wait. And wait. You are almost ready; just have to shower, dress, a bit of this and that. Ah, that's it, you appear. You greet them, and being very polite, they don't comment on your tardiness. Everyone seems fine; but really, it wasn't done in the proper way. You did appear, so all is not lost, but the reception could have been of much higher quality.

A personal anecdote may bring home this point even further. Many years ago, I had a brainstorm. In my desire to entertain my young children inexpensively, I found out where the Goodyear blimp was garaged, hoping we could watch it take off. Sounded like fun and didn't cost a dime. And it was a mere thirty minutes from our home. We arrived a half hour before takeoff and let the children observe and play a bit, waiting for the 12:30 lift off. But something was missing. I looked around and couldn't see anyone else there who could possibly be passengers. I inquired in the office and discovered that the blimp had room for six passengers. Where were they? The staff assured me they were coming. I wondered. Who gets tickets for the blimp and doesn't arrive ahead of time? Sure enough, by 12:30 only four ticket holders had arrived and my two oldest children were able to actualize an amazing fantasy: a ride in the blimp!

Incredibly, no passengers arrived for the 1:30 flight, so they took all of us. Hard to believe, but true. From this unusual episode, I learned a lesson for life. When dealing with a special opportunity, prepare early and wait. Otherwise, one could miss a once-in-a-lifetime chance.

So let's use our imagination and fire up our family with the excitement of welcoming *Shabbos* as befits the *Shabbos* queen. Tell stories; there are plenty and we can create more. Young children will be delighted to hear about how some imaginary family gets ready for *Shabbos*; you can elaborate and add on as your audience's interest allows.

Once the mindset is properly established, using some of these tried-and-true tips may help:

🐾 *Daven* for help! Ask *HaShem* to guide you and help you be successful in this specific area. There is a special *tefilla* to recite, asking *HaShem* for help in creating a calm atmosphere as we prepare for *Shabbos*. Of course, your own words are fine, as well.

🐾 At the same time, *daven* to be *zoche* to keep *Shabbos* properly, even without any unintentional mishaps.

🐾 On a large sheet of paper, write down the time you want to *bentch licht*. It can be the time on the calendar or earlier; it's your goal. Post it on the refrigerator. Besides serving as a constant reminder to you, it will also help your children, who often cannot keep track of time and don't have a good feel for when *Shabbos* will begin. Announce the designated time and how soon it will arrive every hour or even more often, as lighting time looms ever closer. With so many distractions in our lives, we need plenty of reminders!

🐾 Early in the week, make a list of what needs to be accomplished before *Shabbos*. It can include errands, purchases, baking or cooking plans. This would be a list that varies from week to week, but could include the regulars as well. Post this list and don't add to it! Anything new goes on next week's list. Cross off each task upon completion. As you get closer to *Shabbos*, you may need to move some items to the next week's list, but this can help you organize and limit your expectations.

🐾 Do some type of preparation each day. Just have in mind that it is for *Shabbos*. As you do the job, say aloud "*L'kavod Shabbos Kodesh* – in honor of the holy *Shabbos*!" Include your family. Let everyone perform a daily five minute Shabbos job. The beginning of the week is suitable for polishing, cleaning unnoticed areas, measuring and checking recipe ingredients, preparing clothing. Napkins can be folded. Desserts and cakes – and even other parts of our menu – can usually be prepared early, without any loss in taste.

🐾 As you carry out your regular *Shabbos* jobs, try to time them. Keep these times in a notebook and get a more realistic view of how long things take to get done. That will help you decide whether or not you have time enough for a particular job in the future. Don't forget to include clean-up time! Use this notebook to notate successful times, frequently used recipes, any new insights of getting things done earlier in the week as well. Review when you need refreshing!

🐾 Analyze how you spend your Friday and the few hours before *Shabbos*. If a task, or even part of it, can be done earlier in the week, reschedule it. Do you bake? If you need to sift flour or check oats do so earlier in the week. Some prepare the entire *cholent* on Thursday, placing the full pot in the refrigerator. If you choose not to, you can do some parts; check and soak the beans and barley, measure the spices and/or peel the potatoes. *Erev Shabbos*, it goes into the pot in seconds.

🐾 Do your children help out? Although they may be more eager and willing *erev Shabbos* than during the week, try to get them to help for *Shabbos* earlier as well. Enlist their cooperation by whatever method works! For example, set a timer for 15 minutes several times on Wednesday afternoon – whoever completes their assigned task gets to play a game with you, help make cookies or enjoy a treat. Thursday afternoon play a cleaning-up-game. Select any game at all; players take a turn only upon completion of a small task. Picking up or putting away a few things is a good choice. You can even try a race; see who can get their job done first. Hopefully, they will still help *Erev Shabbos*, but in a less pressured and more enjoyable atmosphere.

🐾 Is your *erev Shabbos* so hectic, important things get forgotten? Create a more specific list, and post it prominently. For example, everyone needs to shower, but sometimes it gets late and we are all rushing, and all of a sudden there is no time. Avoid this by setting up a schedule during the week. Do your best to accommodate everyone, rotate if necessary. Indicate starting and ending times. Latecomers simply must shorten their bathing time. Use a timer to ensure adherence. Post this schedule by Thursday.

🖐 *Motzei Shabbos* is not too early to start! Polish *Shabbos* shoes, place any torn clothing in the mending pile, note any items that need repairing or replacing before the following *Shabbos*. *Erev Shabbos* will flow more smoothly without such tasks cluttering up the day.

🖐 Get enough rest! A good night's sleep Thursday night will leave you relaxed and energized to get through your day calmly. It will also allow you to arise early Friday morning, as recommended in the *Shulchan Aruch*, code of Jewish law. Of course, some function better working until all hours Thursday night and getting a lot done. Know yourself and schedule your time accordingly. Just keep your goal at the forefront.

🖐 Consider a private reward/punishment scheme for yourself. Ready five minutes early? Or five minutes late? Select a reward that really motivates you, be it new clothing, time off to read a good book, an excursion or even a facial. Decide how many minutes it takes to earn your reward; keep track of the time and follow through!

🖐 At the *Shabbos* table, give each person a chance to thank another for a task done. Feel free to elaborate or prompt!

I once saw a book on the topic of becoming wealthy. The author said that his goal was to earn millions of dollars. He wanted to be aware of his goal constantly, to never forget. So he hung signs around the house; he even wrote on the inside of his hat: I want to be rich! He succeeded and attributed his success to his single-mindedness.

Lighting candles right on time requires the same qualities: steadfastness, determination, commitment and persistence. With *HaShem's* help, these attributes will ensure that you reach your goal and enjoy the tremendous benefits in this world and the next.

Pesach Tips
Even for Procrastinators

Why do we seem to be caught unprepared? *Pesach* comes around every year and certainly we think about it quite frequently as the months roll by. We are determined to start early and avoid last-minute stress. Unfortunately, the actualization of our best intentions sometimes evades us. In any event, regardless of when we begin, everyone must clean their home for *Pesach*. Where and how to start?

Let's first get an insight from the Torah. In *Parshas Bo,* the Torah tells us how to prepare for the *korban Pesach*. The *korban* was to be brought by an extended family; if this group was too small to finish the lamb, families were to join together.

Would it take too large of a stretch of the imagination to suggest that we use this prototype for our *Pesach* preparations? There are plenty of pre-*Pesach* tips, but many families, blessed with many little children, cannot begin to use them! Neither can the elderly. They can barely get through a normal day; *Shabbos* is hard and *Pesach* seems impossible. So start your preparations with a *chessed*; join up with others! If you are able to assist a neighbor, friend or relative, do so. It may be in shopping, inviting them for a *Shabbos* meal before *Yom Tov*, preparing a meal or sending your children to help prepare.

Don't think, incidentally, that your offspring are only there to help you. Remember that our children are not our personal possessions, but rather a loan from *HaShem*. Since we are all really *areivim zeh l'zeh* – responsible for one another – they are fulfilling a *mitzva* if they help others as well as you. Of course they have a bigger obligation to their immediate family, but keep in mind: Charity begins in the home, but it doesn't end there!

As a mother, you can model this exemplary *middah* of sharing. Bear in mind the *pasuk*, "*harbei shiluchim l'makom*" – *HaShem* has many messengers. You will get whatever is coming to you on every level. Many times, I have found that when I took extra time off to help someone or sent my daughter out, other things fell into place, so that the time was compensated for. See **Get More Done with Chessed**.

Chances are you won't even **appear** to lose at all; your daughter will value your *ahavas Yisroel* and will find time for both. In conjunction with this idea, let your daughter work with a friend; they can *Pesach* clean at her house, and later at yours. The girls will enjoy working together and can also pick up new cleaning methods and other ideas from each other.

Keep the *korban Pesach* model in mind vis-à-vis guests as well. We're all in this together. Although many of us are overwhelmed with our extended families, think about the singles you know. Some dread the arrival of *Yom Tov*, with invitations as hard to engender as *chometz* on *Pesach*. They may also be struggling to get ready for *Yom Tov*. If you can assist them by arranging cleaning help or invitations, great; if not, a sympathetic ear may ease them through this challenging time. Attention singles: if you are in a position to help either families or other singles, the time is now!

~> ***Notebook Tip!*** ~> Keep a *Pesach* folder to be used from year to year; note how the cleaning went, including time spent and ideal times for each job or component. Record your detailed shopping list there – it will be indispensable! As you see adaptable-for-*Pesach* recipes throughout the year, it's the perfect place for them as well.

Now for some well-tested cleaning ideas. Let me begin by sharing another witticism of my Great-Aunt Rose. She used to point out that there are two time slots for washing dishes; when you finish eating or before the next meal. Applying this concept to *Pesach*, we can either clean throughout the year as needed, in which case our *Pesach* job is made easier, or leave all the work for "*erev Pesach*" – the few weeks before *Yom Tov*. Of course, everyone has a different standard to aspire to, so chances are both types will end up working hard. They will just finish with different levels of cleanliness.

As you work, bear in mind that all pre-*Pesach* cleaning is a *mitzva*. Awareness of doing the will of *HaShem* and *davening* to *HaShem* for *hatzlacha* are wonderful ways to occupy our minds as we go through the next few weeks. If you have a lot to do, be thankful for your many possessions. Alternatively, if you have a small apartment and not much in it, your work is that much minimized; this is certainly the time to thank *HaShem* for that! Concerning your belongings, reduce your work by de-junking. See **Organize Now!**

Before you begin, don't forget to turn your liabilities into assets. Your children; even the little ones. Admittedly, if they are under two, you may have to wait a bit, but even very young children can get involved in the *Pesach* fun. Start by sitting them down with a snack such as apples or popcorn, so that they will listen quietly. Elaborate on how big a *mitzva* it is to get rid of all the *chometz* and how they can help. Use a chart or stickers or try a dry-erase board; my children love it! See **Family Time, Family Fun!** and **Children – Keep Them out of Trouble!** for motivational ideas.

Offer them tasks broken down into small parts, according to their ability. If they are helping in a significant way, and you can afford it, be generous with rewards. We need never be thrifty with praise and appreciation. And be sure to let them hear you tell their loved ones about how nicely your *Pesach* cleaning is coming along, thanks to their cooperation!

What can they really do? Children can clean off Lego, wooden blocks, puzzles, books, especially if you are planning to seal them off for *Yom Tov* anyway. If they are old enough, they can clean out their clothing drawers, closets, knapsacks and personal belongings. Of course, you will inspect before all is done, but they will have a feeling of accomplishment and keep busy while you work; whatever they achieve will be better than nothing!

Consider letting them scrub with you. One year, my four and six-year-olds actually did a decent job on refrigerator shelves, while I worked nearby to supervise and help get shelves and food in and out. Children can clean cabinet doors, appliances, corners of the floor and more. They may also be able to clean out bathroom drawers and whatever areas were kept basically *chometz*-free all year.

If you find it difficult to supervise all of your workers at once, arrange shifts. ~>*Warning!* ~> Resting workers, now at play, may demoralize your working staff; send the players off to an area where they are out of sight and sound. Set a timer so that you remember to rotate shifts.

That takes care of your children. Now for you. You must plan your time wisely, according to the many variables of your household. I divide *Pesach* work into two categories: Absolutely necessary – refers to areas to be used during *Yom Tov*. Supplemental cleaning – includes, but isn't limited to, all of the spring cleaning and reorganizing that we must do periodically. While not absolutely necessary for *Pesach*, overall tidying up does enhance our *Yom Tov* arrangements. Look at it another way – it's something we ought to do yearly. When done before *Pesach*, it's part of the *mitzva*; a very worthwhile goal. My yearly plan of action is to begin around *Tu B'Shevat* and get all this superfluous cleaning/organizing done by *Purim*. Then, rinnnggg! Times up! Accolades for all accomplishments, but now it's time to get down to business. With only four weeks remaining, it's imperative to concentrate on cleaning areas that will actually be used on *Pesach*. Some like to start in the kitchen, others like to end there; experiment and work as suits you best. Just don't get sidetracked at this point; focus on ensuring that the absolute minimum is truly done before you tackle any extras.

❧ In the kitchen, make sure to thoroughly clean the areas that will be used on *Pesach*. Topping the list are the refrigerator, freezer, highchair, table, chairs and the drawers and cabinets that will be filled with *Pesach* items. Be aware that some of them may have a lot of built-up *chometz* (depending on when you cleaned them last and how meticulously) and allow enough time to remove the dirt that has been attached for months.

❧ In all likelihood, a treasure trove of *chometz* is lurking in your car. Since you will be driving on *Chol Hamoed*, however, no short cuts here; it must be thoroughly divested of all crumbs, big and small. Even if you allow eating in your car all year long, after it is cleaned out, you must insist on no more *chometz*-eating there before *Yom Tov*. Once enforced for this amount of time, consider making it a year-round rule! While cleaning out your vehicles, don't forget the car seats. Usually the pads can be removed and you may find quite an array of ancient snacks there.

❧ Don't forget strollers, recliners and couches. And purses, backpacks and suitcases, if you will use them on *Pesach*. If you won't, at least make sure that they are free of any significant *chometz*; put them away with the *chometz* you are selling.

Before hastily deciding which areas to ignore, consider these tidbits. I once read of a family that had set the air-conditioner to go on during their *Seder*. It is hard to imagine their shock, as it turned on and began spewing forth Cheerios! In another incident, a family was enjoying their *Seder* when one of the guests looked up at the chandelier and noticed a wad of gum! Granted, most parents never warn their children about such contingencies. It's likely, however, that in those homes, as in many, eating was not restricted to the table. So this is just one of the decisions each of us has to make; whether to be constantly vigilant or to work like our forebears in *Mitzrayim* for a few weeks. Either way, those anecdotes remind us to think of unlikely but possible places where *chometz* may be hiding and not to take anything for granted! We must do our utmost, but maintain balance and normalcy in our homes.

How about tips for *Yom Tov* itself? Food isn't everything. Treat your hardworking family: Invest in new books, toys and games that you can enjoy on *Yom Tov*. Pack them away with your *Pesach* kitchen items, thus ensuring they stay *chometz*-free and can entertain everyone year after year.

Save time, money and calories by preparing simple *Pesach* meals. Whenever you see anyone just sitting around and talking, don't hesitate. Whip out a peeler, bowl and potatoes and put him to work. You have but one peeler? *Pesach* means potatoes, so get extras! And good ones; it doesn't pay to scrimp. As long as you don't throw them out accidently, you'll have them for many years to come. Your helpers can sit, talk and peel all at once! And you will be ready for whatever potato dish you want to make. Don't forget that potatoes cost a lot less than matzo. See the recipes marked with an * in the recipe section; they are all fine for *Pesach* and most are very quick to prepare.

Yes, *Pesach* is a lot of work, before, during and after, but with a little organization and planning, it will be an experience to be **fondly** remembered the whole year long. Of course, if you want to prepare more elaborate dishes, you can, but your family might enjoy having their Mommy spend some time with them and will hopefully realize that forgoing *kugel*s and time-consuming menus is a small price to pay for this privilege.

Homework, not Hardwork 🐾

For me, it's always such a pleasure when my young children first start coming home from school with homework. They tend to take it so seriously and are so conscientious about completing their work, getting it signed and putting it in their knapsack. Perhaps it is due to the teacher's incentive program, or their desire to show how big they are. If only I could help them hold on to that motivation! Unfortunately, as they mature, sometimes their attitude takes a change for the worse.

And consider those children that get stuck from the beginning and are not interested in performing. What can be done to get **all** children on the path of good study habits, and keep them there? Collected from years of personal and second-hand experience, here are tips that can help any child:

🐾 Have a special area for doing homework. It can be a corner of a room, with a certain table or desk, and maybe a very comfortable chair. Make sure there is adequate light. Try to reduce disturbances, be it from other children, the telephone or other activities. It's a good idea to keep track of what distracts your child; one might want music in the background, while another can't work with any noise. If you have a few children, don't hesitate to write down each one's preferences; it will be one less thing to keep track of. You can even show her that you are doing so and she will see that you really think it's important. Once you know what works, follow through. If you need to eliminate noise, but cannot, try earplugs or make an arrangement with a quiet neighbor.

🐾 Set a specific time. When your child comes home from school, give him about an hour or so to relax, eat and play; after that it's homework time. You can let him set a timer shortly after coming home. He will thus feel more involved and responsible, possibly relieving you of the need to remind him to begin. If necessary, point out that the timer has beeped; hopefully, he will cooperate. Of course, maintain flexibility; occasional breaks from set routines can refresh your young scholar.

🐾 Have supplies organized. We know how frustrating it is to prepare dinner only to discover that the can opener is missing, or we can't find our favorite knife or peeler. Designate a box and keep whatever may be needed inside. An eraser, pencil, pen, markers, paper, pencil sharpener, ruler, scissors, tape, glue and glue stick are some of the basics. Make it a rule: Supplies are not to be allowed out of the homework area! Have duplicates in a different area for other needs.

🐾 Of course, you can't just gather the supplies and forget about them. Although it is a good idea for the children themselves to take responsibility for the upkeep of the supply box, it may not always work that way. Before the children come home from school, take a minute to ensure everything is there. You may want to ask one of your children to write a list of the contents and tape it to the box; easy to verify that everything is present and accounted for. You can even attach a picture of how it ought to be arranged; they may enjoy maintaining order. Depending on what else is going on vis-à-vis the children, search for the missing items or replace, without delay. You don't want a situation where your child can claim, "I can't do my homework! I need an eraser!"

🐾 Keep extra supplies in a storage area to avoid inconvenient runs to the store. Although you may get annoyed at the cost of replacing supplies and the lack of responsibility on the part of your children, prioritize before reacting to those faults; we need to pick our fights. Remember, also, that whatever you spend on supplies, it is in all likelihood less costly than even one session with a tutor!

🐾 Set limits on time spent and allow for breaks. If your child is overwhelmed with the amount of homework he has, you can try a few approaches. Allow him a break of about fifteen minutes after a certain goal is achieved, offer to help with part of the work – perhaps only after he has completed a set amount – or use other incentives. If you truly feel it's too much work, contemplate contacting the teacher.

🐾 On the topic of helping your under-motivated child, you may want to try this innovative idea. Tell your child she will get some treat after completing her work; if you do not want her eating at that time, it can be for her snack in school the next day. She may ask you for help, but each request will cost her a small part of the snack. If you shun such negative consequences, employ a positive method; let her earn snacks or some other reward for working independently. Although the first suggestion does have a negative spin, it is very clear and immediate, and can be very effective.

🐾 When age appropriate, encourage your child to study or work with a friend. This has so many advantages; it removes you from the picture, so there is no disciplining involved and homework time becomes a fun social activity. This is actually a fantastic way to encourage your child to build a friendship!

🐾 Make sure to remind your child to get his homework done, especially on off-schedule days. During times when there is a *simcha* in the family, an impending *Yom Tov* or perhaps your child has stayed home for an appointment, you might forget all about homework. So will he. Until you are in the middle of putting him to bed, when he suddenly recalls, "I didn't do my homework yet!" and you are in trouble. You may want to make a firm policy about this issue, with a "no homework after bedtime begins" rule; just remember again, that you need to pick your fights and rules are made to be broken. Try to avoid the whole issue by making sure homework is done earlier. It is especially effective to say, "You need to finish your homework before reading or playing," or "Remember! No staying up late to finish your homework!" If he sees you mean business, he'll take it seriously as well. It may result in his going to school one time sans completed homework, but at least he'll know for next time.

🐾 When older students have exams, they may need some studying tips. The goal is to review **all** the material from all available sources as time allows. They should read through whatever they can – their notes, the material in the book or *sefer*, all the quizzes, homework and the notes of some classmates. Choose from among those that take clear, correct and concise notes, of course! Reading aloud whenever possible will engage more senses and make it easier to remember. And as they review, they can take abbreviated but thorough notes on the important dates, places, formulas, facts that need memorizing. Compressed onto one piece of paper or index card, the facts can be frequently reviewed in minutes, right up until the test. It's bound to help them retain the information!

🐾 Encourage your child to go to sleep on time the night before a test. Last minute cramming will probably not help that much; coming exhausted to an exam will generally prove to be detrimental.

🐾 Teachers often assign projects in advance. When your child is assigned such a project, help him determine how much time he will spend on it each day or week so that he does not have to stay up late and run to the library at the last minute.

🐾 Keep a calendar where tests and long-term assignments are duly noted. Refer to it daily to avoid problems.

🐾 Although it is important for your child to work independently, it's also a good idea to look over what she has written. Offer some corrective suggestions where necessary, only after complimenting neat handwriting, correct answers, well thought out points or any improvement.

✋ If you have a problem that you cannot handle, contact your child's teacher; don't wait until appointments are set up. Sometimes a short conversation or note are all that is needed to get your child back on track, and with the teacher's assistance it can be quickly seen to. If you are unsure about how to approach the teacher in a proper manner, consult with an experienced friend or two. Be careful not to inadvertently cause the opposite of what you intended! If your child needs extra effort or attention from the teacher, you may want to resort to a little inducement. Subtly executed, a small gift can be very effective; truly, the teacher deserves it in any case.

As you think about these ideas, tailor them to your needs; experiment and improvise and develop your own unique system. Just bear in mind that each child is different and that their mood changes from time to time. A technique that worked wonders in the past may suddenly not appeal to your child and a method that never elicited a response may unexpectedly bring about results. So be ready to keep trying varying approaches and keep *davening* for success!

Times Tables
Gift of a Lifetime

Times tables just seem to confound many children. They cannot figure them out, remember them, understand them; they don't even want to look at them. And yet, most of the math they will have to deal with in elementary and high school and throughout their lives is based on times tables. When a child doesn't know them, every math class is torturous, to be avoided, or endured and finished as quickly as possible. The worst of it is the fact that the problem may never go away. I once advised a friend whose child was having difficulty in math, "Ask him some math questions as you drive or walk around with him." She confided in me, "How can I? I do not know the answers myself!" Oh, no!!

I want to suggest that it does not have to be like that.

I want to suggest that times tables can be mastered. It may not be effortless, but it is well within our children's grasp.

Before I put forth my system, I would like to clarify what I believe is a misconception that prevents many from mastering their times tables. Those that have mastered the times tables have done so by memorizing; they are not constantly recalculating them.

Hopefully, when the concept is introduced, the student will be taught what it means to multiply and why it is the greatest shortcut ever invented by mathematicians. And how useful it can be when you need to order supplies, plan for a party, and do anything in multiples. We need this skill to compute *tzedaka* – and to determine the discount at a big sale. Understanding it and working out some problems by way of introduction to the concept is all fine and important, but after that, memorization is a must. See **Train Your Brain** for more on this.

So, let's get into gear and do the following:

Buy, or better yet make, flash cards of our soon-to-become new-found friends, the times tables. When the child constructs the cards, even if done by a computer, he will start to think about the numbers, hopefully with a kinder eye. On the front of each card, put the equation; for example 8 x 7. On the back, the entire filled in equation should appear: 8 x 7 = 56.

Begin by going through the cards, one by one. Show your child the first card. He gets two seconds to think. Does he know the answer? Great! It goes into pile A and you can give him a big smile or quick affirmation. He doesn't know it? Don't allow extra time; let him read the entire equation from the back of the card. He can decide how many times he wishes to recite it, which will give him a feeling of control and partnership with the process. Reading it aloud will allow him to engage three senses: seeing, speaking and hearing it as well. When done, place the card into pile B. The whole process should go very quickly.

When there are five or so (he can pick the number, modify if necessary) cards in pile B, stop selecting new cards; go through your B pile, starting with the first one placed there. Use the same process. Can he answer immediately? Move the card to pile A. If he still can't give the answer within two seconds, let him repeat the equation a few times; the card goes back to pile B. Continue in this way, gradually moving the cards from pile B to pile A. You will see results.

Once a week, review pile A, which should take about a minute. When all the cards are in pile A, continue to review weekly. When the entire review takes about a minute, your child has mastered the times tables.

Although this system can work with cards in a random assortment, if the student finds this too challenging, sort the cards into individual times tables; let him master the 2's, the 3's, 4's, working his way up. Make sure to point out that the higher you go, the fewer equations there are to memorize, because the first few in the group were already memorized. Clarify how, for example, 7 x 3 is the same as 3 x 7, which the student will know by the time he does the 7's if he is going in order.

You may want to share this inspiring and encouraging story with your child. When the *Steipler*, a genius and massive *talmid chochom* was young, he was forced to serve time in the army. Occasionally, he was assigned guard duty. This meant taking a two-hour shift outside, throughout the Russian icy winter. To keep from freezing, a heavy coat was passed from the soldier on duty to his replacement, as the shift changed. One *Shabbos* the *Steipler* came out but the soldier he had to relieve had already gone indoors. Graciously, he had left the coat outside, but it was hanging on a tree. And that made it *muktza*. The *Steipler* knew that for *pikuach nefesh*, to save his life, he could remove the coat from the tree and wear it. However, he decided to remove it only when he would be truly desperate. "I can survive for two minutes," he thought. After the two minutes passed, he thought, "Well, I can last another two minutes." And that was how he spent the entire two hours, never touching the coat.

With this thought in mind, don't expect your child to sit for a long time with the cards; just the thought of it can be very overwhelming. Try three minutes during breakfast, when he comes home, before or after supper, before going to bed. Children love a few extra minutes of "up" time! Use prizes and treats to motivate. This is such a simple method that he can do it on his own, but be ready to work with him if need be. Most children will benefit from a weekly or monthly review. When you are together with nothing special to do, whether on a bus, in a car or out on a walk, quiz him. Use the cards or pitch in a few math problems.

Certainly, it is okay to point out any tricks of the trade – we mentioned that 8 x 7 = 7 x 8 and there are many hints for the 9's. One is to point out that when multiplying 9 by any number between 2 and 9, the answer will always be a two-digit number. The first digit will be that number minus 1 – that's in the ten's column. The second digit – in the ones column – will be 9 minus the first digit. The two digits always add up to 9!

7 x 7 is easy for those who count *sefiras haomer*. Or share this: "Eight hungry tots ate eight pies of pizza (8x8), and they got **sick before** (64) their mother came home." Give him whatever shortcuts you can, anything can work. But don't forget the bottom line: we need to memorize and eventually know it like we know our own name.

Little by little, we can accomplish a lot. Encourage your child with each equation he knows and let him work at his own pace. "Add" some *tefilla* as well and you will both take pleasure in the "product".

Games for the Gang

Rainy days, long summer Shabbos afternoons or long trips in the car can be perfect breeding ground for children's boredom, which can easily develop into fights. But all this can be circumvented with a good family game. Here are a few old favorites that we enjoy as a family. They are also useful for keeping children calm during dinner, in a store or the doctor's waiting room. You may even use them to keep everyone enjoying their time in the *Succah*! Most are educational as well. Play as suggested, or modify to suit your family or group.

Alphabet – This has endless variations. Select a category, such as food or animals, and start going through the alphabet – English or Hebrew. Within the category, each player must think of an item that begins with the next letter in sequence. Or ends with it. Or has the sound of the letter in the word. Decide if you want to limit words chosen to something they can see. It's a great way to pass the time while walking or traveling. Use signs or anything with lettering; players either have to find the letter in print, or something beginning with that letter. Excellent skill builder! For older children, consider reverse order.

Bingo – Begin by calling out 16 assorted, pre-selected numbers; players enter them as they choose on a card with 16 boxes: 4x4. The clue giver, armed with the list of numbers used, must ask questions to fit the numbers, or he can be given a list of questions. Players cover the appropriate number on their cards with buttons or some such. A clue could be a part of someone's age, phone number or even a formula such as, "the number of key chains owned by Penina, divided by two." Preparing the clues is part of the fun and so is comparing the answers! Lots of laughs for all ages. This game can be enjoyed without a winner or apply Bingo-style rules; first to fill in a row in any direction or first to fill their card wins.

❧ *Book Answers* – this is a game only for readers! Each player gets a book – any will do. The organizer prepares a list of questions; usually on a certain topic, related to the purpose of the gathering. Players must find a quote from the book that answers the question. This can be very interesting and is clearly suitable for adults as well as teens!

❧ *Brachos* – Put a few miscellaneous items in a bag. Each person has to say something nice about another person or give a *bracha*, based on an object withdrawn from the bag; no peeking! This game is perfect as recognition for some special deed performed or for a birthday celebration. Past *brachos* include this cute line, given by my seven-year-old grandson. He pulled a toy bus out of the bag and said, "May you have enough children to fill a bus!"

❧ *Charades* – Through pantomime only (no talking!), two or three players act out a well-known concept, story, tradition, historical event, or an idea from *Tanach* or *Pirkei Avos*. The other children try to guess the theme/source.

❧ *Crown* – Players take turns adding letters, trying **not** to finish off a word. The first player starts off with any letter of his choice. The play continues as each player, in turn, says a letter that can form a word with the previous letters in the given order. The player who finishes off a word gets a penalty letter; "c" the first time, then "r" and so on to complete the word "crown." The first player to finish a word five times is out. She can take consolation in knowing that she earned a CROWN! A player who cannot think of a letter to add can challenge the person who said the last letter. If the challenged player divulges a valid word, the challenger gets a letter. If the challenged player has no word or is misspelling a word, that challenged player gets a penalty letter. Suggested minimum word length is four letters.

👋 *Geography* – So called because it is played using names of places, but you can select any category; food, animals or plants are some good options to try. Each player says a word that begins with the last letter of the previous word in the chosen category. Whoever cannot think of a word is out or gets a letter as in *Crown*, see above.

👋 *I Spy With My Little Eye* – Give a hint as to what you see and let the little ones guess what it is. You can use picture books, items in a room or something outside. It just has to be in full sight.

👋 *I Went To Eretz Yisroel And Took Along…* For more fun, add memorization to *Alphabet,* see above. The first player recites this phrase and names an item beginning with the first letter. Each player thereafter recites the phrase with every item listed so far, ending with his new alphabetical contribution. Memorizing this list of words is simpler than appears; restricting the choice of items to a particular category will make the list even easier to remember!

👋 *Jotto* – This is similar to Mastermind, but a little more complicated. It is a great two player game for older children. Each player chooses a secret five letter word; no proper nouns or double letters allowed. The goal is to puzzle out your opponent's word. Each player, equipped with a sheet of paper and a pencil, writes the alphabet on top. On the next line, write any five-letter word; of course it is better to not use your secret word! Players trade papers and each must score their opponents word, according to how many letters of their secret word it contains. Position of the letter in the word is not relevant when grading. When you attain the coveted zero, or by logic eliminate a letter, cross it off on your alphabet chart. When you know a letter is definitely in their word, circle it. When all five letters have been determined, arrange them correctly and write their word. First to do so, wins! Genius level challenge: play without pen and paper!! For younger children, use three letter words.

🐾 *Meatballs and Spaghetti* – Players pick a book and take turns reading aloud, with a twist. Every word beginning with an "m" is read "meatballs"; each word beginning with an "s" is read "spaghetti." You can use any two words; such as elephants and lions. Just decide if you want to have a lot of substitutions or not, and select words that begin with a common or not so common letter accordingly. Lots of laughs with this one.

🐾 *Scavenger Hunt* – Create a list of items that need to be found and define the search area. Children can work individually or in teams. Consider a store or park only if your crowd is mature enough to play without disturbing others. Experiment with putting creative items on your list such as "snack with longest ingredient list" or "smallest leaf, flower or bug" or "least expensive meal." Especially if playing in a store, think about giving each team a small amount to spend on *nosh* afterwards.

🐾 *Singing Songs* – Sing any at all, but it is more fun to follow some type of pattern, be it alphabetical or containing a particular word or idea.

🐾 *Story* – Each person tells a small segment – a sentence or two – and a story is created! You can use various pictures or small toys and each person gets to select one with his eyes closed; the item gets incorporated into their part of the story. Alternatively, let each person say just one word. This can get very funny and creative.

🐾 *Tehillim Round Robin* – Finish the entire *sefer Tehillim* in a fun way. Each player gets a *Tehillim* and is assigned a *perek* sequentially. That is, the first person says the first *perek*, second person says the next *perek*; each person gets started as soon as they receive their assignment. As participants finish a *perek*, they call out the next unassigned *perek* and begin to recite it. Continue in this manner until the *sefer* is done. When there are seven or eight participants, *Tehillim* can be finished in about twenty minutes. You may want to have a moderator to keep track of which *perek* needs to be said next!

👣 *Telephone I* – The first player whispers a phrase or sentence to the next person, who tries to pass it on exactly as he heard it, and so forth. It's fun to compare the final person's version to the initial phrase.

👣 *Telephone I, Broken* – Same idea, however each player purposely changes a detail.

👣 *Telephone II* – The first person whispers a word; the next person passes on a related word and so on. For example, shoe-sock-hole-donut-*Chanukah*!

👣 *Theme* – One player is "it" and must leave the area, while the other players select a theme with which to answer his questions. Sample themes: Reference an event that took place prior to the previous answer, begin with the letter of your name, use a word that the last person included in their answer, and so on. Once a theme is selected, "it" asks each person a question. At the end of the round, "it" guesses the theme. Although the theme may seem simple, it can be quite difficult to determine! Play continues until "it" names the theme.

👣 *Twenty Questions* – One player thinks of a tangible object and the others have to figure out what it is. The players each ask one general "yes or no" question to gather information. After that first round, players can continue gathering information or venture a specific guess. We often play this at the *Shabbos* table. Optional: Announce the topic, such as the *Parsha* or a particular *Yom Tov*. Common questions: Is it of plant origin? Mineral origin? Is it food? Does it fit in a shoe box? Do we have such a thing in the house? Have we ever seen it? Is it mentioned clearly in the *Torah*? *Tanach*? Children really enjoy this, especially when it is their turn to decide on an object.

Family Time, Family Fun!

It's vacation time! In all likelihood, someone – maybe everyone – in the family is clamoring for fun things to do. Unfortunately, most of those fun things cost money and even less expensive ideas tend to add up very quickly. The good news for us budget watchers, is that there **are** entertaining things to do that cost very little or nothing; children can be kept occupied and have fun without expensive trips and toys. ~> *Caveat!* ~> Although these ideas may not cost much in dollars or *shekels*, they will cost in time and patience. So, if you have a lot of those, get ready and psych yourself up for fun as you spend quality time with your family.

As you begin, don't forget this principle: Everything is in the presentation. Much more so when your budget is tight. Preferably, don't mention money at all. Focus on the positive; explain to your children that they are so lucky and will be in "camp-Mommy" this vacation! Start by getting a notebook and work on planning a calendar together with your children. First explain that it is only a suggestion type of calendar and really success is up to *HaShem*. It could be a good time to talk about enjoying whatever we do, turning lemons into lemonade when necessary and so forth. It is always better if everyone expects less and gets more, rather than the opposite.

After that, start to collect ideas from the children, while you introduce some of your own. Hopefully the ideas you see here will suit you or at least "prime the pump" of your own imagination! You can write down each suggestion without approving or disapproving. Expensive or inappropriate ideas can be responded to with a joke, or try to find a redeeming feature and get the submitter to modify. For example, if a child suggests, "Let's go visit our cousins in Switzerland!" you can praise your innovative thinker for being family oriented. Offer to send off photos, letters or perhaps one of the projects you are planning to make. Suggest that you can all plan a Swiss evening after researching what they eat and any traditions involved. A humorous response might also work. "Great idea! And we can get kangaroo rides in Australia on the way home! That would be some trip! Something we would never forget!"

After you have collected ideas, tell the gang that you will review them and put a plan together. Meanwhile, proceed to set up a daily schedule that can be used on most days. You may need more than one for varying ages. Here is a sample schedule that worked for my young children:

8:30-9:00 breakfast, listen to a story tape

9:00-9:30 *davening, Tehillim* or review *aleph-bais*

9:30-10:00 game time: memory, lotto, bingo, checkers, etc.

10:00-10:15 clear away toys, tidy bedroom or bathroom; an easy to complete task that can make them feel good

10:15-10:30 snack – our favorites include juice popsicles, popcorn or fruit/vegetable slices

10:30-11:30 arts and crafts project – see ideas below

11:30-12:00 cleanup from project and prepare for lunch

12:00-1:00 lunch, free play

1:00-2:00 rest time; let non-nappers listen to a tape, read/look at books or perhaps work on a project that is not for the younger ones

2:00-2:30 get up, put away books/project, snack time

2:30-4:00 swimming, water fun or short outing
4:00-5:00 play with blocks, color or help prepare dinner
5:00-6:00 dinner; begin bedtime routine

~> **Warning!** ~> cleaning up first may compromise your ability to get everyone to bed in a timely manner!

6:00-7:00 bedtime routine – review the day with each child and hear what they enjoyed. Take notice of how they would like to have fun next time, but try as best as you can to emphasize the positive. Coax them into listing what made them happy; it can be a really warm ending.

This schedule may sound idyllic, but it is worth posting, even if only part of it works only one day. Children like to know what the plan is and can earn treats for staying on schedule. They can even have a chance to check off each thing done; if you see it goes, make daily copies. If everything is written in the notebook you started with, you'll have some great vacation memories!

~> *Note!* ~> Many of the following ideas mesh well with *Chol HaMoed* and will enable you to spend extra time in the *Succah*, instead of running around!

COOPERATION MOTIVATERS:

🐾 Every morning, fill a little cup with *nosh*, one for each child, for their afternoon snack. Label their cup with a sticker or write their name. Explain that if one child bothers or hurts another, one of the perpetrator's snacks will be transferred to the sufferer. It can be one pretzel or chip, just something to appease the injured party. In the afternoon, the children enjoy their treats; hopefully by that time having recovered from their small losses and learned their lesson. If you find it very successful and want to keep it going constantly, set up the next day's snack right away. Try to vary the treats; you can include sweet cereal and different types of pretzels, chips and cookies. Depending on your *nosh* outlook and what your family is used to, you may want to also include some chocolate chips, chocolate lentils, winkies or other such small treat.

🐾 Use some type of point chart. Even if you find such a chart difficult to maintain all year long, it might be easier during the relaxed vacation schedule; it's worth a try! It's sure to add excitement to the day; see **Try a Point Chart**.

🐾 Let them earn a late night! This can be a big treat no matter what; but especially if you are usually punctual about bedtime, let your crew enjoy a change in routine. Of course, it can be based on behavior and it can be either a once-a-week or a one-time event. It will be more fun if there is an activity planned; put on some music and dance or exercise! Pop some popcorn and play a game or review photos.

🐾 How about earning half a day or even an entire day off from school? They can get a card to hold onto and turn it in when desired. Even if it can only be earned once or twice a year, it's a thrill for any student! Your child is not the best student? One day off will not have a major affect on her studies. On the contrary, it might give her a refreshing break. ~> ***Warning!*** ~> Clarify any restrictions; explain that there may be some unpredictable off-limit days, that they need to ask at least a day prior and that it cannot be used on test days. Delimit as clearly as possible to avoid disappointments.

🐾 Your children will delight in exploring new recipes and ways of setting the table. Let them participate according to their ability. Serve some foods that are new, special or just not what you usually indulge in. If applicable, let them prepare a menu. Or play restaurant and let one child be the waiter/waitress. Use a special apron; give him/her a notepad. Make it look real with a check-off list; use pictures for those that cannot read yet. We did this with a falafel dinner; each child was able to pick how many balls, which vegetables and amount of *techina*. The children enjoyed the entire process, down to the last falafel ball.

🐾 Rearrange furniture or rooms. We find that the children really enjoy this. No matter how limited you are you can usually make **some** change, even if it is as minor as switching beds or letting someone sleep on the couch! We have set up beds under the dining room table; another time we lined up chairs, put a mattress on them and thus created a bed! Even a small change – a different drawer or shelf – can be fun.

🐾 Toys, books, prizes – shop according to your budget; any of these can be used as incentives. Collect a supply from bargain outlets, second-hand stores or yard sales as you pass them by. Stow away the items to present as needed.

🐾 Offer to trade toys, games, recordings or books with a friend for a few days; just make sure you agree on how to handle loss or damage.

PROJECT IDEAS:

🐾 ***Play dough*** – Although there are many recipes for this, this is the easiest. Mix one cup of flour, ¼ cup water, 2 tablespoons salt and a tablespoon of oil. Knead into a dough; add oil or flour if needed. Separate into a few balls and knead a different color of food coloring into each. Give your children rolling pins and cookie cutters and let them have fun. The dough can be stored in a bag for about a week; just refresh with a few drops of water or oil. This can entertain for hours.

🐾 ***Baking*** – Make cookie dough and give your children cookie-cutters and chocolate chips, sprinkles or ground nuts with which to decorate. Or make challah dough. The children can each get their own ball of dough to form into rolls of all types, even pizza. See challah, pizza and cookie recipes.

🐾 ***Snowflakes*** – Are your children old enough to handle a sharp pair of scissors? Get the thinnest paper you can find and fold it in half three times to form a triangle. Trim the open unfolded side; it can be rounded off or scalloped. Cut out all kinds of shapes along either side or at the point; open it and discover a dainty snowflake. Get as intricate as you can; if the paper is thin enough, fold it one more time. Display as is, or on a pretty background. Sharp scissors and thin craft paper will make this a lovely project, suitable for a *Succah* decoration.

🐾 ***Cutting*** – Actually, all kinds of cutting is fun. Give your children old magazines, and instruct them to cut out pictures of food, babies or any type of category. Check out the magazine before suggesting, so that they can find plenty to cut. If they are a little older, they can cut out individual letters or words to write messages, decorate notebooks or scrapbooks and address envelopes. Find some old baby sheets or thin blankets with adorable designs on them. They can be bought second hand for this purpose. Any characters can be cut out to play with on a felt board. Or, they can be easily made into little bags or pillows, doll blankets or toys. They can be sewn, glued or stapled, or used as-is.

Magnets – reuse those business cards and old calendars that are magnetic sheets. Glue on pictures or letters, or stick on stickers. Cut them out for adorable unique magnets! Place as close together as possible to maximize usage.

Coloring – Children love to color. To retain and maximize the excitement, supply them with something different each time. Color by number, tracing, geometric patterns, stencils, crayons, markers, paints and colored pencils afford variety to this basic idea. Color salt with chalk to make colored "sand"; spread glue on a picture and fill it in with this sand. Give your little ones small amounts of clay and they can color with that. They can rub the clay onto the paper; it has quite a nice effect. Or they can fill in a picture with tiny balls of clay. Pictures can be sent to Zaidy and Bubby or other interested people, collected in an album of some type, displayed at your end-of-vacation banquet or hung in a Succah.

Succah decorations – Summer vacation is a great time to get started. Chains can be made out of all kinds of papers – you can even cut up your local advertising magazine! Children love stapling, taping or gluing the chains together. Take care to have good storage, so that their works of art will look fresh and beautiful. Empty suitcases are perfect. Just ensure that dust and dirt stay out and nothing gets crushed.

Fish tank – Put blue-tinted water in a bottle with glitter and let children cut foil into fish and other shapes. Use super glue to seal the bottle and shake it up; watch the fish swim.

🐾 *<u>Portrait</u>* – Trace your children onto shelving paper and let them color in the picture.

🐾 *<u>Design jewelry</u>* – Use fishing line or yarn to string beads. Buy them or create your own, using plastic straws, clay and other craft supplies. Make paper beads by cutting thin strips of paper. Smear with glue and roll around a toothpick. Slide the bead off and let it dry; use as is or paint. It's also fun to create edible necklaces with some type of Cheerio cereal.

🐾 *<u>Make your own "Little People" (menchies)</u>* – Use clay to decorate and recreate. Hours of fun!

🐾 *<u>Record</u>* – During a period of a few days or weeks, turn on a recording device whenever you read to your children. Add in a few singing sessions and whatever else appeals to everyone. Your children will enjoy listening to the recording for years. Hold onto them for long enough and your grandchildren can enjoy!

🐾 *<u>Creative cubes</u>* – This is fun to make **and** play with. Obtain sixteen identical cubes. They can be as small as dice, or as large as you like. You will also need four bright colors of paint to paint each cube identically. Red, yellow white and blue are good choices. Four sides will be solid colors; two opposing sides will be split along the diagonal, creating two triangles on each side. Paint each of the four triangles a different color. When dry, create all kinds of patterns with the cubes. Use graph paper to transpose pretty patterns, fun for children to copy.

🐾 *<u>Paint a room</u>* – Two or three small bottles of acrylic paint, at about a dollar apiece, can be used to paint a room! Simply mix the paint in a container with about four or five times as much water as paint. Next, procure a few sponges, dip, squeeze and sponge-paint! Many types of patterns are possible; play around with it and you will be impressed with the results. The effect can be very artsy and will freshen a room for next to nothing. With throw sheets and good aprons, you will minimize the mess. Of course, your children can help, and voila! It's an activity!

🐾 *<u>Crocheting projects</u>* – Most children do not have the patience to crochet an entire project such as a scarf or blanket. Here are some quick and easy ideas. **Knob covers** – crochet a covering for any round knob, cabinet or door handle. It's just like crocheting a hat, but much smaller. Start by crocheting one stitch and then crochet six times into that stitch. Next row; add a stitch into every other stitch. Continue crocheting a few rows, adding six stitches per row. When you reach the desired size – the diameter of the knob – start decreasing; again six stitches per row. Measure to determine how many rows you need. Add elastic for a snug fit, or use glue for a long-lasting attachment. Use the same method to crochet a hat for a doll, or if you get ambitious, even for yourself! ***Camera case*** – it's so easy to make a small bag for any purpose. For extra padding to protect a camera, use heavy yarn or two yarns together; the result will be pretty and sturdy. Chain stitch about ten or twenty stitches, according to desired size. Then start the next row; when you get to the end, continue by circling around to the other side of the chain stitch. Keep going around and around until you reach the desired size. Make a flap by crocheting back and forth on one side, about four rows. Sew on a button; no need to make a buttonhole, just push the button through some stitches. Make a strap by braiding a few strands of yarn or with a chain stitch. Once your child knows how to crochet, such projects can be completed in less than an hour!

MISCELLANEOUS IDEAS:

 ❧ *Workbooks* – on all subject matters can be very entertaining and useful in the summer time. During the year, clip and save any for-children activities from newspapers and magazines. Check your local library; you will find all kinds of educational material that you can do with your children or that they can delve into on their own. Review and build upon math, spelling and vocabulary skills. Books and magazines contain a variety of science projects and all types of logic puzzles and experiments. Ice cubes, for example, can be made in a variety of shapes, and toys can be frozen inside; it's easy to set up experiments with them and so educational. You may want to set aside a certain time each day for studying, or just have the books available and remind your children to use them whenever time allows. Books can be cheaply obtained from yard sales, thrift shops and library discards.

✋ *__Having company and visiting neighbors__* – can be a fun activity. You can contact a friend that you do not see often and invite her to your home. Assure her that you will return the favor! Everyone will have fun playing in a different setting and you two can either catch up on news or trade off babysitting. Are there some elderly or lonely individuals in your neighborhood? Bring some of the cookies or another project you made with your children and plan a short visit. You may want to bring along some toys or books – children can get bored quickly and you don't know how the visit will unfold.

✋ *__Turn your home into an amusement park__* – This can be a lot of fun and just requires some imagination. Copy some camp ideas and have a blast. Have a blindfolded taste test, search for chocolate chips in beans or flour, ball up some socks and hit a target. Make a version of pin-the-tail-on-the-donkey or arrange a maze with furniture and have your children traverse it blindfolded. Use your play equipment for rides; decorate a wagon, stroller or bike. The children can dress up as well! Sit back – perhaps with some comical attire of your own – and watch them have a great time.

✋ *__Mitzva fair__* – A fun project, only for those who are really ambitious. Older children can really get into this. Everyone can have a good time and make some money for a *tzedaka* simultaneously. Include any of the above ideas, get some prizes donated and sell tickets. Raise a lot or a little, it's surefire entertainment. Of course this takes a lot of planning; it can occupy your entire vacation time.

Lastly, make sure to brainstorm with creative friends, especially those with children older than yours, who have been successfully occupying their offspring throughout the years. Most probably they have lots of ideas to share with you, but you have to ask. Just don't forget to begin each activity with a *tefilla* to *HaShem* for *hatzlacha!* And enjoy your vacation!

Make a Happy Birthday!

When I was a little girl, birthdays were very important to me. Some years I enjoyed a party, other years a nice gift; there was always something to remind me that my parents loved me and that I was their treasure. One of my favorite birthday memories, however, was not a celebration for my own special day. My mother laughs as she recalls...

I was a young girl when my mother, who grew up in a small town in Romania, confessed to never having had a birthday party. My first shocked response was: In that case, how did you get older? When I became a teenager, I decided to take matters into my own hands. My mother was home all the time, so planning a surprise was not so simple. One *Shabbos* when we were all in *shul*, I told my mother I had to leave early. When she and my father and brother came home, the table was decorated, and a birthday cake was on the table. It was a big surprise for her and it became a happy, warm memory we share.

As I matured and listened to various *shiurim*, I discovered that some actually frown upon birthday celebrations. These antagonists point out that each birthday brings a person closer to death. One speaker I heard said, "Imagine being on a train that is hurtling along the tracks, bringing passengers to their grave. Would they celebrate each stop at each station?"

However, since birthday celebrations are not actually forbidden, I would like to plead their cause.

To accept the above viewpoint in its extremity, we could mourn the birth of a child, realizing that eventually his life here will end. *HaShem* has, however, put us here for as many years as He allots to us. We are commanded to serve Him in joy. Perhaps in years past when people led much more austere, serious lives, birthday celebrations were a distraction that they didn't need and probably couldn't afford.

Today, when we live in an era where most people have plenty of possessions but suffer from lack of attention, celebrating a birthday can serve as another tool to grow in our *avodas HaShem*. Somehow, many children feel overlooked in their families or suffer from lack of recognition. Being the center of attention now and then can have long-term positive effects on their self-esteem. As a child enjoys her "day in the sun," she can better accept and share in the joy of others. Children can learn that being happy with another person's happiness allows us infinite opportunities for joy. A *Rebbetzin*-friend of mine summed it up nicely when she shared this precious thought with me: "In my husband's family there is a rule; if there is some reason to celebrate, celebrate!"

~> **Warning!** ~> Going overboard can have serious, deleterious ramifications! Spending a lot on special paper goods, expensive food, costly entertainment, party favors and more can have the undesired effect of causing a child to become self-centered and spoiled. In some communities, "How much is too much?" can be a thorny question. It can be a very fine line, but following the rule of "don't be first, don't be last" can help parents keep things in perspective.

Keep in mind as well that we want to avoid spiraling celebrations. When my oldest was in second grade, she came home one day very upset; a classmate was having a sleepover party and she wasn't invited. I didn't realize that the girl's parents were trying to minimize; I only saw that my daughter was left out. I told her that she could invite her entire class to a

Motzei Shabbos sleepover party. I thought that such an oral invitation, issued *erev Shabbos*, would have very few takers. Boy, was I wrong. Her whole class showed up; it was a night I'll probably never forget! And a few days later, the father of her friend who had made the small party confronted my husband. "Upping the ante?" he inquired. We realized that we had not properly evaluated the entire situation.

There is not a simple answer to this dilemma – inviting the entire class is too much; inviting just a few causes many to feel left out. Those with large or extended families can easily put together a crowd and celebrate, but that is not an option for everyone. Each case must be considered and dealt with sensitively. Weigh all the factors when planning your child's special day and try to make it a unique event that will become a cherished memory, without arousing jealousy. Be careful not to arouse envy within the immediate family as well – if you decide to splurge one time, you had better explain well or you will be on the hook for every future event! A one-time overindulgence easily becomes the future norm.

Here are some ideas for making a birthday a special day, while hopefully avoiding the above-referenced pitfalls.

🐾 Lots of birthdays to remember? Ruchel *a"h*, my older cousin, a great-grandmother and a great-aunt, liked to send everyone a card and a small gift. She would sit down on the first of each month and mail the entire month's-worth of birthdays! No one was forgotten and she avoided having to check her calendar on a daily basis. Creating such a birthday calendar takes some amount of work but is an excellent investment. Let one person be in charge and make sure to update everyone (grandparents, married siblings, cousins and other interested relatives) with a copy, including all new additions. If nicely done, it can be a thoughtful and appreciated gift; it's also a wonderful way to stay connected!

🐾 Let the birthday child select all or at least part of the menu. You can get a cute tablecloth and keep it under plastic so that it can be reused for future parties. It can be a family tradition! Alternatively, arrange photos or pictures that the children have drawn or cut out letters spelling his name and tape them onto a paper tablecloth. Scatter confetti or metallic shreds, cover with plastic and it can look very attractive.

🐾 With young children, snack bags are often prepared so that everyone gets a treat. The birthday child should be allowed to select at least part of the contents. To ensure that the birthday girl feels special, perhaps she can get one item that no one else received. A friend of mine who does this told me that the celebrant invariably gives a small piece of her special treat to all attendees to share. A beautiful occasion for demonstrating good *middos* and a great opportunity for parental follow up. "You're sharing your special cupcake! I feel so good when I see that!"

🐾 Encourage family members (especially young ones) to give homemade gifts. Consider making a collage or writing a pretty message; then turn it into a puzzle! A wrapped band-aid/tea box makes a pretty presentation. Sew a simple pocketbook or water bottle holder, adorn a new towel with beads or with markers; there are many inexpensive craft ideas.

🐾 One of our favorite gifts, do-able by any verbal child, is a coupon book. They are appreciated by young and old. Compose several coupons, offers that you know the recipient will appreciate. These are some that have been well received: "Good for one time cleaning your room." "Good for typing three pages." "Good for one trip to the store, buying up to six things." "Good for three times first choice of music to listen to." Everyone will have a good laugh and the offerings can be enjoyed for a long time.

🐾 Use the occasion to express your thanks, especially if it is an older person's birthday. I read a lovely article by Rabbi Jack Kalla of Aish.com. At first, he didn't know what to give his mother for her 80th birthday, when inspiration hit him. He simply wrote 80 "thank yous", ranging from "thanks for diapering me" to "thanks for my bar mitzva party" and so on. She loved it and shows it to all her friends!

🐾 A favorite birthday game in our home is "hot potato." Give the children some small toys and prizes and let them start wrapping. That will keep them busy for a while, and it is half the fun! ~> **Bonus** ~> Put the old wrapping paper you have been saving to good use! Magazine or newspaper pages will do admirably as well; remove the center staple of the magazine to obtain large pieces. The first toy is wrapped alone. The second toy is placed on top of the first and they are wrapped together. Wrapping continues with a toy in each layer, until the finished product resembles a small pillow. During the party, this toy package (called the hot potato) is passed around while music is played or someone sings. When the music stops, the child holding the hot potato gets to unwrap one layer and keep the prize! (Feel free to subtly cheat and strategically stop the music so that everyone wins a prize!) For more game ideas, see **Games for the Gang**.

🐾 Take pictures during the party; of course with a special picture of just the birthday boy. Print them out. He can get an album and will be able to relive his happiness later. You may want to get a large album and keep adding to it each year. The special pictures will be an interesting record of his growth.

🐾 If your time/energy level allow, consider a mini-celebration on "half-birthdays." We have found that to be well appreciated.

🐾 Put a lot of thought into deciding whether or not to make a surprise party. Anticipation is half the fun and there is none of that with surprises. More than that, many children (and adults) get rather sulky as their birthday approaches and no one says a word. It may not be worth the brief wonderful experience of being surprised. The best of both worlds may be to do what a friend of ours did. She planned the party with her daughter, but surprised her by having it a few days early! Any aspect of the party can be a surprise, while most of it is planned together. This way the birthday-girl knows way ahead of time that you are thinking of her.

❧ On the topic of anticipation, it can be a very good idea to take some private time with your birthday child, about a month before his birthday, to discuss the big day. Tell him you can't wait to celebrate and are wondering what he wants, or how he would like to commemorate the occasion. If you are afraid he may suggest something out of bounds, offer choices right away. "Would you like to go to Bubby or do you prefer the park?" "Do you want a new ball or game of checkers?" That will give him an idea of what the boundaries are. Hopefully, he won't respond with an outlandish request, but if he does, a bit of humor may rescue you. Something like, "I would love to get you a private helicopter to travel around in, but there is no room in our garage!" may make him laugh and become more realistic. If you wait and he comes to ask you before you offer, the whole event can come off with your child believing that he pried something out of you, without feeling that you wanted to give it; what a loss.

❧ I once read about a family planning a party. One parent said to the other, "Something may go wrong at this party; it happens sometimes. If you ignore it, no one will remember the mistake. But if you lose your temper, no one will ever forget it." It's a good idea to remind everyone that we plan, but *HaShem* decides what will actually happen. "*Gam zu l'tova*" is what we have to say.

As always, maintain flexibility and try to see it all from your child's point of view. With *HaShem*'s help, you will create many happy memories.

Join the Cut-Down-on-Candy Club!

I caught up with a friend of mine as she was pushing her toddler in a stroller with a couple of little ones walking alongside her. This was an opportunity to wish her a Good *Shabbos* and catch up on the news. We chatted amiably while we proceeded in the same direction. As we strolled along, I noticed that each of the children had a small bag of little candies; I couldn't hold back. "Do you really think that even your toddler needs a bag full of candy?" I questioned. "Wouldn't he be happy with a candy or two?"

"Oy," she responded. "You're so right. But it's too late for me to cut down. I have older children – young teens – they will never listen to me and give up on any candy. It's too hard to limit the little ones when they see what the older ones get. I'm just out of the groove of even thinking about it."

Perhaps monitoring our children's sugar intake is not the burning issue of the day and maybe many mothers simply do not want to deal with it. May I just present various benefits, some of which may not be so obvious? That information, coupled with a few "how-tos" that may not be so excruciating to implement, may convince you to try.

The nutritional payback is well known, but there are plenty of other advantages as well. For example, a little self-control added to our routine can be a useful habit to acquire, one that will prove to be valuable in other realms of our lives as well. We live in an age where self-restraint is not heavily stressed and it is to our detriment. It crops up in our inability to control our weight, our spending, even in our difficulty in disciplining ourselves to get enough sleep! As you control the amount of candy your child receives, teaching him to be satisfied with less, you will strengthen your child's ability to achieve self-control.

Another plus is that by denying ourselves during the week, we can increase our pleasure of *Shabbos*, as we enjoy those delicacies reserved for that special day.

And as is well known, sugar is not helpful to our attention span, general health or minimizing our dental bills!

So, there are some good reasons to sidle over to the health-conscious crowd. ~> **Disclaimer!** ~> I am not going to suggest foregoing all sweets. Adults can and should consider that route, but children spend a good part of their day with their peers; eating and *noshing* are fairly frequent activities. An absolute withdrawal is too restrictive. Especially today, when we are admonished on the importance of maintaining a high happiness level with children, asking for total abstinence could fall into the cruel and unusual category. So, let's see where we can cut down while keeping everyone from feeling overly deprived in the process.

Some "let children enjoy themselves" proponents claim that at parties, the children from sugar-restricted homes go berserk in an effort to compensate. If only a real survey could be done to prove or disprove this theory! All I know is when candy is thrown at a *simcha*, seems like every kid races around getting what they can; are we to believe that **all** of these children are candy-deprived? Let's face it; generally speaking, children (and adults…) greatly enjoy treats and will make an effort to get what they can when they can, no matter what their normal diet consists of. Of course, there are always exceptions and special cases, but we are referring to the norm.

An important first step is modeling. Let your children see you snacking on fruit and vegetables. Talking about it is something that should be done irregularly. Explain the importance of cutting down on sugar, referring to points mentioned above. Fortunately, there is so much material around; as we peruse newspapers and magazines it's easy and interesting to share nutrition-related articles. Delineate the cost/benefit ratio for them. Encourage them to join you in this crusade. Bring in some humor to the equation; suggest they form a club! Listen to their ideas. When offering rewards, select non-sugar incentives. See **Family Time, Family Fun!** and **Children – Keep Them out of Trouble!** for motivational ideas. Look for and appreciate incremental improvements. My children know that I want them to be happy and enjoy life but at the same time want us to keep the *mitzva* of guarding our lives.

It's a great topic that has a lot of angles and can be discussed on a regular, "irregular" basis. That is, bring it up often although not constantly. Sometimes just a bit of information, other times a discussion. The other day while reading a biography of the *Chazon Ish*, a very worthwhile endeavor for many reasons, a particular paragraph captured my attention. "Listen to this," I told my children, excitedly. "The *Chazon Ish* has a list of five recommendations for *yeshiva* boys, aspiring *talmidei chochomim*. Can you guess what the first one is?" No one had a clue. "Scrupulously avoid overindulgence in food… an exceedingly low mode of conduct and a hindrance to learning." Rather than lecture, just quote what others have said.

On another occasion, my son wanted to take a fruit drink to school instead of his usual: filtered water. When I told him he couldn't, he begged, "but everyone else brings flavored drinks!" "Really?" I responded. "Do me a favor, look inside their mouths as they speak to you. Notice the condition of their teeth." That stopped him in his tracks and he didn't mention it again for quite a while.

Continue your offensive by cutting down on the candy and other assorted sweets brought into the house. Expecting guests?

If they bring a gift, candy is a common choice. Let them know ahead of time that you prefer cookies, flowers or wine. As you bake and prepare desserts, notice that all recipes are not created equal; look for those that contain proportionally less sugar; the amount really varies. Have plenty of popcorn, juice popsicles, fresh fruit and vegetables available for *noshing*.

When your children ask for "junk," try to gently and pleasantly wear them down. A modified version of the broken-record technique can be a handy tool; here is a sample.

"Mommy, can I have some candy?"

"I bought the most delicious apples today. Can I cut some up for you?"

"No. I want those sour sticks."

"How about some cucumber slices? Crisp, cool, delectable…"

"No Mommy, can't I just have a little chocolate?"

"Perhaps later. How about if I pop some popcorn for you? Yummy!"

Heavy sigh. "Hot air?"

Aha! I am getting somewhere. "I'll pop popcorn with the hot-air corn popper, then sprinkle on some salt and oil. Here are some apple slices to eat while you are waiting."

Mission accomplished. My child makes a *bracha* and digs in, waiting for the popcorn. Later on, I may offer her a small square of chocolate or some chocolate chips – my favorite choice of candy, due to its (albeit limited) nutritional content.

Another successful technique is encouraging children to eat their *nosh* s-l-o-w-l-y. I occasionally recount the time I gave one of them, about two years old at the time, a small candy winky. We were out on a stroll, about twenty minutes away from home. This adorable toddler sat quietly in her stroller, holding the candy in her hand and licking it the entire way home. She spent more time enjoying that tiny treat than most children would spend on eating an entire pack! Sure, that was a bit extreme, but it really happened! Another favorite stretcher-outer is a race. Each side gets a winky or chocolate lentil or some such small treat. We see who can keep it in their mouth the longest. Yes, the winner gets another one and we may play a few times, but the total candy consumed is significantly small.

Time to confess; on occasion one can employ another method, albeit a radical one. Offer to buy their candy for cold cash, or offer some small toy or points toward something more major. Alternatively, propose to trade it for a less offensive indulgence. It's their decision, especially when it is a candy they have received out of the house. Don't force them, just encourage and educate them to make good choices.

Can we always be successful? Of course not. But can we at least serve much less candy? I think so. Look for small gains and be thankful for each one. Clearly, my children eat a great deal less candy, and conversely more fruits and vegetables than most. And just possibly, they enjoy the unhealthy treats they occasionally receive all the more.

Re-use with Relish

Have you ever experienced angst when relegating possible treasures to the circular file? Torn between your desire to clean and your knowledge that this container/paper/bag may prove useful in the future? Concerned about all the waste?

While not the top priority in our busy lives, these thoughts might buzz around our heads as we tidy up, especially if we have help from our children. I don't know about yours, but mine are all too happy to toss everything out. Of course, they are also all too happy to run out and purchase whatever they think they need!

Accordingly, if you want to be a part of the "re-use" society, but not drive your family batty in the process, you must be organized about it. Start by choosing a storage location for your soon-to-be-stowed treasures and direct all such items to that area. When you see that you have more than you can handle, your local pre-school or babysitter will probably be thrilled to accept donations. Yes, they will be overjoyed to receive containers, buttons, bottle caps, rubber bands, cardboard inserts from shirts or hosiery and more. At least they happily accept my contributions!

As you entertain your children, send food or packages to neighbors and friends, or need some accessory to complete a project, think about your treasures. They may expedite and ease your task! Alternatively, appraise your loot occasionally and see what you can use.

Here is a true to life sample:

Diary of a Cereal Box

July 1: Hooray! I get to leave this stuffy market and go to someone's house! Can't wait to make new friends!

July 2: This kitchen table is sure interesting... Hey! Everyone is shaking me around and emptying me out!

July 9: Today the last few crumbs were eaten. Hope they don't toss me into the trashcan!

July 10: Is this my new home? Inside a box on top of the dryer? B-o-r-i-n-g-!

July 12: Today was fun! I was a hat on a little girl's head for a while. She even decorated me! But now, I am back in the box.

July 17: zzzzzzzz

July 21: Yummy! I'm full of pretty cookies, wrapped in a bag. I heard them talking about a *Kiddush*!

I'm traveling! I'm trying to shake as little as possible, so these cookies arrive whole and beautiful!

They're removing the cookies and everyone is admiring them.

Close call! I was in the garbage, but luckily I got rescued. I guess I need to spend *Shabbos* in this stuffy suitcase. But at least I'm safe!

July 23: Finally home again; back on top of the dryer. I wonder what my next adventure will be.

July 25: I guess this is good-bye for me! I'm getting trimmed down to a small size... with a nice picture glued onto me... ooh, that tickles... a little girl is covering me with tiny balls of clay... gosh, now I get to hang on the wall... this is nice... people are looking at me and smiling... good-bye...

This is the animated real-life history of a cornflakes box of ours, although I must admit that some do get thrown out! The point is that you never know exactly what you can use or will need. We have re-used boxes to enclose gifts, send packages to children in camps and dorms, bring meals to friends and store small items. We once even turned a band-aid box into a pretty present by decorating it and covering it with clear contact paper; a handmade puzzle placed inside made a special gift for a friend. We just missed one opportunity; the puzzle would have been more durable had we only made it out of a sturdy cereal box!

And we can do more. How about salvaging leftover crumbs and drops of food in containers, which commonly get thrown out? We can save a bit of money, enhance our recipes and avoid *bal tashchis* with just a bit of planning.

🐾 Set aside some small containers; old condiment or spice jars are perfect. Take a minute to mark them. It's so annoying when people try to help themselves and discover pretzel salt in the garlic powder container. If your family is not as magnanimous as mine or if you are a drop less than totally dedicated, such errors could sabotage your entire program!

🐾 Crumbs in the bottom of your biscuit or cookie package? Put them in a container marked "sweet crumbs" and use them in a cake or cookie recipe. If it's a small amount, no need to adjust the recipe. Of course, don't add it to a delicate sponge cake or meringue, but rather some type of bar or cookie recipe. Alternatively, use it as a topping for oatmeal or ice cream. It can even become part of a fancy ice cream dessert, with layers of ice cream, cookie crumbs, nuts, chocolate syrup. If you won't get to the crumbs within a few days, freeze them; but not for too long or they may get stale and/or freezer-burnt! These ideas are also great for leftover chocolates and candy; they can transfer your plain cookies or ice-cream into a gourmet treat for special occasions.

🐾 Do you indulge in pretzels with sesame seeds? You can offset your expense by saving all the yummy toasted sesame seeds in the bottom of the bag; there is usually a decent amount there! Of course, you have to get to them before they get spilled or thrown out, so you may want to put the pretzels in a container as soon as you open the bag and squirrel away your treasure. Mark this container, "savory sesame seeds," and you are all set to season pasta or a vegetable dish, raw or cooked. They are also a great addition to homemade crackers!

🐾 What about plain pretzels? I hope I don't sound off-the-deep-end when I point out that there is usually a spoonful or more of salt on the bottom of each bag. Mark your container "pretzel salt" and use in *kugels*, *cholent*, soups or salads.

🐾 Some leftovers are best harvested straight from the container. Just a bit of salad dip left? Put your salad in the container and mix; that's one less dish to wash! You will have the satisfaction of getting each last drop. Small amount of cottage cheese left? I actually introduced a new dish in our house: Rice cake crumbs mixed right into the cottage cheese. It's a real double header, since I salvaged both cheese and crumbs. A bit of salad dressing left in the bottle? Use it for your next marinade, which will include some other liquids. Simply pour one of those liquids (vinegar, wine or juice) into the dressing bottle first, shake it and then add to the other marinade ingredients. Chocolate syrup bottle seems empty? Pour in some milk, shake well and enjoy a yummy surprise! Ketchup or mustard bottle not willing to part with the last of its contents? Pour in a bit of water, shake it and empty it into your *cholent* or marinade recipe. This applies to cleansers and shampoos as well. Just add some water and continue using. Shampoo will actually lather more easily and quickly this way.

🐾 Transferring leftover soup from the pot to a container? Take advantage of the fact that soup tends to thicken; empty it into a container, then pour a little water into the pot. Swish it around a bit and add it to the container; you will have transferred every drop. You can do the same with a food processor, after processing vegetables. If you have no immediate use for it, make a note of what it contains and freeze it. Next time you are cooking soup, just pop it in. If the food doesn't loosen from the processor, turn it on for a few seconds.

🐾 A big favorite in our house is "Fake Pickles." Thinly slice some cucumbers into your leftover pickle juice, marinate for an hour or two; less, if you are a real pickle *nosher*. Presto!

Enjoy "Genuine Fake Pickles." To avoid any bug issues, strain the pickle juice or rinse the pickles off before consuming. Unfortunately, we have found that they don't keep their taste or texture for more than about a day in the fridge. Additionally, you can only use the juice once or twice; additional batches didn't pass our quality-control board.

🐾 And still another favorite is hot air popcorn. Put the popcorn into a plastic bag and sprinkle in a bit of oil and salt. Shake the bag and enjoy a tasty, high fiber, low-calorie treat. Then, give all those kernels that didn't pop a second chance. Put them aside until you have popped four or five batches; don't mix them with fresh kernels. You will have enough for another batch of popcorn. Don't worry about the little pieces mixed in with the kernels – the popper will blow them right out. The good news is that this batch is the yummiest, as it is made out of toasty kernels. Sorry, but any kernels still left un-popped are not really worth collecting, as they are somewhat burnt and will not usually yield much.

Is it worth it? You may not save big bucks with such a system, but you can enjoy the good feeling of knowing that you have avoided *bal tashchis*. You may have those special stored crumbs come to the rescue when you are in the middle of a recipe and do not have the specified ingredient. And bottom line, you might even save enough for… for an extra bottle of… dressing, ketchup, or chocolate syrup!

Love Laundry Day

Most of my friends just hate doing laundry. Dealing with all kinds of soiled, malodorous clothing is simply not perceived as **fun.** And what makes matters even worse is the fact that although it can be pushed off a day or two, it is something we just cannot neglect, no matter what. Laundry is always there, never ending. The entire enterprise is just like the inescapable "death and taxes." Is it really possible to turn this distasteful chore into… A bearable burden? A pleasant pastime? A truly gala event? Well, let's not get carried away. Rather, let's see if we can aim for something more tolerable; a system which will allow us to get the laundry quickly done and out of the way **and** be a positive experience.

Start out by developing a perspective that can get you on the road towards a positive attitude. Remind yourself how fortunate you are to have running water, a washing machine, perhaps even a dryer, as well as all kinds of detergents. You do not need to do what your great-great grandmothers did and, actually, as millions of people in other countries are still doing today. Appreciate your preferential situation! Consider as well how fortunate you are to have so much clothing! Are you washing for your family? Be grateful you have one.

As you perform this mostly mindless task called "laundry," you can exercise your "gratitude muscles," listen to a good *shiur* or converse with a friend.

Let's get practical. We would like to have our clothing last as long as possible. Unfortunately, however, laundering shortens the lifespan of clothing! So whenever you can re-use something without washing it, you will prolong its longevity, besides saving yourself a chunk of work. I once saw a very funny poem, about how when one is desperate, one can go through the hamper, pick out a soiled item and put it on backwards, inside out, with a vest or some cover-up. Well, I am not recommending that, but just mentioning it to help us enlarge our horizons and open our minds to consider some less than perfectly-clean ideas. With questionable food, the rule is, when in doubt, throw it out. With laundry, use the opposite tack. When in doubt, wear it again! So, prepare for a paradigm shift; we will lower our expectations from "perfect" to "tolerable" – aka *l'chatchila* to *b'dieved*. No need for commitment, you need not obligate yourself to operate in a "tolerable" mode all the time. Use it when you need to; after a baby, before *Pesach*, while preparing for a *simcha*. No, no; not when your mother-in-law is visiting! Personally, I always have something more important to do than laundry, so "lightening my load" is my usual method of operation.

To do the same, be on the lookout for ways to minimize. Consider bedding. Changing linen weekly is for newlyweds or those with housekeepers! The rest of us can hold out at least two or three weeks, if not a month. If you think you cannot tolerate such an idea, perhaps compromise by washing just the pillow cases, but not the whole set. Incidentally, if you have a set of linen with embroidered or decorated pillowcases, keep an additional pillow with a plain but matching pillowcase underneath. Do not sleep on your fancy pillowcases; you will thereby enjoy their beauty for many more years! If that doesn't work for you, at least invert the pillow to the plain side.

If you have a bed wetter, naturally you will need to wash the linen as soon as possible. Help your child stay dry by giving him fewer fluids and water-based foods such as soups, fruits or vegetables when within two to three hours of bedtime. When putting this child to bed, use a double diaper or a larger diaper. Remember to *daven* that your child matures and outgrows this problem quickly.

Back to laundry. Let's tackle typical cases and focus on the hardest first: our youngsters' clothing. Minimize that by preventing clothing from getting soiled in the first place. Let's start with the following old fashioned, albeit unpopular, advice: BIBS/APRONS! When used regularly and properly, they will save you lots of time on laundry day; no need to elaborate on that! Unfortunately, not all cover-ups are effective. When the clothing is not adequately covered, the only accomplishment is another item to wash. If you are serious about this, you may want to do what a friend of mine did. She went to a seamstress and had bibs custom-made that covered her children's clothing more effectively than the store-bought ones! Sound expensive? Perhaps. But they perform admirably; she recoups her investment in saved laundry detergent, work and durability of clothing. And her daughters always look picture perfect!

Bibs just won't work for you? Take this tip from another friend of mine. When her babies sat down to eat, she simply removed their shirt or dress. Upon completion of the meal, she quickly re-dressed them and they looked great. Contrast that with changing your children into fresh clothes after a meal and putting a lot of stained clothing to soak.

It's certainly true that children seem to eat nonstop and these ideas are a hassle. Bibs get pulled off and you may not feel comfortable with them eating with only an undershirt. If you can pull it off, however, you'll be delighted on laundry day and pleased to give away or pass down the clothes that have stayed in excellent condition. Could be worth it!

Two other habits that can really keep clothing clean are to check for a clean seat before sitting and to lean forward over a plate or table while eating. Although it may take a while to become routine, these relatively simple practices work!

As your children grow and are responsible for some level of neatness in their room, watch out! They will find it much easier to toss clothing into the hamper, than to return them to their closet. A mother I know was preparing a load of wash and saw a bunch of tights. They didn't seem in need of washing at all and actually looked awfully familiar. When questioned, the children admitted – sheepishly, to their credit – that when they found them on the bed, they weren't sure whether they were clean or not, so into the hamper they went!

And how often do girls try on a few outfits before deciding what to wear? Tried-on clothes look a bit rumpled, so into the hamper they go as well. Once in the hamper, they could absorb odors; then they **will** need to be washed. So, instruct your children that clean clothes do NOT go into the hamper.

Inspect your children's clothing as they change into pajamas. Whatever is still passable can be worn the next day or simply returned to the closet/drawer when no one is looking! Freshen any borderline cases by hanging them outside in the fresh air for a few hours before returning them to the closet. As a backup, keep a small hamper in their room that you can frequently check. Bottom line, you need to ensure that clothes stay clean as long as possible and that only soiled clothing gets washed.

The hampers are full, the drawers are empty; we are ready to wash. Although many are successful with throwing in a load whenever the hamper fills up, here is the system that works for me: One day a week – I prefer Sunday – gather the contents of **all** the hampers into one area and begin to sort. Fill one basket with white undergarments only. Since this load will go straight into the dryer after the wash, I do not include tights or slips that I prefer to air dry. The next basket gets all the light-colored shirts, dresses, blouses and tights. Towels, tablecloths, linen and darks can be grouped and laundered as needed. Alternatively, if you have room for a few hampers, save some sorting time. Mark them and train your family to put each item where it belongs.

If you choose to soak shirts and such items, fill the machine, add the soap and select the soak cycle. This can be done the night before or early in the day. After a few hours, end the soak cycle and complete the wash.

I usually launder the dark wash second, hanging the larger items out to dry and holding the wet socks in a separate container. ~>*Warning!* ~> When drying dark clothing outside, hang them inside-out, to minimize any fading effect from the sun. Remember that any additional time spent outside, needlessly increases the chances of clothing fading or falling on the floor. Possible mishaps abound; it could rain, or worse yet, birds or insects may surprise you. Avoid all these mishaps by retrieving the clothing as soon as possible. Don't rely on your memory; use an alarm or timer.

Indoors or out, hang out the clothing as tidy as possible to minimize creases. Fold the pants neatly seam to seam, smoothing out as many wrinkles as you can. Straighten out sleeves and collars.

White underclothes fill the machine next. When this load is finished, you may want to leave them in the machine. Add the wet socks from the dark wash and do an extra spin cycle. This will remove the extra drops of water and shorten the drying time. Either way, all of those items can go into the dryer together. Afterwards, I do the other loads if I have enough to make a full load; otherwise they'll wait. If I really need one of those items, I'll make some type of combination. Later in the week, I will wash more, but NOT socks or underwear; they will wait to join their cohort of like items on Sunday.

Yes; wash (not change!) socks and underwear only once a week. Of course, this means you must have enough changes for an entire week. You probably already do; after all, how do you manage in the nine days and *Chol HaMoed*? If you were skimping or laundering, it really doesn't pay. Once you get all the extra underwear and socks, you'll be set for a longer time. When one of my sons was in *Yeshiva*, he felt bad washing just a few pairs of socks each week; the machine was mostly empty; it was so wasteful. I bought him lots more pairs and he simply washed them all on a monthly basis. Very efficient; saved **him** time and saved **us** laundry money. And he had socks for years.

On the topic of socks, to avoid spending a lot of time pairing them, buy as many as possible with the same pattern. If it is too late for that, supply your sock-wearers with safety pins. Prevent holes in the toe area; instruct your family to pin them elsewhere. Although attractive and neat looking, I find that the plastic sock-lock rings are only good for very thin socks; regular socks cannot dry well around the plastic ring.

Here are some additional tips:

🐾 Try to presoak particularly soiled shirts, either in a tub or in the machine with detergent and/or a laundry booster. When tackling little boys' white shirts that tend to be covered with actual dirt and grime, and any clothing that is soiled in a few areas, presoaking is an easy solution.

🐾 Wash fewer items at a time for cleaner results; try just five shirts at a time, and compare!

🐾 If you are using liquid detergent, put small amounts of it directly on the soiled areas of the clothing and wait a while to start the wash; the soap will get right to work. You can leave it on for hours or days; I have not noticed any damage from the detergent. Remove stubborn food stains with lemon juice or dishwashing soap; simply pour a bit on the spot.

🐾 Use a lower temperature of water, a shorter washing cycle and don't overload the machine; these ideas may help clothing emerge with fewer wrinkles.

🐾 Hanging dirty shirts instead of stuffing them into a hamper, where they will languish for a few days, can cut down on wrinkles as well.

🐾 Put a few at a time into the dryer, preferably with a low temperature for a few minutes; complete the job by hanging them out until totally dry.

🐾 Alternatively, partially air dry, on hooks or hangers, then spin in dryer for a few minutes.

🐾 Either way, when you hang the shirts, even after ironing, take care to hang them properly. Close the top button and straighten out the collar. Center the shoulders on the hanger; make sure each shirt looks as neat as possible. Put the garments in the closet without squashing them. You'll avoid undoing all that you worked so hard to accomplish.

❧ When you cannot remove stains, give the dry cleaner a chance. I was pleasantly surprised when I picked up a lovely tablecloth that I had soaked and laundered but just couldn't get clean. They really renewed it beautifully.

❧ A lot of clothing marked "dry clean only" can be safely machine washed; experiment at your own risk!

When the rest of the laundry is all dry, it's time to fold. It's a bit hard to describe a neat folding-method, but the idea is that when you are done, you have a neat square or rectangle, sized according to your storage area. You should also have one "smooth" side; that is one side where only the last fold shows, no insides or edges or inner folds. This next point may sound obvious, but surprisingly few people do this – at least among those I have hired for housework! Fold everything the same way. Don't ask me why, but people just seem be innovative when folding laundry and towels! Save your creativity for a different project; here simply select one method and be consistent. Finish the task by stacking like items. All of this is, of course, the best way. When you are pressed for time, towels, socks and undergarments can just be tossed into the proper drawer, and no outsiders need be the wiser. As my friend's husband once commented to his wife, "I'd rather have just **my** items in the drawer, albeit in a messy fashion, than everything folded neatly, but not strictly my things!"

Which is part of the next point: The most important step of completing laundry is getting everything back into the proper drawer. Since in a busy household, things tend to not be static, distribute it all as soon as possible. Delays may result in your needing to re-fold, re-sort or worse yet, re-wash!

Here are a few more general laundry tips:

❧ Wet or damp items have no place in a hamper. Left there even just a day or two, mold may appear and you will be hard-pressed to remove it. Hang such items out; it's safe to toss them into the hamper after they have air dried.

🐾 Tip from a drycleaner: The longer you wait to remove stains, the harder it is to remove them. This rule applies to items washed at home as well. So this is one area where you definitely should not procrastinate.

🐾 If you cannot get to a stain quickly, soak the item. Change the water daily until you are ready to wash.

🐾 Remember to empty the dryer's lint filter after each load. ~> **Caution!** ~> Ensure that nothing falls into the filter during this maintenance process. That can break your dryer.

Keep in mind that as with many household tasks, children **can** help; you just have to figure out how to motivate them. If you can make it fun, even your little ones may be willing to help. Toy strollers, shopping carts and other such playthings can make it entertaining for your child to transport clothing to and from the laundry area. At one point in time, my toddler would roll up the paired socks and deliver them to his siblings' rooms via his dump truck! We enjoyed a shared activity and he actually helped me. And who knows? When children are more involved with all that goes into keeping their clothing clean, they just might be more careful with them.

Apply these techniques and you may really find yourself loving laundry day; you'll surely love those empty hampers!

Delight in Doing the Dishes

Unless you eat out all the time or use disposables regularly, washing dishes is a perpetual task. If you have someone performing this chore for you or have a good machine, realize how fortunate you are. It's still worth checking out these tips, even if only to train your children and/or hired help. And as you do, you might realize that it is not such a daunting task.

Although it seems to be a fact that standing at the sink and washing dishes immediately in hot water is the most efficient way to go, I would like to challenge this so-called truism. Friday night, after the *seuda*, I am **done**. The dishes simply must wait for *Shabbos* morning, even though at that point they may be encrusted with dried up food. To make matters worse, we may not use hot water. Much to my delight, I discovered that with the following method, I am able to get them completely clean, with a minimum amount of effort, soap and water. Sounds intriguing? Read on.

Before the first step, here is a real energy-saving idea. Try **sitting** at the sink on a step stool or bar stool. Or stack a few chairs to obtain the proper height. Although it may take a while to accustom yourself to this position, you **can** work at the sink in this manner. Check it out. Your legs will thank you!

Although this first step is not necessary, if you keep the dishes in the sink, the water running over them as you wash your hands or rinse off a fruit or some such item will soften the food residues. ~> *Tip!* ~> It is not necessary to wear gloves, but doing so will not only protect your skin; it will actually make the job a bit easier. Added bonuses: You can easily use very hot water when washing dishes during the week, feels wonderful in cold weather and transfers very easy from meat to dairy dishes. There is no need to carefully wash in between, just switch gloves! Again, it takes getting used to, but it pays.

When you are ready to begin, stack your dishes on the counter, as many as will fit onto your drain board. Prepare a little bowl half-filled with water and add a small squirt of liquid soap; it really doesn't need much. Next, dip your hand into the soapy water and go over the entire surface of each plate, bowl or piece of silverware, with your soapy hand. No need to rub; the soap will do the work for you. Just make sure it remains soapy.

Wait about ten minutes. Not less because the grime will not be softened yet. Not too much more or it will re-harden. You can use the waiting time to soap up glasses, silverware or serving pieces. By the time you are done, the first stack may be ready. Run your hand over the dish to see if it feels dirt free; occasionally re-soaping is required. Now turn on the water and wash off the dishes. Notice how much water was saved? Many leave it running while they soap up the dishes, but that is wasteful. With this method, your dishes will quickly sparkle, even if they were encrusted with congealed foods such as *kugel*s and *cholent*!

If you have a stubborn dish or two, re-soap them; try again after a few minutes. Before attempting to rinse, rub the surface to detach any clinging bits of food. If you cannot tolerate the waiting time, soap up the dirtiest items first and begin rinsing the cleanest items, so that the soap will have maximum time where needed. Usually that means soaping the dinner dishes, followed by the silverware, which can easily be kept in a pot of water overnight; lastly the glasses. Complete the job with a good rinse; first glasses, next the silverware and finally those dishes.

Clean glasses by pouring this much-diluted soap into the first glass; rub it all over inside and out; pour the soapy mixture into the next glass and repeat. Avoid breakage by holding the glass toward the top, with a finger on the rim. If the bottom of the glass has crumbs stuck to it, place it on a soapy plate. Wait a few minutes and rinse off.

If you are not comfortable using just your hands, try a plastic sandwich bag or a piece of the plastic net bags in which onions or potatoes are sold. Ask your *Rav*; I was told that since it is plastic (which doesn't absorb) and not made for that purpose, it is a permissible choice for *Shabbos*. Although you may be so enamored with that free scouring pad you will want to use it daily, it's a good idea to have something stronger for during the week. The type of scrubber made from what looks like springy, shredded steel is especially useful. Cut it into small pieces; each one lasts a long time. You can attach colorful twisters to differentiate between dairy, meat and *pareve*.

To clean pots, pans and baking dishes with baked-on food residues, try this innovative idea. As soon as you have removed as much of the food as possible, cover the pot and store it away; baking pans can be placed in air-tight trash bags. Twenty-four hours later, the bulk of the mess will easily slide out. To remove any remaining mess, the tried-and-true soak method is really effective, but soaping can work as well. If you choose to soak, using boiling hot water will accelerate the process. Burnt-on food? Scrape off as much as possible using a spoon or spatula; throw whatever you can into the trash, not down the drain. Next, soak or soap up. Attend to some other tasks for about a half hour; come back and re-soap. After a five-minute wait, try to scrub, with steel wool or one of those above-referenced foil scrubbers. If the burnt remnants are not easily removed, pour in some undiluted bleach for half an hour or more. ~> **Warning!** ~> If you do not have a high-quality pot, set a timer and just leave the bleach in for a short time or skip it and keep scraping; the bleach may ruin your pot.

~> **Bonus:** ~> While you wash the dishes, you can just think. It's a fact: Our days are so busy with family members, phone calls, MP3's and maybe an occasional book or magazine, we often don't get a chance to actually reflect and consider major or even minor issues. Dishwashing goes very well with thinking – try it!

How about some silverware tips? Here are a few:

🐾 After making a s*imcha* or a large meal, do not throw out your trash until you have counted the silverware.

🐾 When eating out of the house, or bringing food to someone, please use disposables!

🐾 Multi-process. Polishing silver is the perfect mindless task to do while doing anything else not requiring your hands.

~> **Sink tip!** ~> Buy some screening and cut out a small piece to fit into the drain. You'll be surprised when you see how much garbage was going down the drain. Yes, it's great for shower drains as well. Of course, this is not needed if your sink is equipped with a garbage disposal system.

You may be thinking, why bother with dishes and all that washing, at all? Sure, you can save yourself a lot of effort with disposables, but there is an aesthetic difference between china and plastic or paper. The pros and cons are obvious and shall not be belabored here. Just remember to prioritize according to your current needs and always be ready to re-analyze. And as you deliberate, please realize that this choice is a relatively unimportant one. Enjoy your meals and the ambiance, whatever you decide!

If You Can Read, You Can Sew

When I began high school, my family moved to a new community. As we drove around the neighborhood, we passed a fabric/sewing store where an ad caught my eye: "Learn to sew! Six three-hour lessons, only $18." Yes, this was years ago! Even back then, as a teenager, I was of a very practical bend, and begged my parents to enroll me.

"I really want to sew!" I pleaded. "I'll make clothing for myself and for Mommy! I want to learn how!" In our previous house, there had been an old sewing machine in the basement. One day I had sat myself down and somehow created a wearable skirt. I reminded them of this fact, to prove that I wasn't just talking! That assertion clinched it. A little while later, I took the six-day course and made myself a dress. After that, I spent a good part of my free time sewing, creating a variety of clothing for many occasions.

When I became a *kallah*, my mother-in-law *a"h* suggested I make my *chassan* a *kittel*. At first, I was surprised by her suggestion and apprehensive. Upon consideration, however, I wondered if a *kittel* pattern existed. Could I possibly make such a thing without one? I took the plunge and asked my *chassan* to borrow a *kittel* his size from a friend. I bought a flat white sheet and started cutting and sewing. Much to my great surprise and happiness, a *kittel* emerged. And it's still in use!

Clearly, sewing is a great hobby which has so many advantages. It would be wonderful if basic sewing classes would be taught in every school! Until that happens, however, I'll complete my sales pitch and offer a few helpful tips; hopefully you will concur.

BENEFITS OF SEWING:

🐾 Creative outlet: Varieties of things to be sewn are endless. Clothing certainly, but also curtains, toys, pillows, pillowcases, pocketbooks, bibs, potholders. And much more!

🐾 Time well spent. Today, when we have more leisure time than ever, many people do not really have a good way to spend that time; it's often spent shopping. When one can sew, there is **always** something to sew!

🐾 If you are not an easy-to-fit size or just can't find outfits that flatter you, sewing is a life-saver.

🐾 Money saver, and how! Unless you receive hand-me-downs, sewing will save you a lot. If you feel that making an entire outfit is beyond your capabilities, think about repairs and alterations. Most clothing is mended in just a few minutes. Hems, split seams, even holes in tights – these types of fixes are really quick. If you are more ambitious, extend the lifespan of outfits by changing the size and removing or adding trims. Also, many types of gifts suitable for all occasions are surprisingly simple to create.

🐾 Most importantly, dressing modestly is a snap when you sew. You decide on the style, the length, the width, the sleeve, the neckline. It's easy to follow the *halacha.*

How to start? Here is the good news: If you are really interested, there is a wealth of information to be found right on the patterns. In my pre-married years, I once heard a friend's older sister flippantly remark, "If you can read, you can cook!" I was relieved to hear that. I hadn't spent much time in the kitchen growing up and now I didn't have to worry! When I got married, I didn't know a pot from a pan, but her words were firmly engraved in my brain. She was right! I opened recipe books and learned to cook and bake. Thinking about all that I have sewn using regular American patterns, I can conclude that this adage equally applies to sewing. The instruction page that comes with each pattern is very clear and specific, defining each term and showing how each step is accomplished. If you can read, you can sew.

Certainly, as with cooking, professional instruction will aid and facilitate making projects with ease. Without some guidance, the well-illustrated steps may seem confusing and unclear. However, equipped with desire, patience, a superior grade sewing machine and a pair of sharp, high-quality scissors you can get started on easy projects and repairs. Of course, one can sew with a mediocre machine and scissors, but they are harder to work with and may frustrate beginners.

REPAIRS:

- Some patch-ups are very obvious, like a split seam. Just line up the seams and sew, right on top of the old stitching line. While you're at it, sew it again. It will withstand more stress and won't pop open as quickly as one set of stitches.
- Most other repairs need a bit of investigation. Although it may seem obvious, I discovered this precious tidbit from a fix-it man that used to come to my home from time to time for various repairs. He seemed to have magic hands! One time, my baby carriage was broken and I wondered how he would fix it. He took the carriage, studied it, flipped it over and twirled the wheels. I saw what the problem was myself. I marveled at his simple yet brilliant approach. Use this idea for repairs! Study the garment or item, see what is wrong and just try to put it back together. Remember: You can always pull out your stitches if it you aren't happy with the results!
- When you need to **cut**, however, do not be hasty. If you cut in the wrong place, you might have great difficulties in repairing your error. My daughter was adding a piece of material onto a jacket

to lengthen it and asked me for some help. I lined up the piece with the jacket, seam to seam, and saw that it was way too long. Wanting to help her finish quickly, I grabbed the scissors and trimmed it. Whoops! Turned out that in my haste, I had lined up the wrong seams! She had already cut it to size, and was asking a different question. Luckily, we just laughed about it. Since we had extra material, we were able to repair the error and the jacket was successfully lengthened. But don't rely on this happy ending. There isn't always surplus material and even if there is, people do not like to redo their work. Take a minute to verify that you are measuring the right section; then re-measure. Afterwards, you are ready to cut.

🐾 Do you need a bit of material to repair a tear? Check the pocket lining, the hem or a seam. Or perhaps there is a flap of some type and you can cut the material underneath. Alternatively, a bit of contrasting material or ribbon might be the answer. Try to consider all kinds of solutions before giving up and trashing the garment.

🐾 Boys pants with a hole in the knee? You can try a patch, but if that doesn't work for you, don't despair. If your boys are young and you just cannot keep replacing their pants, use the following idea, providing the pants are a bit longer than needed or have a hem to let down. Make a horizontal seam at the knee enclosing the hole and continue the seam all around the width of the pants. Sew a matching seam on the other pant leg, even though it isn't torn. If that doesn't work, the only alternative left may be to turn the pants into shorts!

🐾 Has someone outgrown a jumper or skirt? Found some clothing that is not quite in the height of fashion anymore? It is very possible that with a few minutes of sewing, you can 'downsize' it for a young child. Elastic at the waist, a hem and/or moving buttons can make a hand-me-down suitable for a smaller size; perfect for a less style-conscious "customer."

🐾 Want to lengthen a skirt, but the hem is insufficient? Try the following. Find a nice contrast/matching material. Cut a piece that is as long as the amount you wish to add, plus two inches (5 cm) and as wide as the circumference of the skirt at the hem, plus an inch. Sew it together so that you have a band of material as wide as the skirt. Next, cut off the bottom of the skirt, a few inches above the hem. Use pins or a marker to cut straight. At this point, you may want to finish off all the cut edges with a zigzag stitch. Now simply sew the skirt to one side of the band and the bottom of the skirt to the other side of the band. It may look even nicer than the original version!

🐾 Is the Velcro on a shoe no longer staying closed? Use a fresh piece of Velcro to determine which part is defective and replace it. Cut the new piece of Velcro to size and sew on the replacement. Machine stitches are stronger and it is faster, but your machine may not be able to handle such thick material. If it cannot, simply sew it by hand. Although not absolutely necessary, use a razor blade to remove the malfunctioning Velcro if it will be too bulky otherwise. Simply cut the stitches that attach the Velcro to the shoe.

🐾 When machine-sewing heavy material, don't use the reverse option; the needle is more likely to break when used that way. Rather lift the pressure foot and rotate the material.

🐾 Does someone's jacket no longer stay well on a hook? Probably the small loop on the inside back is torn or missing. Take some type of sturdy ribbon or rickrack and sew on a new loop. Same can be done for the loop on the back of a tie, although you will need to sew it on by hand. Towels falling off their hooks? Get some nice ribbon and sew on little loops.

🐾 Small doll strollers sometimes need refurbishing. Often, the frame stays in serviceable condition, but the dolly's seat becomes torn and unusable. Don't toss the stroller! Simply study the seat and you will see that it is quite easy to replicate and replace. Take a fresh piece of material (old crib sheets with a cute pattern are perfect) and cut it as wide as the stroller, with a length three times the width. Finish off the edges with a serger or sew a zigzag stitch. Next, create loops to slip around the handles. Use a sturdy piece of ribbon about six inches (fifteen cm.) long and fold it in half; sew it onto both corners on the top of this material. On the bottom of the material, fold up a two-inch hem to the inside, but do not sew it all across. Generally, it needs to fit over the two metal extensions, one on each side. Just sew it closed on each side and again about an inch away from the corner you just sewed, creating a casing for the extension. Be extra fancy; fashion a belt to keep dolly safe! Attach two ribbons, about eight to ten inches long on either side, a little more than halfway down. Sew on a third ribbon in the middle of the bottom, with a small one-inch loop at the end of it, for the belt to pass through. Now dolly can be safe and comfortable. Guaranteed fun!

🐾 Are your sheets coming off the mattress regularly? Sew about 6 inches (15 cm) of elastic onto each corner. Stretch the elastic as much as possible and sew it onto the sheet so that the middle of the elastic is attached as closely as possible to the corner of the sheet where there is a seam. Don't bother to remove the old elastic, it is not necessary.

🐾 How about renovating pillowcases? Find a suitable lace or ruffle, or design your own. Stores have a stunning variety of yarns; they can be used as trim. You can turn a simple inexpensive ruffle into a fancy one by sewing the yarn at the edge of the trim and again at the point where it is sewn to the pillowcase. Or make a ruffle! You need three yards of material, a couple of inches wide. You can sew a few smaller pieces together to get this length. Make a small hem along one side. If using trim, sew it on at the same time. Form a ruffle by sewing a zigzag stitch right over a contrast-colored thread all along the edge. Pull the thread, gathering the band of material as you do. Match and pin it to the pillowcase; sew it on along the edge, again over the trim.

🐾 Need to cuff a pair of pants? Study a pair of pants with a cuff and see how it's done; you need to do the same. Here are the directions, but consult those spare cuffed pants to see what is actually needed as you read. First get the correct length; this is most easily done by lining up the pants with a pair of pants that are the proper length. Put a pin through the pant leg, marking the length. Measure three-and-a-half inches under that point; trim off the rest. Finish off the bottom of the leg with a zigzag stitch or serge if possible. Next, fold up a hem to the inside, two and a half inches from the bottom (an inch away from the pin); tack it down all around with pins. Sew it down about a half inch above the first pin, which marked the length of the pants, or about an inch and a half from the fold you just made. Now make the cuff. Fold up the pant leg bottom all around at about one inch from the bottom towards the outside. Finish by sewing a couple of stitches along the side seams, up and down, on each side of the cuff. Voila! Iron the hem and it's done – with a very professional look.

🐾 ~>*Reminder:* ~> Certain materials such as men's pants may get shiny when ironed. Prevent this by placing a thin sheet of material or some ironing cloth on the garment. If you aren't sure whether or not you need such a cloth, check by ironing an interior area or use an ironing cloth just in case. An old worn sheet is good for this purpose or purchase a special guard that attaches to the iron.

🐾 Is your son's long-sleeved shirt frayed or stained at the cuff? Turn it into a short-sleeved shirt by cutting and hemming the sleeve. For professional-looking results, measure the sleeve length against a store-bought shirt. Notice there is usually a one-inch hem; sew yours in the same way.

MISCELLANEOUS TIPS:

🐾 Threading a needle is actually one of the few things in life that is easier than appears, even if you do not see so well. Simply follow these steps: Cut the thread so that no wisps at all remain. Wet the end and hold the thread as close to its tip as possible, leaving about a quarter of an inch (half a centimeter) exposed. With a sewing machine needle, bring the needle to the highest position; lower the pressure foot. It should slide right in within seconds. When sewing by hand, beware. The eye of the needle may simply be too small; it pays to get needles with large eyes. Alternatively, buy self-threading sewing needles or a needle threader.

❧ More on hand sewing: Knotting the thread can be annoying. Sometimes you tie a few knots, yet it just slips through the material anyway. Try this: Leave a bit of the thread hanging out with the first stitch and sew the next two stitches loosely; start tightening with the fourth stitch.

❧ When you finish machine-sewing an item, wait to cut the thread; start the next piece to be sewn right away. After a few stitches, cut the bit of thread that attaches the two. This will save you from having to rethread your machine when it becomes unthreaded due to your having left too short a "tail" of thread. Working on a few repairs concurrently will ease the flow of sewing when using this method.

❧ Tape a small bag to your sewing surface, so you can immediately throw away bits of thread and material. Otherwise, they often land on the floor!

❧ A sharp razor blade, used carefully, is a very useful tool to remove buttons and zippers, open seams or buttonholes and more. ~> *Warning!* ~> Remember to store it in a safe place, as with all sewing supplies.

❧ Filling a bobbin? If it is a frequently-used color, load several while you're at it.

❧ Bobbins and spools getting all jumbled? Take a piece of Styrofoam and cut it to fit a container. Cover the Styrofoam with a piece of material and staple the material onto the bottom. Take some long, small-headed nails, toothpicks or pieces of skewer and push them in, leaving about an inch exposed. Place them far enough from each other so that a bobbin or spool can be placed on each one. Use the in-between areas as a handy pin cushion!

❧ Keep a variety of sewing supplies organized; purchase a clear, over-the-door shoe holder and load the pockets. Neatly displayed and easily accessed.

Can everyone become an expert sewer? Well, not everyone will excel in baking, cooking, organizing or any skill. But everyone **can** learn to perform these tasks on a basic level.

Sewing is a skill truly worth acquiring.

Be the Hostess With the Mostest 👋

Are you planning a s*imcha*? A special *Shabbos*? Guests make it special. Our *simchos* would be pretty *nebby* without them! Maybe some relative or friend would like to join you for a meal, or pops in for just a quick visit to spend some time together. Whatever the hosting situation, bottom line is you would like a pleasant time for all; your visitors as well as yourself.

Here are some guidelines and suggestions, with a caveat. In this realm more than ever, it's very individualized and a lot depends on the depth of your relationship and the sensitivities of the guest. Review these ideas, think about your particular situation and even consult others to try to ensure that all goes well. Good luck in performing a very important *mitzva*, dating back all the way to *Avraham Avinu*.

👋 Start with the proper mindset. Although you may have a variety of reasons for entertaining, remember that it is a *mitzva* and that will enhance your entire viewpoint. A well-known *Rosh Yeshiva* once told a pharmacist, "You are so fortunate to have such a job. Dispensing medication to people, helping them feel better. What a *zechus*!" The surprised pharmacist replied, "I never thought of it that way. Really, it's just my job." But he took the *Rosh Yeshiva*'s insight to heart and took on this new attitude. Little by little, he began observing more and more *mitzvos*. He later attributed his success in life to this paradigm shift.

❧ Is your guest offering to help or bring something? If you are not certain of the sincerity of the offer and can manage without the help, reply graciously that it is not necessary. If the visitor insists or if you are in need, accept graciously. When food or a gift is brought, try to put it to immediate use. If you cannot for some reason, politely explain and apologize. Of course, use your intuition. Sometimes, the less said, the better.

❧ Are you having a few separate guests? Especially if you have invited someone that does not exactly fit in, make sure she has someone to talk to. If you cannot, you may be better off inviting this guest at another time.

❧ There are lots of ways to entertain. Any of them might prove successful. Sometimes it is difficult to predict what your guest will prefer. When in doubt, ask. When you must decide on your own, do your best according to the circumstances. There are times when you can turn your home into a five-star hotel and other times when you can only offer the minimum. ~> **Remember!** ~> Don't let the best be the enemy of the good. If you can do the best, great. But don't be afraid of offering something mediocre when that is all you can do. It may still be much appreciated. Your guest might even feel more comfortable!

❧ Accordingly, if your guest is sleeping in your home, surely you will strive to have the bed made with fresh linen, have a fresh towel, a neat and clean room, space in the closet and a surface such as a dresser or a chair for them to arrange their things. Perhaps some *nosh*, a drink, even fresh flowers. Most guests would certainly be very appreciative of such attention. However, if you cannot provide all of that, it doesn't mean you cannot host a guest! If they really want to come and you are in overload mode (lots of little children in the house, working overtime or tired) your guests may not mind bringing their own linen, making their bed and helping out in small ways. Just know who you are dealing with; relate to them and provide accordingly.

🐾 One of the most important questions to ask when hosting is whether or not your guest suffers from allergies of any type, be it food, pets or plants. See what accommodations are needed and decide whether or not you are capable of providing them.

🐾 Unexpected callers or a short visit? It's always mannerly to offer refreshments. If you cannot find out about any restrictions ahead of time, try to have a variety of foods, so that hopefully, there will be something they can eat. It can be simple; rice cakes, fresh fruits and vegetables or some other basic staples that can accommodate almost anyone.

🐾 When you invite company, try to be clear about what the invitation consists of. For example, if you are inviting someone for *Shabbos*, let them know what is available for them to do in between meals, especially if you plan to nap or have some class to go to. If the invitation is just for *Shabbos* lunch and you do not want to entertain all afternoon, it's best to let your guest know. You can say, "We'd love to have you for lunch, but when we finish I need to take a nap. Will that work for you?" If you can handle more, say, "Would you like to relax or read while I nap? Later on in the afternoon you can join me for a class." This way they know what to expect. I once heard a guest complaining about the meal ending quickly; he felt very unwanted. If the family's routine of speedy meals is delineated ahead of time, it sounds much nicer and the guest can plan accordingly, without feeling driven out.

🐾 On the same note, if your guests will be joining others for a meal or spending time elsewhere, be sure to let them know how to get back in. Provide a key or show them where you have one hidden; explain any quirks. If they need to lock up afterwards, clarify your preferences vis-à-vis the lights and any other information. And do it as soon as they come or you may miss your opportunity!

❧ If you host often, consider writing a friendly house rules list; be sure to leave it in a prominent place in their room.

❧ Do you need to leave the meal in the middle to tend to children or some other pressing matter? Clue in your guest. Years ago, my husband and I were deserted at the *Shabbos* table without any warning, abandoned by our hosts for the greater part of an hour. Newlyweds at the time, we couldn't figure out what had happened! Why not explain before you rush off and offer your guests reading material, along with some snack.

❧ Just as you provide food and accommodations, don't neglect yourself – or your children! Part of preparing for a guest is being well rested and in a good mood. Sometimes this may mean preparing fewer courses or not cleaning to your desired standard, but overdoing it is not worth the cost.

❧ Don't leave the conversation to chance; it needs forethought as well. Even if you know your guests and feel certain that the conversation will flow in a comfortable and *halachically* permissible manner, it is still advisable to take out some insurance. Think ahead; it's always wise to have some *divrei Torah* in your pocket. Kosher current events, anecdotes or anything that has caught your interest lately can also be utilized. Discussing a book or class is usually perfect; just be sure to avoid controversial topics, any kind of criticism and *loshon hora*. Always be prepared to re-route the conversation if necessary.

❧ Never force anyone to eat. Offer once or twice and let them help themselves. People have all kinds of personal preferences and dietary restrictions that they may not want to explain. Excessive offerings may embarrass them.

❧ If your children are not very accustomed to having guests, or you are expecting an unusual individual, prepare them. Review rules, remind them to not stare or ask personal questions. Encourage them to behave their mannerly-best. It would also be wise to mention in a casual way that they should quickly and privately report any disturbing behavior.

❧ As children mature, they may need to be re-educated on

the topic of hosting. Review even common-sense rules. For example, no eating anything without offering guests first. Sometimes there is not enough; wait for another time to enjoy that food, and instead select something that you have in abundance. And so on. Children are impulsive and tend to forget. Friendly reminders before the arrival of guests will save you embarrassing moments.

🖐 Above all, stay calm; remember your goal is to enjoy your guests – and for your guests to enjoy their visit – and leave warm, happy memories. Do your due diligence and leave the rest to *HaShem*. Our job is to be *b'simcha*!

To sum up, take some time to consider your guest's needs and communicate well to make sure everyone is prepared and knows what to expect; stay calm and cool. You'll probably all have a wonderful time. Enjoy your guests and your *mitzva* – and don't forget to leave the welcoming lights on!

Be the Best Guest

It may be a *bar mitzva*, wedding, *Shabbos*, *Yom Tov* meal or maybe even a few-day getaway. At one time or another, we are invited out. *Hachnosas orchim,* hosting guests, encompasses many *mitzvos* and most are incumbent upon the host. Consider, however; a guest is actually enabling her hostess to perform these *mitzvos*. Clearly, without a guest, one cannot host! Just make sure not to overdo or impose more than necessary! So gratitude is in order all around and so are good manners. Here are some tips that can help maximize this delightful opportunity and allow both guest and host to enjoy.

- Most invitations issued are sincere. If you will enjoy going, accept and don't overly analyze.
- Warn your host as early as possible if you have any food restrictions; when they invite you or at least when you accept the invitation, is not too early. As you do so, you may want to offer to decline due to the difficulties involved. Alternatively, let your hostess know that you are not a big eater and limit your eating to your allowed foods; just be aware that some hostesses will get upset with this. There cannot be a hard-and-fast rule, as it depends on so many factors; simply use your best judgment and learn from your previous experiences.
- If you prefer not to accept an invitation, but feel

obligated, try offering a weak excuse and see how that is received. If your hostess asks you to please change your plans and come, you will know that your presence is truly sought. If, however, your pretext is accepted, you can assume that they are willing to manage without you. Please do not write off this friend! On other occasions you may feel differently and she may as well.

🐾 How about if you feel that the hostess really wants you to come, but you definitely do not want to go? If it is to a large gathering, such as a bar mitzva or *sheva brachos*, the best way to handle it may be to tell her that you are not sure you can come, but will try to work it out. Don't be in a rush to decline. When I was younger, I once received a *chasuna* invitation and was certain that I could not attend. Not wanting to push things off, I responded on that day, with a "sorry, cannot attend." I realized afterwards that my response must have been one of the first to arrive. My quick rejection was not very considerate, I understood belatedly. Additionally, you may even change your mind or circumstances will change, so that you decide to participate after all. As long as you respond a week or so before the event, you will have caused no harm. Added advantage – at that point, the hosts are so busy with last-minute details, they will probably not agonize due to your lack of attendance, as they might have with an earlier refusal.

🐾 In a similar vein, a friend of mine was invited to a wedding that she felt she absolutely had to attend. Problem was that attendance involved an expensive and time-consuming trans-Atlantic flight and lots of stress on her husband to run the house while she was away. She told the hostess that she really wanted to come and even made a reservation. On the final day to pay for her ticket, she still didn't know what to do. Surprise! One of her children woke up sick; what a relief! Now she couldn't go. And no hurt feelings were engendered! Although we would not hope for a child to get sick and couldn't arrange it if we wanted to, sometimes things happen at the last minute and we clearly cannot go. Other times, we must use our intuition and "create" such happenings, if that is the best way to maintain *shalom* all around.

🐾 When you do want to accept, let the hostess know as soon as possible. Many *ba'alei simcha* have an added task – and not a very pleasant or easy one – of calling the invitees that didn't respond, for one reason or another. Try to keep out of that group.

🐾 Your host will often be willing to accept assistance. Especially when it's a *simcha*, there is much to do. State your availability, how when and where, and if they pick up on it, fine. Some hosts are a bit more reluctant to accept sweeping offers; being specific has its advantages. Try "Can I make phone calls for you? Pick up or drop off something?" A friend of mine was making a bar mitzva; I offered to bake a cake, which truthfully I was not anxious to do. Perhaps she deduced that (although I hope not!) but her response was music to my ears. "I really do not need any more cake, but could you help me find accommodations for my guests?" That was a cinch for me and I found her some apartments. There is almost always some way of helping out, you merely need to find it! And even if the people making the *simcha* do not accept, they are bound to appreciate your thoughtfulness.

🐾 Helping in the house, especially in the kitchen? Don't make any assumptions; your guess may cause them much aggravation. Ask before moving things, plugging in chargers or other such items, placing food on counters or in refrigerators, using appliances or washing dishes.

🐾 Clarify exactly what the invitation encompasses, especially if it is for more than a few hours. Even more so if it is for a few days. Does the invitation include all meals? Will they provide a bed, a private room or apartment? Will they expect you to entertain yourself between meals or are they counting on you to join them in some venue? Will you be given a key or do you need to plan your schedule around theirs? Don't assume; ask and you'll be prepared.

🐾 If you are invited to their home, try to come on time or just a few minutes late. Avoid coming early, since they may not be ready and could be embarrassed. If a specific time was not confirmed, it's considerate to call about an hour before your arrival.

🐾 Rather than surprising your host with chocolates (they may be diabetic or health conscious) or wine (may not be the flavor they like) or flowers (for sure not a great idea if you are coming close to *Shabbos*!) see if you can bring them something they will really appreciate. Just ask!

🐾 If you **do** bring flowers *erev Shabbos*, be sure to offer to arrange them in a vase; your hostess may not have time.

🐾 Is there a host you visit often? They deserve more than occasional flowers or cake. Reciprocate by inviting them out to eat, shopping for them, hosting their children. Perhaps you noticed an area of need in which you have some expertise; show *hakaras hatov*, and help them out.

🐾 Can you easily bring your own bed linens? Offer to do so; your hostess may accept!

🐾 Prepare a list before packing; if you are a frequent guest, you will use it again and again. My niece added this clever idea: Hold onto that list and consult it when re-packing at the end of your visit. Hopefully you will return home with all your possessions!

🐾 Do you plan to shower at your host's home? Ask first; you do not know her schedule, and it may be very difficult for her to squeeze you in. Thus informed, you and your host can plan accordingly. On two occasions, when I was a guest using someone's apartment, I did not follow this rule. I could not figure out how to get hot water; a very unpleasant situation, to say the least.

🐾 Is your style of clothing in variance with that of your host? Avoid embarrassing them. Show your appreciation and respect by complying with **their** dress code. If you just can't, it would be in good taste to ascertain that they are aware and don't mind.

🐾 In a self-serve situation, start with a small portion. There may not be a sufficient supply or you may not care for the way it is prepared. Taking less than you normally would, will alleviate either circumstance. After the dish has circulated, you can always take seconds while complimenting the cook!

🐾 Don't monopolize the conversation. When there are children present, do not assume that any given topic is safe. You can't be too careful in this area; err on the side of caution.

🐾 Do not discipline your host's children or ask them to do anything for you, other than minor requests, without your host's permission. It may take a lot of self-control, but that's life. If you witness truly alarming behavior, speak to the parent privately or check with a *Rav*.

🐾 It's always nice to bring something for the children, but again – obtain clearance from your host. People often have all kinds of ideas as to what their children should and shouldn't eat, read, play with and so forth; don't risk creating problems.

🐾 Consider very carefully before criticizing in any way. For many, even an "I just want to understand…" or "I'm just curious…" or "Why don't you…" can come across as a condemnation. Unless it is a matter of utmost importance or *halachic* observance, you are probably best-off refraining from such comments – especially if you anticipate future invitations. Re-invites not coming your way? Discuss it with a friend, be prepared to change.

Although thank-you notes are mostly out of style, they are a delight to receive; of course, even a phone call is always appreciated. Mention something specific that the host said or did, especially if an extra effort was involved. Sometimes you may be hosted by someone that you do not really know, such as when your friend finds an apartment for you to use. In such situations, expression of gratitude goes to both your hosts. Perhaps the most important aspect of gratitude is making sure to leave everything as you found it! Do your best, and you will be a sought-after guest!

Moving Day

It was a day I was eagerly anticipating. And dreading. The excitement of moving to a new home and all the changes and adjustments that come along with it, was permeating our family. In our case, we were buying an apartment in *Eretz Yisroel* for the first and hopefully last time, which made the whole experience all the more thrilling. But that doesn't mean that it was all smooth sailing. Friends reminded me that the privilege to live in *Eretz Yisroel* is only earned through enduring afflictions. Considering what people have gone through in the past, my trials were really a piece of cake…

For various reasons beyond our control, we were unable to set a moving day until the last minute. We were not even sure if we would be able to move into our new apartment when it would become available, due to problems in breaking our current lease. We didn't know whether to pack, find a temporary dwelling or what. Our new apartment would be available on a Tuesday, but as late as two weeks prior to that date, we still didn't know when we would have the *zechus* to move in!

Monday, eight days before our new apartment was to become available, an agent called to tell us that the landlord had accepted a new tenant, who wanted us out as soon as possible… could we move by Thursday? We went into high gear to complete our packing, throwing things randomly into cartons, just trying to get everything packed. Unfortunately, the moving company could not move us on Thursday, yet we had to be out; we were stuck with an *erev Shabbos* moving day. The only *gam zu l'tova* I can make of that nearly fatal error is that now I can let everyone learn from our hardship. **Do whatever you can to avoid moving on *erev Shabbos*!**

The mover arrived bright and early on Friday; he assured us that we would be done by 1:00. Perhaps he would have been had we handled things differently. Not only was the move completed quite a bit later, but when the movers walked out, our precious possessions were strewn throughout the new apartment, almost without rhyme or reason. The following week we spent an inordinate amount of time reorganizing before we could begin to unpack. Here are some tips to avoid all the problems we experienced.

🐾 Obviously, the more you organize before the move, the easier it will be. Writing "bedroom #2" in small letters on your boxes will probably not be noticed or understood, since many workers are foreigners and cannot easily read your notations. Instead, color-code your boxes: Use large colorful stickers, markers or crayons or tape/glue a large colored swatch on each box. You may even want to do more than one side – if you have little children, this is a great job for them! Put a matching color patch on the door or entrance of the intended room, *daven* a lot and you will greatly increase your chances of getting your belongings to the desired locations.

🐾 If you have storage or wardrobe closets, ask the mover to put your dismantled closets into the truck last, on the first trip if there is more than one. That way, they will be the first objects unloaded. If your carpenter is ready and waiting for them, he may be able to assemble them before the room becomes overcrowded. Generally speaking, closets are first assembled on the floor and then placed up against the wall; much floor space is required. Similarly, plan for dressers and other storage units, to be among the first unloaded items. If you are moving perishable food, your refrigerator should also be among the first items unloaded. Don't expect the mover to figure out what you need!

❦ Using suitcases or specially marked boxes, pack clothing and other essentials needed for the first few days. It may be more hectic than you anticipated and you may not be able to unpack everyone's possessions immediately.

❦ For the most part, the less time the actual move takes, the better off you will be. Ask your mover how many workers he intends to bring and request that he bring an additional one. Ideally there should be at least four. If he charges you more, it's worth paying. Don't forget, the longer they work, the more he may charge you and certainly the bigger a tip they will expect. You may also want to offer them a set amount as a tip for finishing in a reasonable, but shorter than projected amount of time. This scheme will most probably not cost you additional expense and you'll be done with the move that much sooner.

❦ Have cold drinks, cups and some snacks available for the workers. They really do work hard and will appreciate your kindness.

❦ If you can, prepare some meals ahead of time. It may take a few days or even weeks until you can start cooking again. We subsisted on microwaved potatoes for quite a while, as well as cereal and milk, sandwiches, fresh fruits and vegetables. Perhaps if you pack your kitchen in an extremely organized way you will avoid this, but don't forget: life is always full of surprises!

Will everything go smoothly if you plan enough? *HaShem* reminds us from time to time that He is running the world. If anything goes wrong, remember it's a message from Him, and make the best of it. If you have done all of your proper *hishtadlus*, you'll be able to say *gam zu l'tova* more easily.

Wishing you *hatzlacha* in your new home!

Re: References

Your child recently told you that it is time for a *shidduch*. You experience elation, anticipation, excitement... and dread. Will suggestions come through? How can you get information? How are you to analyze it? Once you have determined which characteristics are best for your precious son or daughter, how can you be assured that the prospective match has them?

First, remember that it is all with *HaShem*'s *hashgacha*. I once heard at a *shiur* that we use the term *bashert,* preordained, so often with a *shidduch* because there is so much *hashgacha* involved. Stories abound of people that had crucial information, but weren't home, didn't hear your question clearly or forgot to mention something... Sometimes valuable information is garnered just by "chance." You mention a name to a friend just in a "by the way" manner or to inquire about some minor aspect. It turns out that she knows **everything** about them! You see that a Hand from above is guiding the entire process. Keeping that idea in mind, we still must do our *hishtadlus*. *Hishtadlus* requires us to make calls, ask questions and, with *siyata dishmaya*, make choices.

Let's start with a general reminder for any reference giver ("referencee"): Check with a *Rav* if you are unsure about what you may say, what you must say and what should not be said.

If you get a call and are unprepared, the tried but true, "I would love to help you, but I am running late for an appointment. May I return your call?" can be employed. Soon as possible, be sure to speak to your *Rav* and clarify the *halacha* as it applies in this case. Highly recommended: The *sefer, Chofetz Chaim, A Daily Companion,* with a section on *shidduchim* included at the end. Thus armed, promptly return the call.

But why wait for the call? If you know of someone close to you with a marriageable age child, prepare yourself. My daughter's teacher imparted some very clever advice at the end of high school. She pointed out that in all likelihood, they would get calls about classmates. Take the time now, she advised the girls, to write down a few nice comments about each girl. That way, when you get **the** call, you are ready. Sure, if your classmate is a great girl, no preparation is needed. You can easily sing her praises. But if she isn't… stammering, stuttering, telling the caller that you are about to jump into the shower and you'll return her call may be your only options. When prepared, you can happily and graciously say, as you open your notebook, "That girl? Oh yes, a very nice classmate. She wasn't my best friend, but…" by then you are on the right page and can naturally recite what you have written. We can all use this excellent idea. Do your *mechutonim* have children in *shidduchim*? Your neighbors? Your siblings? Be ready for that call.

Back to the information seeker. I'll start with this warning: If you do not organize yourself, you are headed for a lot of unnecessary work. And more. Be kind to yourself, it's a big enough task as it is. Get a notebook and take notes as you call people to check out a *shidduch* suggestion; after a few such interviews you may no longer remember who said what. Moreover, you may want to rethink your decision a few days or even months or years after making it; your notes will save you a lot of time and embarrassing phone calls! You may also want to clarify a remark made by a referencee; nearly impossible unless you noted who said what. On the subject of notebooks, may I fast forward briefly to the culmination of all these inquiries? When you meet with your *mechutonim* for the first time, before the *vort*, come equipped with a notebook to record clearly who commits to what. That will help avoid all types of disagreements and misunderstandings!

Keep in mind as you begin all of these inquiries, some **do** go overboard, asking about relatively unimportant matters; this can prevent them from finding **anyone** for their dear child, thereby prolonging their child's search. *Talking Tachlis*, by Rosie Einhorn and Sherry Zimmerman, recommends selecting five priorities, no more. Check it out; this book contains an overabundance of guidance.

Although you may ask many questions in order to form an image, don't get caught up in trivialities. A woman that I didn't know (and I am quite sure I was not given as a reference!) called me to inquire about a *bachur*, in his mid twenties. I would guess that she had already been seeking a match her daughter for a few years. After a few general questions, she asked, "Who wears the pants in that family? Who makes the decisions?" Considering she was a total stranger, calling me about my friend, I thought it was a very inappropriate question. (No, I did not tell my friend about the call!) It could be that my friend is a bit on the opinionated side, but do I know who makes the decisions? Would I tell a stranger? Should she write off all boys from homes where the mother makes decisions? Make a list of what is **really** important to you and concentrate on finding a candidate that fits your criteria. Remember that no one has it all! And shouldn't we leave room for *davening* and *HaShem*'s guidance?

On the other hand, to make no inquiries at all and say, "let them meet each other and decide," is unfair to all concerned. Minimally, make a few calls and see if in general the couple can be compatible. If you refuse to do even that, at least do not complain about the inappropriate people your child is meeting. (I actually heard this comment from such a parent!) If you do feel that the suggestions coming your way are clearly unsuitable, be brave and speak to a *Rav* or mentor who knows you well. It may be time for a reality check.

~> **Beware!** ~> Do not make the mistake of deciding based on reported personality. Every two people interact differently. Many individuals are quiet in one set of circumstances, but not in others. There are countless stories of happy couples that don't seem to have matching personalities. Just think of people you have met over the years and perhaps wondered how they get along, yet they do amazingly well. *Hashkafos*, *middos*, goals, attitudes and desired lifestyle are the real areas that need to be researched. It's of utmost importance to verify that there exists strong common ground. If that is in place, let them meet and decide the rest on their own.

Let's revert. The best referencees are clearly people who are close to you and will feel compelled to tell you if there are any problems or such; that is, to give you "real information." If you have access to such people, by all means call them. In any event, the *shadchan* should furnish you with a list of friends, neighbors, *Rabbonim*, *mechutonim*... Although generally speaking, this group will be looking out for "their side," you can still get information, especially by asking specific questions.

~> **Caution!** ~> Phrase all questions carefully and politely; it's worthwhile to work out the wording and write it down. Often these inquiries are to people we do not know, who are close to the other side. We have to realize that their loyalties are to their friends, not to us; total strangers. We also must recognize that although our intentions are good, our questions may be considered offensive to some. Also, we cannot expect people to reveal private details of their good friends. So consider carefully before plunging in.

When calling a referencee, start out by requesting complete confidentiality. I have heard stories of referencees telling the prospective match all about the phone calls they received and the questions they were asked. They may be doing this out of a desire to cheer the person and to hearten them. Letting people know that inquiries are being made can be a kind and encouraging thing to do; it's revealing the detail of the conversation that is probably *ossur*. Bear in mind that your request may not be honored, but it doesn't hurt to try.

If you are having trouble obtaining referencees you truly trust, try some of these ideas:

🖐 As you speak to the referencees given by the *shadchan*, they can generate more names. Request the name of the candidate's closest friend, mentor, roommate, co-worker, most influential teacher or *Rav*. They may be worth a call.

🖐 If you know someone in the city they live/d in, give that person a call; they may be willing to research for you or provide you with additional sources.

🖐 Ask the *shadchan* if the family has any friends in a city you used to live in or where you have a lot of connections. I was once checking out a *bachur* and couldn't find any friends of mine who knew his family. Turns out (we found out only after the engagement!) that they are very close with a family who lives in the city we used to live in; friends of ours! The right question would have yielded us that information.

🖐 Find out if the seminary/*yeshiva*/school they attended has/had any students from your neighborhood; if so, you have another source.

Once you contacted a referencee, let them speak; usually, whatever they say first has the most significance. Of course, it may be most significant to the referencee, but not a reflection of your target, so as with all information, try to keep it in perspective.

If they give that frustrating response of "ask me questions," you must ask about the things that are important to you. It may be a hint that there is some problem in the family that they will only reveal if a direct question is asked, so be specific. As an example, I heard that some *Rabbonim* say that one should not reveal that a *bachur* smokes, unless asked that specific question. We need to remember, "Buyer, beware!"

To my mind, one of the most important questions is, "Does he have a *Rav* he is close to and takes guidance from?" If he does, check it out. Call the *Rav* and ask point blank when this *bachur* called last and if he takes *hadracha* from him. I know of a *bachur* who was having a difficult time in *shidduchim*. Since I was somewhat involved, I called his *Rav* and asked him why this *bachur* was so stubborn about certain relatively unimportant issues. The *Rav* told me, "I have spoken with him many times, but he is just holding steadfastly to his list!" Did the *bachur* have a *Rav* he was close with? Yes. But. Each person can draw their own conclusions, but I prefer a *bachur* that **follows** the *hadracha* of his *Rebbi*. That training of oneself to follow *Da'as Torah* can be very important if there are problems in the future, *chas v'shalom*. You would never know unless you make the specific inquiry. Having said that, it would be misleading to omit the end of the story. That *bachur* married a wonderful young lady and they appear to be very happily married. So there are no hard and fast rules, we can just do our best and *daven* for *HaShem*'s guidance.

For girls, their mode of dress says a lot about them. If you agree, ask very specific questions. Since this is a matter of *halacha* and *hashkafa*, you may want to work hard on getting a good feel for this. Of course, you can and will inquire about her behavior, friends and grades, but beware of a lot of exaggeration! How she dresses and comports herself is of a more factual nature.

How about your side? You will have to furnish references for your family and your child.

Here are some pointers:

✋ Ask your intended referencee for permission to offer her name. You may feel awkward, but you'll thereby avoid many of the problems cited here. If necessary, coach them. When people are not expecting a phone call, they can give answers that do not reflect well on your child. I have heard some that made me cringe. From a sister-in-law: "My husband and I do not give references for our siblings." What is that? A poor reflection on someone, you can decide whom! At least declare, "My sister-in-law? She is a wonderful girl! So helpful! Smart! Great *baalabusta!*" Have a few such words prepared and end with, "I really can't say more; for personal reasons we do not give references…" Not great either, in my opinion, but better than a flat "No references!" From a teacher: "I don't really know her, why don't you call the principal." Oy! Why did this family give such a referencee, without calling first and ascertaining they would get a rave review? And how can a teacher of seminary-age girls give an answer like that? Sorry to overburden anyone, but if you are involved with single young men and women, it would be a great *chessed* to keep a record or note of something nice to say. Although these are extreme examples, they did happen!

❧ Do you have married children? Warn them as well. Could be they do not know how to handle such calls, yet may get them whether you list them as references or not. Prepare them; elaborate on the good points of your child and family and see if they have any questions. One girl asked her mother-in-law, "but he eats chicken with his hands. Do I mention it?" "Lots of people do. Why talk about it, unless you get a specific question?" answered the mother-in-law. Explaining what should be emphasized and what needn't be mentioned will make them excellent referencees.

❧ On the topic of coaching others, it's a good idea to let people know that your child is in *shidduchim.* Including, but not limited to, all your family members (*mechutonim*, daughters/sons-in-law) and some neighbors, even though you didn't list them. If you need to, spell it out. You would like them to be prepared for **the** phone call. No misrepresentation is being suggested; the fact is that if people are alerted and can organize their thoughts, they can think of some good things to say. If they are caught off guard and you haven't returned the sugar, eggs, milk and books you borrowed from them, you may be heading for trouble. Of course, you may not want to tell everyone; the choice is yours. Just be aware that people's feelings about you can subconsciously, for the positive or negative, affect how they respond. If there are people with whom you have unresolved issues, think about this seriously. For this and other reasons, take this opportunity to make *shalom*. ~> **Bonus!** ~> Once you let them know, they may have a name to suggest!

Additionally, don't forget this crucial point: Determine what your child is looking for and what he needs. Don't be afraid to offer *hadracha* and encouragement; but don't be aggressive. Avoid pushing your agenda. They have to live with the choice, not you! Getting married is a big step. Talking about marriage, good communication techniques and responsibilities are all part of preparing your child. Yes, it is a fine line, but that is life. Make sure they realize the consequences of what they think they want. Consult with your mentor, a *mechanech* close with the candidate or whoever you feel can help you; determine what lifestyle really makes sense. Once you determine the requirements and desires, let those be the focus of your inquiries.

Bear in mind as well, when researching, that you and your family may have your own "skeletons"; don't be quick to reject a prospect. Someone took the time and trouble to make a suggestion, meaning they thought it had merit. Take an honest look at your child and family, and be realistic. If you have been looking for more than a couple of years, and/or reach the stage where your child's friends are all getting married while yours hasn't found the right one yet, it's time to re-evaluate.

~> **Beware!** ~> As we check out prospects, different "negative" pieces of information surface that may initially disinterest you. Many *shidduchim* are rejected due to non-essential factors, and young people suffer from Delayed *Shidduch* Syndrome. Focus on the candidate – we never really know how their family and upbringing impacted on them. We have all heard of children who follow their nurturing to a "Tee" and others who blazed a totally different path for themselves. Automatic rejections due to age, locale of upbringing and even height can also be unnecessarily limiting.

I once saw a *shidduch* application from the organization *L'Chaim*. One question read, "Tell us about this person. Make the candidate come alive!" I like to ask for anecdotes. When someone tells me, "This girl shows up at each friend's *chasuna* with an updated class list!" or "One day, just by chance, I saw her on the bus with her nieces; I was so impressed by the way she handled them," I feel that I have gained an insight into the uniqueness of this girl.

On the other hand, as in many issues, people have different feelings even on this type of question, so it's an individual decision. I found myself in hot water once when inquiring about a girl. A referencee told me how fantastic the girl was, but I couldn't discern whether or not she was suitable for my son. When I asked for an anecdote, some telling story about the girl, my source became quite agitated and said, "I will not reduce this wonderful girl to a story! I told you, she is just great!" I apologized and got off the phone, no closer to knowing if she was suitable for my son or what differentiated her from many other girls. I couldn't even understand what had upset this referencee, but re-learned, "different strokes for different folks!"

And lastly, how about a big thank you to the *shadchan*? Of course, you will pay her if the match goes through, but if it doesn't, don't neglect her. She thought of you and she tried. She may have spent hours on your child.

By speaking to acquaintances and relatives with married children, you can gain a lot of understanding and perspective and thereby do your best in this quagmire called *shidduchim*. When I am stuck, I almost always gain some insight through such consultation.

And *daven*. May we soon wish you *Mazal Tov*!

Simcha Savings

Mazal Tov! Whether it is your first *bar mitzva* or your third *chasuna*, you want it to be special. But what makes a *simcha* special? Arousing jealousy of others? Going into debt? Driving yourself crazy, agonizing over each detail, demanding perfection? A non-Jewish painter once shared this beautiful story at the *shiva* house of a *Rav*. "I showed up one morning to paint this Rabbi's apartment. The first thing he did was made sure I had some breakfast. That was unusual enough, but I will never forget what he said next. 'Listen,' this Rabbi told me. 'You can't do a perfect job, because only G-d is perfect. Do a good job, the best you can.'" As we try to prepare for our *simcha*, let's keep that in mind. Let's focus our time and energy on making sure our guests will enjoy and the couple – or *bar mitzva* boy – will continue to grow in their *avodas HaShem*.

Is it possible to have a beautiful *simcha* and stay within a budget? Some may say, "It's a one-time event, it will throw our finances out of whack no matter what, so why get nervous looking for relatively minor savings?" Well, actually, the savings can be rather major. Of course, you need to know yourself and your family – and in the case of a *chasuna*, your *mechutonim* – **and** your true budget to decide this. Here are some cost saving ideas that you may be able to sneak in regardless; *Mazal Tov* and enjoy your *simcha*!

🐾 Get a notebook! And get to work. Professionals are booked well in advance; the longer you wait, the more limited your choices will be. Although you may be floating on air, land quickly – before you crash! And get those reservations in as soon as possible. If you delay, you may be forced into a more expensive alternative, due to lack of choice.

🐾 Start with an estimated guest count. First, write down everyone you can think of. Go through your phone book and consult with close friends, neighbors and relatives. Ensure you haven't forgotten anyone. Don't forget those in the lonely crowd, who seem to live for attending *simchos*; invitations mean so much to them.

🐾 Now review your list, paring it down if necessary. *B"H* it has become quite common to invite people only for the *chuppa* or *Simchas Chassan V'Kallah*. Of course, the cost of this method must be determined as well; depending on your caterer and guest list, it may actually cost you more to do this. That fact surprised us, but when you invite a lot of people for "just dancing," it is still customary to serve cake and even some food. Although cheaper than an entire meal, many more portions are needed; it can add up to a significant amount. Analyze all the numbers and needs, and proceed accordingly. Since you are making a decision based on information, you'll hopefully avoid surprises.

🐾 Your choice of location will be restricted, depending on the size of the anticipated attendance. Some halls have a minimum; all halls have a maximum. Once you clarify your needs, start calling: halls, musicians, photographers, caterers. Write down all relevant information. Minimum charges, extra charges, number of waiters provided, cut off dates, time and method of payment are some of the details to collect. Once you have gone through the time and trouble of phoning, may as well write it all down, even if you are fairly certain that you will not use this provider. Plans change and input comes from many sources; you may have to reassess. You'll be glad to have notes to refer back to.

🐾 When you finalize with the hall and caterer, try to ensure that everything is all spelled out. Menus, quantities, times, leftovers, cost for additional servings; try to be very clear about each point.

🐾 Gifts for *chassan* and *kallah* are standard – and they are not. I have heard of *chassanim* that requested more *sefarim* in lieu of a fancy watch, and *kallahs* that ask for a high-quality appliance instead of a bracelet. So before you buy, it pays to ask. If you are on a strict budget, be honest with your *mechutonim*. Offer them the choice of spending the same amount or some other plan. Consult and compare; you will see that there is quite a range in the bottom line.

🐾 Will the *kallah* be happy with a cubic zirconium? Although there is an obvious difference between bracelets costing a couple of hundred dollars and those costing thousands, only an expert can differentiate between a real diamond and an imitation. Why not save big time with this purchase? One *kallah* I know had heard so many stories about lost rings, she insisted on getting an imitation. And has never regretted it. Incidentally, there are diamonds and there are diamonds – imperfect ones can sometimes look lovely in a nice setting. In any event, if your *kallah* is clever enough to want to economize here, let your *mechutonim* know as soon as possible. Hopefully they will be delighted. If not, they can always shower their wonderful *kallah* with more jewelry or gifts in the future.

🐾 Although discussing dollars and cents is not pleasant, it's unavoidable. Bite the bullet; work it out beforehand and avoid problems and bad feelings afterwards. A young couple called me when they heard that my daughter became engaged. Turns out that each side had bought expensive quilts and pillowcases, so they were offering a set to me, at a reduced price. Another couple I know found themselves without some basic appliances. Avoid such scenarios by clearly defining the shopping list and spelling out who will actually purchase what. How everything is to be financed should also be discussed as soon as possible. In one innovative solution, both parents deposited all the money they were planning to spend for the *simcha* – gifts, *chasuna*, gowns, apartment needs – in a joint account, and gave it to the young couple. "Go ahead, spend as you see fit. Whatever remains is yours. If you are short, you'll need to economize somewhere." Hopefully the parents were there for consultation! This method allowed the young couple to decide where they preferred to spend and where to save. Such a plan could be a blessing or source of much conflict; consider it only if the couple is very mature and sincere.

🐾 That being said, try to stay calm and enjoy the time spent shopping and preparing. It can easily turn into arguments and worse. If you see yourself heading toward stormy seas, take a break. Announce that whatever decision you are grappling with will wait; call for guidance as soon as possible. A *Rebbetzin* or friend with many married children may be able to rescue your situation. Look upon this entire adventure as an honors course in "thinking before speaking." If you pass, you will be all set for your new role as mother-in-law. Needless to say, a sense of humor will come in very handy as well.

🐾 Try this innovative plan and you will save a lot of time on seating, avoid hurt feelings ("Why did she seat me here?") and save money as well. Did you know that about one out of ten people who respond positively to your *seuda* invitation will not actually attend? Ask the caterer. Problem is, you do not know in advance who these no-shows will be. Generally, there are three categories of guests: relatives, friends of the family and friends of the *chassan/kallah*/bar mitzva boy. Let's say you have thirty relatives; write on each of their cards, "You are seated at table 1, 2 or 3." That way seating is not totally open, but not totally rigid either. I have found this bit of freedom to work out very well. At one *simcha* a relative asked me, "Did you do this because you knew I will not sit with my mother-in-law?" No, I hadn't. But she was thrilled. Here is how this system also saves money. Statistically speaking, only 27 of the 30 relatives will come. So simply set nine seats to a table. The advantage with this scheme is that you are spreading out your estimate. The entire explanation is a bit complicated, but if you analyze it, you will see that this system hedges your bet. You may want to ask one good friend to help make sure everyone has a seat, and to be on the lookout if it is necessary to move a chair and setting. With this system in place you can safely order ten percent fewer meals.

🖐 Wondering where to find clothing for all the girls? A dress for the *kallah* and other relatives? Special candles for bringing the *chassan/kallah* to the *chuppa*? *Benchers*? Emergency items package? All these and more are available in *gemachs* in many communities. Some charge a small amount, others are free. ~> ***Note*** ~> If yours is missing one of these chessed organizations, think about starting one!

🖐 Anticipating many young children? Bring some toys, books, and games. Help them coordinate to hire a babysitter. Yes, this is an expense, but might save your peace of mind and more! So it is a good investment.

🖐 Make an arrangement for gift deposit. Many *simchos* have had a 'puncture' when the gifts disappeared, were clearly stolen or forgotten. In one believe-it-or-not episode, one of the *mechutonim* supposedly made off with all the cash and checks! Check out the hall, see if they have a safe – if so, get the key and assign a trusted, responsible friend to be in charge. Forewarned is forearmed!

How to finance everything? If you have kind and generous relatives or friends, or money squirreled away, lucky you. Otherwise you will need to borrow and/or take advantage of *gemachim*. The best counsel is to start saving early on and keep expenses within your means. This may entail a *vort* in your house, a *chasuna* in a *shul*, small guest list; there are many economizing opportunities.

Will people be upset with a simpler, smaller *chasuna*? I hope not. I would trust that guests who are true friends go for the purpose of sharing in a *simcha*, and do not really care about how fancy the hall or food is; they are genuinely coming to celebrate with the *chassan* and *kallah*. As these ideas begin to germinate, will people get offended upon not receiving an invitation from every distant relative and casual acquaintance? Perhaps some will – and perhaps, as we scrutinize our guest list, those are not the people to eliminate! The bulk of a typical guest list consists of people that get many invitations. After getting used to the idea, I trust they will begin to appreciate the precious savings.

Yes, they will not need a babysitter, may decide to forgo a gift or bring a small one, and won't need to spend so much on the various accoutrements of *chasuna*-going. But more than that, they will regain their time. Evenings with family and learning programs can now be salvaged. After all, that is a big part of the cost of attending all these *simchos*. As this idea hopefully snowballs, people will realize that the hosts are simply doing the right thing in cutting down; everyone will enjoy the smaller, simpler and more intimate *simchos* they **do** attend that much more.

~> ***Special request!*** ~> Although not an economy issue strictly speaking, **please** ensure that the band will not blast out their music. Not only does it preclude conversation, loud noise actually causes PERMANENT hearing damage. You may want to put this request in writing in the musicians' contract, offer a bonus for cooperation or predetermine an enforcement method. Until this idea becomes more popular, there is some resistance to overcome, but truly much is at stake!

Last but not least, keep *davening* for *HaShem's* help. And again, *Mazal Tov*!

Grandparenting — Make it Grand!

Many of us are either grandchildren or grandparents during different stages of our lives. As with any relationship, there are expectations, wishes and hopes. What is *l'chatchila*? What is reality? Where do the responsibilities and obligations belong? How can we make the most of these potentially powerful bonds?

The Torah (*Devarim* 32:7) tells us, "Ask your father and he will tell you; your elders and they will say." The *Gemara* teaches that when a grandfather learns with his grandson, it is as if the grandson is receiving the Torah from *Har Sinai*. Rabbi Avigdor Miller felt so strongly about the positive influence that grandparents can exert that he spoke out against young couples going to live in *Eretz Yisroel*, away from their families!

We know that throughout the ages grandparents have played strong roles in families, whether they lived together or through visits and letters. Although in many cases, they were not able to provide financial support, they were **there**. There with an extra pair of hands, to proffer valuable advice, to comfort and to tell stories. Many lucky people treasure memories of grandparents and all the love, help and *hadracha* they received from them.

Today, that role has changed in some families. Perhaps because grandparents are younger; many are still occupied with jobs and other activities. Some are even raising younger children. Others have the time, but do not seem to have the same needs and interests that previous generations had; involvement with their grandchildren is not an over-riding concern for them. They have their exercise classes, study groups, hobbies and vacations; their lives are full. A quick gift or phone call may be all their grandchildren are getting. It's simply not like the "good old days" when grandparents didn't have many entertainment opportunities, and family was their life.

Correspondingly, grandchildren may not be exhibiting the same level of interest in spending time with their grandparents as did their counterparts of long ago. As they mature from adorable, easy-to-please babies to young children, they too become part of this new world of entertainment and comfort. As in all relationships, each side's behavior affects the response of the second side. A grandparent calls or visits and the grandchildren are busy. The grandchildren show their projects and special treasures to their grandparents who give it a quick look and put it aside. Little by little the relationship can deteriorate.

Our perceptions of what relationships are about begin in our observations of real-life situations; first in our homes, later in the homes of our neighbors, relatives and friends. Even our reading material imparts ideas. Although much can be gained from all of this information, the opposite can occur. These insights may arouse the avaricious part of us, increasing our expectations, and thus further aggravating the problem. A child sees a friend with a new toy or outfit, and hears that she received it from her Bubby. Or reads about a generous Zaidy and wonders why his does not ante-up. An idea forms in his mind that his Zaidy and Bubby owe him "stuff."

A shift can occur in the whole nature of the relationship, from one of love to one of demands, dissatisfaction, disinterest and complaints. It isn't only toys; there are trips, restaurant dinners, hotel stays and more. Somehow, children hear about all kinds of indulgences, and these can create grand expectations in their minds. One grandmother was asked why she didn't sell her large home so that she could buy or rent something smaller. "Are you kidding?" she exclaimed. "If I do, all of my grandchildren will be after me for a hand-out or a loan." An extreme scenario, perhaps, but how uncommon?

Although this description may be exaggerated and is certainly not the case in all relationships, how can we get to a more ideal relationship? How can we encourage a stronger bond, a situation where everyone emerges a winner? Here are some suggestions that can help. Of course, if it isn't broken, don't fix it! If you are enjoying a warm and loving relationship, *yasher koach* to you! Thank *HaShem* and share your successful ideas with others.

~> **Warning!** ~> Employ these ideas to improve the relationship from your side, not to raise your expectations of the other side. Most people do a lot of wonderful things for their loved ones, according to their abilities; we never really have a full picture.

Let's start at the top, with the grandparents. Here are some inspiring portrayals shared by various individuals that can provide us with reachable goals:

🖐 "For many years, my parents were a long-distance Bubby and Zaidy. When they were well into retirement age, we found ourselves living within driving distance. Luckily, I still had young children and a new relationship developed. My father *z"l*, would tell them *divrei Torah*, ask them riddles and toss them coins to catch; whatever they caught, was theirs. My mother enjoyed their frequent phone calls, and always kept a steady supply of cake and cookies. If my children misbehaved, she would beg me, 'Don't punish him while I am here,' or 'She is so young, she didn't mean it, just let it go.' She continues to encourage them and tell them stories while she laughs at their jokes. It's awesome to watch the relationship flourish at this stage."

🖐 "Our Bubby loved us, and always wanted us to visit. One Sunday she called to see if we could drop by, declaring she missed us. My mother was very busy, and responded that we had visited her Thursday evening, three days prior. "That was last week!" Bubby protested. She always made sure to have delicious cookies on hand, and always wanted to hear all details of our lives. School, friends, books we were reading; she reveled in hearing it all."

🐾 "My children felt the love of their grandparents for them, so they naturally loved them back. My parents shared themselves with my children. Of course, there were limits. The children were not allowed to run around in the house or even sit on the couch, but there was always time for them. And always a treat. My parents didn't just hand them a chocolate bar and wave them away. No, they would put the piece of chocolate right into their mouth! And always praise, always repeating how proud they were of them. When a child would disappoint them, they would remind him of how much they valued him and how this behavior didn't fit in. As a follow up, they would talk to him about something positive. Maybe his birthday was approaching and that a surprise was on the way, or some such 'pick-me-up.' The message of love and value kept coming through."

🐾 "Every birthday got a card and a phone call. Before the cold weather came, coats and sweaters were bought. I told my children time and again, that they didn't have to worry about basic necessities; Bubby had planned for their needs way in advance. The children knew that their Zaidy and Bubby were always thinking of them. They got love – they gave it back."

🐾 "My Zaidy and Bubby had many children and grandchildren, but each child felt that he was the special one. My Bubby always made a special point to remember what each grandchild liked and to have it ready when they came to visit. One didn't like onions with her fish; all of us got fish with onions, except for her. Bubby had a wonderful chocolate chip cookie recipe and always had plenty on hand. Even when we were married, no one visited Bubby without getting some. A grandchild was going to *Eretz Yisroel*? Studying for a year in *Yeshiva* or seminary? Bubby arrived with a bagful of their favorite cake or cookies. As busy as she was, she would rise at five in the morning to make sure that her offering was fresh. Each of us knew how much she loved and cared for us. As we matured, a hint from her was enough for us to correct any behavior that was not her *l'chatchila*. We didn't want to take a chance on causing her any pain."

❧ "We had special 'Bubby behavior'; the children were taught and reminded that Bubby would get nervous and upset if they were even a little wild. They would try their best to keep the rules. But there were never any demands made of our Bubby. It was just a giving situation."

❧ "Our Zaidy was always there to discuss *hashkafa* with us. He kept it general, never criticizing us, but always anxious to teach us the proper way. He would quote to us the *pasuk*, 'Ask your elders…' One day I told my mother that I couldn't understand certain issues in *Yiddishkeit*. I was really feeling bothered with troubling thoughts. I couldn't believe my good fortune when she responded; my grandparents were going to be our guests next *Shabbos*! *Shabbos* afternoon, my Zaidy spoke to me for more than an hour, and later even made a tape for me, which he suggested I listen to whenever I feel confused. I only realized years later that they had come just to speak to me."

These anecdotes bring out some of the important roles that grandparents can play in their offspring's lives. For those grandparents that have been less occupied with their grandchildren than they could be, consider revamping your style and increasing your involvement.

Of course, if there are roadblocks that have been set up, you may need to work things out with your children first. Sometimes, however, actions speak louder than words. No matter what the history, everyone welcomes cards, letters, criticism-free phone calls and gifts. Playing games together, sharing stories, asking about what is going on in their lives – and listening to their answers – can all open the door. When in doubt, find a good *Rav/Rebbetzin*, preferably experienced grandparents themselves, to consult with. With their knowledge and *Da'as Torah*, they can provide guidance in improving most relationships.

How about a couple of practical tips? Never miss out on an opportunity to dish out compliments. Sincere praise directed to your grandchild and/or her parent is always welcome.

Did you spend some time with your grandchild? Try to deliver at least one *nachas*-gram. Avoid disciplining, unless there is some real danger. Remind yourself: However, they manage when you are not around, they will manage this time as well. Do you want to offer a suggestion to the parents? Do so by sharing your childrearing experience. They will probably get the hint and hopefully will not feel lectured. Close your eyes and daven to *HaShem*; asking Him to guide the parents properly, especially regarding your concerns.

At the risk of being accused of parent bashing, which I most empathetically do not want to do at all, I want to suggest that a lot is in the parents' hands; they hold the key. Parents set the tone for how loving and respectful the multi-generational relationship is.

We parents have our work cut out for us. The first step in forming a closer relationship between the "grands" is to work on the relationship with those in the middle. Children will notice the way their parents speak to **their** parents and parents-in-law. Behave in a respectful manner, show consideration and never argue. Simply stated, children should see their parents conducting themselves with the grandparents in the same way the parents desire their children to behave toward them. With this outlook, a lot of clarity can emerge.

Modeling a non-demanding and appreciative rapport would be the next thing to work on. If children hear their parents asking or *chas v'shalom* demanding from **their** parents, of course they will do the same. A *Rav* counseled, "Teach your children to expect nothing from their grandparents; just to be grateful for what they are."

A very basic, lost opportunity for honoring one's parents and in-laws is presently swept under the rug in many homes: Addressing them by their proper title. "Mommy" and "Tatty" (or some such type of name) should be used at all times, even when they are not present. Unfortunately, some find this difficult to do… so they manage somehow until the first baby is born; now they feel that they can call the in-laws "Bubby" and "Zaidy" or some such title. Many grandparents do not appreciate this nomenclature but don't feel comfortable making an issue of it. These names can be perceived as a lack of closeness, love or respect. Certainly, referring to parents-in-law by their first names, any euphemisms for "hey you," or using other types of avoidance techniques ("Oh, hello… [no-name]; what's doing?") are not recommended! As a husband tells his wife, "I'm calling Mommy (NOT 'my mother') will this be a good time for you to say hello?" he is accomplishing so much. Especially if the children are listening. It's worth the momentary confusion that may arise occasionally as she asks, "Do you mean your mother or mine?" Usually, however, it is obvious from the context. It may seem like a small matter, but it can have great ramifications.

A friend of mine was going away and brought her children to her parents for *Shabbos*. "Remember," she adjured them several times, "you are here to help Zaidy and Bubby. Do not think that it is their job to take care of you and be busy with you." Through example, stories, modeling and actions, this point must be gotten across.

Zaidy and Bubby are coming for a visit? Review do's-and-don'ts. Try to convey how Zaidy and Bubby love them and how everyone is so happy they are coming. Give them rules, according to their age and temperament, and plenty of praise and reward for those who comply. Although it can get tricky when there is more than one set of grandparents with very different styles, the basic idea is the same. The children have to see the grandparents accorded love and respect, and should be encouraged to make the most of the visit.

Prepare your children by telling stories about their grandparents and encouraging them to ask for more, directly from their Zaidy and Bubby. Talk about diversity among people, judging favorably and finding all kinds of good qualities in these special people. Offer specific and crystal-clear directives: "Let's wait outside to greet them as they arrive," "Remember to keep off the recliner; Zaidy loves to sit on it, but won't if he sees you want to," or "Bubby gets upset when we eat junk, so enjoy your *nosh* while she is resting."

These ideas and more apply equally when children visit their grandparents. Remind them that "please" and "thank you" are rarely overused! Prepare them by playing a game in which you make up a situation and challenge your children to come up with an ideal response. Use scenarios that have occurred; if you select one where your child behaved exemplarily, he will be thrilled to hear about it. Using the opposite type can be valuable as well.

Be on the alert to not undermine your parents' efforts. You may not realize the impact of any negative remarks that your children hear circuitously, such as while you are on the phone, discussing an issue with your sister-in-law. Even worse, they may hear comments made directly. Remarks such as, "Bubby doesn't understand," "Zaidy is old-fashioned," or "They always worry about everything" and worse, can ruin years of effort.

What about the grandchildren themselves? If you are reading this, you are old enough to work on the relationship, if it needs attention. You can start by calling your grandparents weekly, being home when they visit and/or visiting them when possible. Notes and pictures – don't forget to identify all of the faces! – will be very much appreciated as well. See **Conversing with *Kavod*** and **Be a Loveable Child** for more specific "how-tos".

How about some real-life illustrations?

👋 "I'm so proud of my grandson. He called me the other day, asking if I could help him buy a home. When I asked him if he wanted a loan, he told me that he would never be able to pay me back, since he lives on a shoestring budget. I told him that I did have some money, but what will be if I will need it for my old age? His response thrilled me. 'Don't worry, Bubby. If you ever need money, I'll get it for you somehow!'"

❧ "I love birthdays – anyone's, but especially mine! One year I invited my married children to join us in a restaurant for a birthday dinner, asking them to come this time without their children. When they came, they brought me a lovely gift – a beautiful collage of photos that my teenage granddaughters had spent hours putting together. I couldn't believe how nice a job they had done and was so delighted with their thoughtfulness. Especially since they had not been invited this time. Of course it hangs in a prominent place in my apartment, giving me much *nachas* whenever I see it."

❧ "My Bubby lived in a *frum* community about an hour away from us. Although there were stores in her area, she preferred to get her fish from a store near us. She told her friends how the fish was so much cleaner, yet cost the same price. The truth was that when we bought it for her, we cleaned it and re-wrapped it before bringing it to her. Bubby never suspected a thing and was always thrilled with her clever daughter-in-law's shopping."

❧ "I grew up knowing we had to do whatever we could for our Bubby. My parents didn't have to spell it out; I simply saw what they did. For example, my mother used to shop for my Bubby, getting her nice clothing and other items. She knew that Bubby didn't want her to spend any money since we were a *kollel* family. With care and wisdom, my mother never let on that she had purchased anything at a store for full price. She would make numerous vague remarks about generous neighbors, close-out sales or hand-me-downs. My Bubby was delighted with her daughter-in-law's thoughtfulness and thrifty purchases."

❧ "My siblings and I followed our parents' example. When we visited Bubby, we would eat whatever she prepared, never commenting when the food was bland or tasteless. We would listen to her stories over and over again, never letting on that we already knew them by heart. When my Bubby reached the point where she needed company for *Shabbos*, we would take turns going to her, bringing the meals and keeping her company. We loved our Bubby."

How about this wonderful phone call a friend of mine received? "Bubby? Hi! I'm calling to give you *nachas*. I was walking outside with my umbrella – it had just started raining – and I noticed a mother pushing a stroller, without an umbrella. I thought, I know exactly what my Bubby would do, even though this lady is a stranger… I approached her and shielded us both with my umbrella, until we reached her destination. I felt awkward at first, but was so glad I did it! Thank you Bubby!"

Although learning new patterns in our relationships can take a lot of effort, we are the ones who will gain, both in our newly strengthened bonds and in our *middos* in general. After all, *kibud av v'em*, honoring parents, is recognized as one of the most difficult of *mitzvos* – keeping it successfully requires a lot of attention. May we all be *zoche* to enjoy *nachas* from our children and parents and grandparents and ourselves, together!

Handy Tips

Babysitting Basics

Whether you are leaving one child or several – whether it is for just for one hour, an entire afternoon, all day long or daily – here are some guidelines that will help smooth the way.

- Hiring a young girl? Until you establish a relationship with a particular teenager, always speak initially with her mother to verify that she gives her permission. Asking the teen first can put a lot of stress on the mother if she doesn't want her daughter to babysit for any reason. Once you get the go-ahead in general, deal directly with your employee.

- When arranging babysitting, double check all the details: date, starting and ending times, address and phone number. Let the babysitter read back the information to you, to verify accuracy. When arranging help a few days or more in advance, reconfirm the details a day before the agreed upon date.

- It's always a good idea to label everything but especially important if your baby will be out of the house. Get a quality permanent marker; put your phone number on baby's jacket/sweater, pacifier and bottle. In short, anything of value. ~> *Caution!* ~> True valuables are best off left at home.

- Post a list of rules and emergency information in a prominent place. Phone numbers, including a close-by neighbor that is usually home, allergies, medicines and any unusual requirements should all be listed.

🐾 Take a few minutes to discuss safety issues such as how to avoid choking hazards. Do you want the babysitter to buckle-up your little one whenever he is in a highchair or stroller? I hope so! If you too deem this safety measure as important, let the babysitter know. If the care is at your home, make sure that you have properly baby-proofed the area; she may not be as vigilant as you. If the babysitter will be out, review additional do's-and-don'ts, including **never** leaving the baby unattended or with anyone not pre-approved.

🐾 If you are exacting about what your little one eats or does, take a few minutes to write down the schedule and food particulars. Of course, don't count on this written note alone, especially if your babysitter is young or inexperienced. Review it together to make sure it is clear.

🐾 If you have any unusual or uncommon specifications, clarify that as well. For example, if you do not want the babysitter to bring books or *nosh* for your child, without your review, let her know. Does your child eat exclusively with a bib? Do you expect her to clean up in any way, put toys away? These and other such requirements should be clearly stated. She may not think to ask; many do not insist on such things. Don't take anything for granted; spell it out!

🐾 But keep everything in balance. Don't overwhelm her with too many requirements. It's wiser to relax some rules when transferring the reins to a babysitter.

🐾 If you are leaving the house with the babysitter in charge, let her know if you keep your door locked and where you keep the key. Do you want her to answer the door? The phone? Are you expecting someone to come by or call? Make sure she will know what to do.

🐾 Discuss payment ahead of time; make sure to have the correct change and pay on time. Although the babysitter may say that she does not mind and can wait, it is a *mitzva* to pay on time; some girls may be too shy to admit that they really do want to get paid right away. If you are expecting to receive this service as a *chessed*, verify that as well. Simply ask, "How much do you get per hour?" If the answer is a clear, "Oh, no, no charge for neighbors!" then fine. Otherwise, be prepared to pay the going rate; if the babysitter is not forthcoming with that amount, a bit of research will yield that figure quickly enough.

🐾 Let your babysitter know what your children enjoy and give her a few tips that work for you. It will make the time spent together more satisfying both for her and your children.

🐾 If your child has something in particular that calms him down, make sure to have it available. Pacifiers, baby blankets, bottles; don't plan on the babysitter managing without them if you can't!

🐾 Show her where you store the diapers, wipes, change of clothes and any supply she may need. Specify that she check the diaper at a certain time; people not involved in regular child-care can forget. She may not notice and your baby could remain in a soiled diaper the entire time!

🐾 If you have a babysitter you truly like, don't forget to show your appreciation. Regularly administered compliments can mean a lot, and occasional notes and/or gifts have their place as well, even if you are paying her.

Car and Travel 🐾

🐾 Assemble emergency items to store in a clearly marked location in your vehicle. Include first aid paraphernalia and some small "just in case" objects, such as a spare key, small tool kit, garbage bags. Of course, there are many items that you can also store for all kinds of road emergencies.

🐾 Avoid emergencies! Maintain your car properly.

🐾 Your car uses gas more efficiently when the tank is full and the tires are properly inflated.

🐾 Regularly review car and road safety tips with your children. Teach them to look carefully when walking near cars, especially in parking lots and such areas where drivers tend to be less cautious. Be vigilant near driveways, before crossing streets and before opening a car door.

🐾 Keep far from the curb and traffic when walking.

Keep a small suitcase or backpack in your car, with different items that you may need. Pens, snacks, baby-wipes, diapers and water are some common staples. Include items you have wished for in previous outings. Don't forget to update your provisions periodically!

🐾 Remember the inside of a vehicle heats up quickly. **Never** leave children in a car, even if unlocked, even for just a few minutes! Be careful with food, especially chocolate, plants and heat sensitive equipment. Many other items can get quickly ruined as well. If you must leave something inside, insulate it with a blanket. **Never** leave a car with a motor running, either, especially with children inside!

🐾 When going out with children, be prepared with some entertaining, perhaps even educational, way to pass the time. Since there tend to be fewer interruptions while traveling, it can be the perfect occasion to spend quality time with your loved ones. For fun ideas, see **Games for the Gang**.

Children – Keep Them Out of Trouble! 🐾

🐾 Start out by keeping your true goal in mind. To raise children is to teach ourselves to be givers, and to train them to do the same.

🐾 The home must always be more warm and welcoming than the street; you can never say, "I love you" too often!

🐾 Seize every possible opportunity to talk to your children. Excellent times are when working on mundane tasks, traveling or walking together. Discuss all matters of value, any aspect of *avodas HaShem*, appreciation of nature, basic knowledge. Use as a high a vocabulary as you can, and be prepared to explain any concepts or exact meanings. Share ideas, stories, anything interesting. If it is hard for you to recall appealing material, a quick look in a book can remind you of a story to tell or topic to discuss. Making up stories is easier than you think. Your undiscriminating little ones will delight in anything; just start, throw in a few familiar names or animals, and have fun. Great for teaching and subtly reprimanding. Don't delay; even babies can pick up information and the more they hear the quicker they can absorb. My friend's toddler knows left and right; those terms are used when dressing or guiding him. When you can't speak, take advantage of the many wonderful recordings that can educate and entertain.

❦ Make your job with your little ones a bit easier; limit their space and maintain a safe environment. Babies and toddlers need not have access to every area. Make use of child/baby gates, lock cabinets and appliances. Baby-proof!

❦ Accustom your babies to spending some time in a playpen. Entice them by reserving certain playthings for use only in there or in such restricted areas. Although they may cry at first, babies will usually settle down and occupy themselves. This actually forces them to play with their toys, which they tend to ignore when they can tear the house down instead! Start with fifteen minutes a couple of times a day. As they grow accustomed to this venue, they may come to enjoy it; their caretaker certainly will! And a playpen is a wonderful place to quickly store toys.

❦ Toddler bothering older children? Let the big ones play in the playpen or restricted area. Two benefits with that; they can play un-harassed and the toddler may be intrigued enough to want a turn there as well!

❦ Children squabbling over something? Try distracting one or the other, offer a different toy or set a time limit. Announce that each child will get the desired item for a specific amount of time and set the timer accordingly. Keep setting it, giving each one a turn, until they move on. For very young children, count to ten. Train them to pass over the toy when they hear you say "TEN!" ~> ***Bonus!*** ~> While learning how to share, they will learn to count!

🐾 Make it a habit to harness your baby/child whenever she is in the stroller, even if it is just for a few minutes; it takes only seconds to tumble out. And save your back – use a stroller in the house to transport non-walkers.

🐾 Get a child harness and use it in your high chair; most high chair belts will not effectively restrain your child. Now it's the perfect place to put him in when he needs some time-out. Alternatively, use it when you need a short break or to keep him out of harm's way. Once he is sitting securely, you can provide him with some type of leisure activity. Offer time-consuming snacks: frozen juice or ice cubes, frozen vegetables (not defrosted) or cereal. Alternatively, give him some toy he enjoys; my son loved playing with our dreidel collection, and this was the only venue for that form of entertainment! Even if you get five or ten minutes at a time, it's worth it!

🐾 Feeding a little one? Limit messes and waste; put a small amount of food on their plate, it's easy enough to refill.

🐾 This may sound illogical, but if it works, you'll do yourself – and your neighbors – a favor. Invite some young children to play in your home. Needless to say, do not invite the most rambunctious ones on the block! Try a couple of mild-mannered seven to ten-year-olds. Girls tend to go for this type of arrangement more than boys, but it depends on their personality. Chances are that they will enjoy playing with your toys and they'll keep your toddler occupied at the same time. And your neighbor will be delighted!

🐾 Consider this very effective timesaver: Young children can sleep in tomorrow's clothing. Normally, youngsters don't sweat, so no one will be the wiser. (*Erev Shabbos* too hectic? Bathe the children Thursday night, dress them in Shabbos clothes, with an *erev Shabbos* vest on top. The clothing stays clean, and they will be all ready for *Shabbos* in a snap.) In the morning, you'll be very pleasantly surprised. They wake up, and you only have to wash their hands, brush their hair and put on their shoes. Don't worry about the long term; as they mature, they'll switch to pajamas. Of course, if your child is not dry at night, this tip will probably not help you.

🐾 Depending on the age and temperament of your children, they can be big helpers in the kitchen. Empty a bag of pretzels or any snack into a big bowl, and let your children make small snack bags. They can use a measuring cup or count the pieces. Let your children check beans or rice; of course, you will surreptitiously re-check it, but it really **is** a help if they remove the obvious discolored and broken pieces. My five-year-old actually found a teeny tiny bug one time!

🐾 Another task they can tackle is setting and clearing off the table. Design a chart; when they see a rotation in progress, they will feel big, and cooperative about taking their turn. Even a three-year-old can put a cup and/or a napkin by each place. They can wash the dishes, although you may wish to give one more rinse when they are done. When using disposables, they surely know what to do!

~> **Warning!** ~> You may want to check the garbage or at least remind them to clear off non-garbage first.

🐾 Motivate your children and make helping more fun by incorporating a game into the job. It can be a treasure hunt, a regular board game, craft activity; anything can work. The idea is that in order to take a turn with the game, a certain small task must first be done. Give a specific assignment as a function of their age; for example, let them pick up and put away as many items as their age. Vary the game or let the children figure it out; you'll be amazed!

🐾 Inspire your children to speak softly and kindly, do acts of *chessed*, and all the wonderful things you would like them to do by modeling the behavior yourself. A friend of mine once came to a *shalom zocher* after the guests had already left. As she spoke to the mother, she began clearing away the trash and organizing the leftovers. Her toddler didn't say a word, but started gathering the toys strewn around! Bear in mind that they may copy you right away or it may only surface years later. Regardless, it's the way to go.

🐾 Keeping your children playing happily frees up lots of time for you. Occupy them with ideas easily found in books and magazines. Rule of thumb: Be proactive. Offer a game or toy or project **before** they begin to fight! Especially when you need to take them somewhere, it pays to bring some entertainment along for them. Whether at a *simcha* or at a store where you need time to select and ask questions, save your sanity by bringing along some basic entertainment. Crayons, stickers, paper and coloring books fit the bill perfectly.

🐾 Can't get your child to cooperate, despite offering various incentives that you think are fabulous? Could be your offerings totally don't interest him. Brainstorm together; be ready to think out of the box. You just might find the key.

🐾 Occasionally, but regularly, remind children about all kinds of safety tips. Crossing carefully and not walking close to the curb; being careful in parking lots, etc.

🐾 We must also carefully warn them about interactions with adults. Not speaking to strangers, not opening the door when parents are not home – even to those they know. Being wary of any adult trying to engage them in conversation when parents are not around and more; all of these activities need to be avoided or at least minimized. It's distressing that this is necessary and children may be scared to hear about it, but that is a price we need to pay for their safety. Warn them that unfortunately there are sick people who appear perfectly normal, but who can try to take advantage of them. Except for their close friends, no one has a secret to tell them or a reason to pull them aside privately. Stress that they need to inform you of any unusual or uncomfortable behavior they encounter, even if told not to. Tell them that under strange circumstances, it's okay to say, "NO!" and get away quickly, even to the safety of a passerby they don't know, when that is the only option. As a form of extra insurance, encourage them to avoid going out alone whenever possible. Once a year or so should be sufficient to discuss these topics. End the warnings in an upbeat manner. As with all unpleasant topics, early in the day is the preferred discussion time rather than toward nighttime, when such talk could generate nightmares.

🐾 Teach your children to play board games and with other ignored toys. My cousin shared this tip with me; it didn't occur to me that such a thing needed to be taught. She sat down with her children one afternoon and played her favorite with them. Once they were hooked, they managed fine without her. Get your children started on some good games: Chess, Risk, Stratego, or Candyland. Interest them in puzzles and other toys in the same manner. It's time well invested.

🐾 Don't ever forget! Whenever anyone cooperates, thank them; preferably by describing what you see. Teach them to be proud of their contribution towards running the home and maintaining *shalom*.

Careful with Computers 🐾

Is your computer, printer, telephone or other such appliance not working? Turn it off; if unable to, remove the batteries. Open your *Tehillim* while you wait a few minutes; try to turn it back on. There isn't an easier or cheaper fix and it actually works sometimes.

🐾 Save yourself untold anguish by making sure to keep a backup. Consult your computer expert for options.

🐾 Need to access the internet? Ask a *sheila*. For extra protection, ask *HaShem* for help; recite *Tehillim*, chapter 25:15 it's very apropos. This entire chapter is easily understood.

🐾 Follow the example of a fire-fighter. Run in, get what you need and scramble out.

🐾 When accessing an unfamiliar website, cover the screen with a sheet of paper **before** their page appears. A misspelled word may reveal a website you are not expecting. Slowly lower the sheet; back out as needed.

👋 Avoid aches and pains. Sit with your elbows and knees at 90° angles. Intersperse short, regular breaks.

👋 Consider carefully before checking your spam or other such garbage. Is the possible gain truly worth skimming through trash? Would you go through yesterday's vegetable peels and leftovers searching for a lost coin? What's the downside to not checking it out? Make an educated decision.

Diet – It can be Delicious 👋

👋 There are so many good books on the topic of nutritional eating and weight loss. It is worthwhile to go through them, even if you retain only one idea. You never know what can help you.

👋 Create your own diet tips list. As you come across something that makes sense to you, write it down; review the list as often as you can handle. Something that may not have initially appealed to you may be just the thing at a different point in your life.

👋 Although healthy eating is an important part of life, that too should be done in moderation. Overeating healthy food can be worse than restrained eating of unhealthy food.

👋 The *Rambam*, Maimonides, has many suggestions that can improve our lifestyle. One is to cut portion size by a third.

👋 Don't graze. Bring your food to the table, wash your hands, sit down and make a *bracha* with concentration – preferably from a card or *siddur* – and enjoy your repast in an elevated manner. Don't forget the *bracha achrona*!

👋 Eat s-l-o-w-l-y. Put your fork down in between mouthfuls and fully chew your food.

👋 Compile a list of activities to occupy yourself with when challenged with the urge to eat or *nosh*. You can recite *Tehillim*, dance or exercise, work on a puzzle or craft project, read a book.

Stand steadfast; often your hunger pangs will cease after a few difficult minutes.

❧ Maintain a stock of low-calorie foods; those that are low in preparation time but take a while to eat are ideal. We simply eat more of snacks that are quickly consumed. Our list includes the customary choices: tomatoes, cucumbers, peppers, hot-air popcorn. How about nutritious frozen treats? Corn and peas, eaten straight from the freezer, can be enjoyed slowly. They really have a good refreshing taste and less is eaten due to their frozen state. Once you're in the freezer, don't forget popsicles or even plain ice cubes; they are small and delectable and take a while to eat! Although most soups are not speedily prepared, blended vegetable soups can be very low calorie, nourishing and filling; see soup recipe section.

❧ Try a bowl of oat bran; simply pour boiling water onto the bran, according to the consistency you prefer. Stir, cover and wait a minute; goes well with yogurt or cheese. Lots of health benefits and very filling.

❧ Don't sit down to *nosh* with a full bag. Take a portion and stow away the rest, preferably in an inconvenient location!

❧ When preparing foods, many calories can be saved, often without great loss of flavor. For example, vegetables can be water-sautéed or prepared with a small amount of oil; soups can be prepared without any oil at all. When you try a recipe that does call for a lot of oil or sugar, experiment. You may be able to get by with less.

❧ Cut the calories of store-bought products by mixing in other ingredients. Love fruit yogurt? It's loaded with sugar. Buy a plain yogurt at the same time, combine them and refill each container. Now there are two portions, each still delicious, yet with fewer calories. Sweetened drinks can be watered down as well. If you are brave, as soon as you open the container pour half into another bottle and add water to each. You can apply this concept to many different foods.

❧ Enjoy salad dressing? You can use less yet still enjoy the taste: Put a small amount of dressing in a bowl. Before taking a forkful of salad, dip your fork into the dressing; it will be the first taste to reach your tongue! And you won't have to inundate the entire salad with all those calories.

🐾 When faced with tempting food, you may be better able to restrain yourself by taking a small portion rather than none at all. Of course, you must learn from your past experiences; some are more successful in maintaining control when they just don't even start.

🐾 Strengthen your will power and control by getting enough sleep. Although it is individual, six hours is a minimum to strive for.

🐾 Try accustoming yourself to using this bon mot, quoted by Rabbi Avi Shulman from his father. "I like it, but it doesn't like me." That's a polite refusal that can come in handy with a well-meaning but persistent host/ess.

🐾 Try to keep away from food situations. Attending a meeting with refreshments? Don't sit near them. Getting together with a friend? Restaurants are not the only venue; you can stroll together or sit in a park. Try to organize your home so that you needn't constantly pass through the kitchen.

🐾 Don't stock up. A friend with a large family told me that although it is more time consuming, she shops daily for what she needs. The more food in the house, the more that is eaten. She claims to actually save money in this manner.

🐾 Getting treats for *Shabbos*? Buy them as late in the week as possible – it is actually praiseworthy to shop for *Shabbos* on *erev Shabbos*! Open them at the last minute and quickly store them away to avoid pre-*Shabbos noshing*.

🐾 Use this joke: While passing a bakery, a woman hinted to her stingy husband, "Smells delicious!" His reply? "Would you like to pass again?" I take this joke seriously. Whenever I am accosted by a delicious aroma, I remind myself that I can enjoy it for free! No cost, no calories, no unhealthy repercussions. After a few such messages, I found myself truly enjoying the smell, without missing the food.

🐾 Remind yourself that you will save money by consuming less. Of course this only applies if you eat less, not if you substitute more expensive food for cheaper, fattening versions! If you do find yourself spending less on food, use the savings to reward yourself; preferably with non-food items!

🐾 You may find yourself spending less time in the kitchen when eating less. If so, reward yourself for self-control with some special activity that you don't usually find time for. Did you take less time to eat your meal because you ate less? Use that time for some yoga, special reading, working on a project. If the time is too short to be useful, add up the savings and cash in once a week!

🐾 Entertaining with lots of special tempting dishes? Tell yourself that there may not be enough food, so you had better not take too much. When we have many people around our table, typically during *Yomim Tovim*, I always worry about this. It really curbs my desire to indulge and overeat!

Health and Hygiene 🐾

Here is a collection of important, yet not so standard, ideas. As you read any health-related information, keep in mind that "figures don't lie, but liars figure." Health claims can be very biased and exaggerated; educate yourself from a variety of sources. Check with your doctor before following any questionable procedures. Most importantly, don't forget to consult the head specialist; *daven* to *HaShem*, especially before attempting any cure.

🐾 Getting ready to say *asher yatzar*? As you fill your washing cup, use the time to picture your body functioning properly. Your heart is pumping, your blood is flowing and all organs are working at peak performance. Wash, continuing this stream of consciousness. Read the *bracha* from a prepared card, wall hanging or *siddur*; concentrate on the words. The whole procedure takes less than a minute – time well spent.

🐾 Keep up to date. Many newspapers and magazines have a health page. It's a good idea to read it through.

🐾 Before taking any medication, read the information enclosed. If your situation is complicated, research even more. If you cannot, get the help of a second doctor or try your pharmacist. The fine print is there for a reason.

🐾 For any aches and ailments, one of the first doctors to consult with is Dr. Sleep. Your work can wait, everyone else will manage. Take the time to refresh and allow your body to heal itself. In general, a body's foremost maintenance work takes place during sleep. Although healing goes on during the day as well, digestion takes priority, so regeneration and recovery get the back burner during our eating/waking hours.

🐾 Another effective cure-all is deep breathing. Inhale deeply and slowly exhale. Try this at the onset of headache.

🐾 Or try this alternative headache remedy: Massage both temples with your thumbs in a circular movement and/or the skin between your thumb and forefinger.

🐾 One last headache suggestion: Fill a pillow case with five cups of coarse salt; sleep on it or place it near your head.

🐾 How about diaphragm breathing? Inhale, relax your shoulders and puff out your abdomen; exhale, pulling in your abdomen. It's how you probably breathe when lying down. May help digestion, voice/hoarseness and can cure hiccups!

🐾 Don't forget to exercise. Walking is wonderful, the advantages are well known. Consider swimming, especially with specific health issues. You'll also enjoy social benefits.

🐾 Try this exercise for posture and more. Stand as straight as you are able to with your back against the wall. Lower your shoulders. Keep pressing each part of your body to the wall, including the heels of your feet. Try to do this for a few minutes once or twice a day. Perfect opportunity for mentally reviewing your deeds.

🐾 Stomachache? Try placing a hot water bottle or even just a pillow on the stomach. In my family, it has proven to be very effective all through the years. Incidentally, a pediatrician said that children get stomachaches in the same way that adults get headaches; usually it is nothing serious. Another magic trick that worked for us is antacid pills. Give children half a tablet as needed. It's high in calcium, so it's actually good for them. Actually, sometimes any vitamin pill at all, administered as a medicine, has worked wonders.

🐾 Massage is another cure-all. Whenever your hands are free and a child – especially a baby – is available, pamper them. Back, shoulders, arms, legs; touch has been proven to be very beneficial. They might even return the favor!

🐾 Experiencing pain or discomfort in the toe area? Shoulder pads found in jackets and some shirts contain thin foam that is easily cut to size. This padding performs excellently in the role of toe-protector.

🐾 Pink eye? Try all or any of these cures: * Rinse with water as often as every half hour. * Brew some non-herbal tea, remove the tea bag, let it cool and place it on the eye for a few minutes a few times a day. * Get some milk from a nursing mother; the younger the baby, the more full of antibodies the milk will be. Put a few drops on the eye.

🐾 Suffering from a wart? Suffocate it; cover it with a piece of duct or masking tape. It may actually shrink and disappear within a few weeks; easy enough to try. Rubbing fig juice on a wart is reputed to work within days.

🐾 When in a rush, use baby wipes to refresh quickly.

🐾 Using a cordless phone? Although they perform wondrously, there are claims that they release too much radiation. The same warning applies to cell phones, but more so. In particular, the radiation from a cell phone used in an elevator, car or bus can be very concentrated, as it is all trapped in the vehicle, even with open windows. (This does not apply to phones with exterior antennas.) All in all, it makes sense to use the speaker function or some type of headphone, and to minimize usage, especially for children and young adults. May even be wise to revert to corded phones!

🐾 Ears are sensitive to loud noises and hearing loss is generally permanent. Use ear plugs at noisy events and protect your children as well; this may mean leaving babies home when attending *simchos*. Never kiss an ear; the suction can cause pain and hearing loss as well.

🐾 Minimize use of aerosol and spritz products and cleansers; the air becomes loaded with chemicals and you will be breathing them in. Instead, spray plain water and use a soapy solution with a sponge or cloth. Powdered laundry detergent mixed with water is very effective. If you must spray, keep people out of the area until the air clears.

🐾 Avoid having even small puddles or pools of standing water for an extended time, especially in the summer. They are perfect breeding grounds for mosquitoes.

🐾 Avoid potential burn situations; turn pot/pan handles in, away from children's reach; don't leave matches, boiling coffee, tea or soups unattended. If someone does get a burn, hold the area under cold running water or immerse in icy water. It may take hours until the pain is gone, but in my experience, while my burn was submerged in icy water, I was pain-free. More than once I have suffered a small burn; I kept it submerged with icy water for several hours and finally fell asleep. In the morning I was pain free and did not require any further medical attention. ~> *Notice!* ~> You'll need a lot of ice cubes; they melt quickly.

🐾 Feeling very tired but no time for a good nap? If possible, close your eyes as you speak or even perform certain tasks; you may be surprised at the many things you can do without looking! Alternatively, force yourself to get up and exercise for a few minutes. It can really energize you!

🐾 When sitting, especially for long periods of time, remember to stretch out your legs; at least do not pull them under you. Bent positions can lead to blood clots.

🐾 Beat the heat; spritz water on the back of the neck.

🐾 Train everyone to wash hands with soap often; at least upon entering the house and before eating. You'll cut down on germs, colds and enjoy some cleanliness! Try this method: Keep a sponge in a small container with some watered-down soap; simple to lather. Proceed by rubbing palms together; then each palm onto the back of the other hand. Finish by pushing fingers through each other. Do each step while counting to ten. Finish off with a rinse; then dry. True, takes half a minute, but it is a wise investment.

🐾 Using raw eggs, chicken or meat? Prevent possible illness; before you begin, put a bit of soap onto a spoon and keep it on the side. Be careful to touch as few surfaces as possible until you have finished. Immediately soap up your hands, as well as any utensils and areas that were in contact with the raw food.

🐾 Cool off hot liquids and foods before storing in plastic containers; the heat could leach off toxins. Do so as quickly as possible and refrigerate, to avoid growth of bacteria. Similarly, don't use warm water from the faucet; if the pipe contains lead, high temperatures can result in contaminated water.

🐾 If you enjoy ice-cold drinks, you may want to limit them. Internally, our body is 98.6 degrees; 32-degree drinks cause a shocking impact.

🐾 Take care of your teeth by brushing after meals and snacks; use a medium or soft toothbrush to avoid triggering gum disease. It's most effective to brush for two minutes; not so challenging when you are prepared. Take your toothbrush, sit down, open a book; now you can brush and read in comfort. Set a timer if you really want to be strict about this. And don't forget to floss! Just take about six inches of floss, about half the usual amount, and knot the ends well to use less.

🐾 Can't brush? Try eating a crunchy vegetable and/or using your finger; it's better than nothing! While you have your finger there, massage your gums.

🐾 My friend, attending a course on healthful eating, expected to hear an earful about organic food, when to eat what, what to eliminate and many such ideas. Although all worthwhile and valuable, following such guidelines can consume a lot of resources and make meals very unpleasant. To my friend's surprise, the instructor started the course with an important caveat, claiming that it was the most important health tip and totally free. Avoid anger. It impedes with our delicate chemical balance, interfering with the work our bodies must perform. See **Igeress HaRamban** for help in achieving this level.

Remember that it requires fewer *zechusim* to maintain our health than to obtain a *refuah shleima*. Take heed and keep *davening*. May we all be blessed with good health.

Household Help

🐾 This time of year, most of us want to hire extra help. If you can afford it and have a good worker to hire, or give extra hours to, lucky you! But keep this in mind: you are very fortunate. There are those that cannot afford regular help, and adding salt to their wound, cannot get any hours at all Pesach time. Keep this thought in mind, and think of your housekeeper-less friends. They would probably be thrilled if you offered them a few hours of your housekeeper's time! Naturally, they would pay her on their own. If you have any special warnings or pointers about her, be sure to alert your friend to that as well.

🐾 Before hiring a worker or housekeeper, try to check references. It is sometimes very awkward or even costly to fire an employee, so it's worth investing a bit of time before employing someone new. Needless to say, be realistic about the value of the referencee. If you do not know the person you are calling and have no common friends, take the information with a grain of salt.

🐾 Clarify wages, days and hours of work and your expectations as much as possible. What is obvious to you may not be to her, so spell it all out ahead of time.

🐾 Of course, if you are having a hard time getting good help, be prepared to settle or do the work yourself!

🐾 Tell your employee how much time you want her to spend on a particular project. Otherwise, she may spend much more time than you intended on one area and will not have time for the rest of your needs. And make sure to have all cleaning supplies readily available before she arrives, so she can get right to work.

🐾 Unless you have access to lots of applicants, don't bother testing, that is, inspecting her work afterwards for completeness. Rather, as she begins her work, point out areas usually neglected and clarify your expectations.

🐾 Let her put all the trash she collects in a specific container; you can go through it to ensure that it is truly garbage. I have found that household helpers carelessly throw out all kinds of things, admittedly usually of negligible value but at other times costly. I have found cash, earrings and even silverware in the trash! You may not enjoy sifting through it, but it's next to impossible to train someone to recognize your valuables, and people make mistakes.

🐾 On the topic of trash, you may want to inspect it for another reason. Putting desired items in the garbage is an excellent method of stealing, as your workers leave the house with the bag in tow; be wary and check it out.

Kashrus — Keep it Clear in the Kitchen 🐾

🐾 Have separate pitchers, salt and pepper shakers, ketchup bottles; whatever goes on the table. Although this duplication may not be *halachically* required strictly speaking, it is still advisable. While you are at it, assign separate dishwashing soap dispensers as well.

👋 Label whatever you can with stickers, tape, permanent marker or nail polish. You never know when someone else will come to work in your kitchen. As long as you are labeling, may as well make it clear, either with the word "dairy" or "meat" or a large enough symbol; a drop of nail polish that is barely noticeable may not do the trick.

👋 Keep the stickers, or whatever you use, in a kitchen drawer or some convenient place. If the symbol becomes unrecognizable, you can refresh it on the spot. Of course, thus prepared, you can also mark new items immediately.

👋 Try to keep separate shelves in the refrigerator. Food and drinks tend to spill and can cause all kinds of *sheilos*.

👋 Using pots, containers or dishes, especially ones that haven't been used in a while? An insect may have popped in. Rinse or check carefully before using.

👋 Be careful when shopping; we live in a constantly changing world. Always verify the *hechsher* before putting any food item in your shopping cart.

👋 Keep your *pareve* items *pareve*. You may be using them to prepare *pareve* ingredients for a non-*pareve* meal, which is fine. Just make sure to put them away as soon as possible, before you move on to preparing the dairy or meat part of the meal.

👋 Do you have *pareve* knives, spatulas, peelers and other inexpensive items? Consider getting additional ones for meat and dairy, even if you only use them for *pareve* foods that will subsequently be added to meat and dairy. It will cut down on *sheilos*.

👋 Don't pour onto meat or dairy directly from a *pareve* tea kettle – it may thereby lose its *pareve* status.

👋 Don't be afraid to call a *Rav*! Most community phonebooks have a listing of *poskim*, sometimes even with their hours. Why rely on your friend or neighbor, when for the cost of a brief phone call you can get a definitive answer and proceed guilt-free?

Make it Modest

👋 *Tznius* is a precious gift given to us by *HaShem*. Studying all aspects of it will allow you to observe it proudly and properly, and maximize its benefits.

👋 Modesty is not just a matter of how we dress; it's our entire way of speaking and behaving.

👋 Carefully observe those you admire, noticing their behavior, dress, speech patterns, eating etiquette and other behaviors. See what you can implement.

👋 On the other hand, when you notice someone appearing immodest, ask yourself, "Is it possible I sound/behave/look the same?" We don't really see ourselves, especially as we engage in all kinds of activities – reaching, getting into vehicles, conversing. Beware of bending, which can actually result in indecent exposure in many areas. Band together with your friends. Agree to let each other know when clothing, tone of voice or behavior is amiss. Don't forget to judge the 'immodest' person favorably; she may not know any better. *Daven* that she learn.

👋 Use a buddy system when clothes shopping. Select a partner that is on a higher level of modesty than your current state, if possible. At the very least, let her be on your level!

👋 Trying on clothing? Don't stand still. Move, bend, reach; climb up a stair. Let your buddy verify that you appear refined in each position.

👋 Beware of short-ish tops; if the overlap with your skirt is less than generous, wear a long shell underneath.

👋 Shirt puckering between buttons? You can sew up most of a blouse, leaving the top few inches open as needed to pull it on. Alternatively, add hidden snaps in between the buttons; a safety pin might do the trick. Again, use a shell for a back-up.

🐾 Once dressed, check yourself in a mirror. Keep one near the front door as well; check potential problem areas before exiting. For example, are you carrying a bag with a shoulder strap? It may lower the neckline.

🐾 Avoid tucking in or adjusting clothing in any way in public.

🐾 When wearing clothing that you have not worn for a while, be extra alert. You may have changed sizes.

🐾 Be prepared. Always have safety pins with you for emergency repairs; a small sewing kit can be a lifesaver.

🐾 Train yourself to speak softly. Especially when in public. Especially when conversing on a cell phone.

🐾 Take the warning found in *Pirkei Avos* (1:5) to heart: "Do not converse too much with women…" Conversations with the opposite gender should be kept as businesslike as possible, even amongst relatives. True, it's not easy, but consider how much heartbreak would have been avoided had we all adhered to this *hadracha*. It's not too late!

🐾 Dressing daughters in fashionable, flashy clothing when young can be a difficult habit to break as they mature.

🐾 As your girls get older, make sure you continue to shop with them. Saving time by sending them out with friends can easily turn into an irrecoverable error. Don't be fearful or fearsome; be loving, yet firm, in upholding the standard of modesty you adhere to.

🐾 Discuss this topic with your children occasionally. Praise modest dress and behavior as the opportunity appears.

🐾 All people, but especially young girls, should avoid going out alone; buddy-up whenever possible. And don't loiter; walk purposefully and get to your destination quickly. Socialize in homes or properly designated areas.

🐾 "Don't blend in," was the advertising slogan of a mall, full of stores with outrageous fashions. Modesty is defined by the opposite. Blend in by refusing to go along with attention-attracting clothing, hair styles and behavior.

Miscellaneous Matters

🐾 Timers are a fantastic adjunct to almost any task. Use them to avoid burning food, to give children specific time to play or read, to remember tasks… the list is endless.

🐾 Going out for an errand or appointment? Expect delays; bring along snacks, tissues, a water bottle, books. My favorite is a *sefer Tehillim*. You'll be calmer as you wait or just be pleasantly surprised if you don't need any of them.

🐾 To remove hot glue, use a blow dryer. Wipe clean.

🐾 Does your glue gun seem broken? If you removed the glue while it's still hot, there may be some residue build-up inside that is clogging the gun. If this happens, try the blow dryer. Avoid this problem by keeping the glue in the gun.

🐾 Cold toes during winter nights? Use a hot-water bottle or try this trick: Get hold of a thermos that does not retain the heat that well; unfortunately, common enough. Fill it with hot water and place it in a strategic position. Under the blankets an hour before bedtime is perfect. What a treat to get into bed!

🐾 Do you need a really loud and unbeatable alarm clock? Simply take a *Shabbos* timer, set to the desired time, and plug in a tape or CD player. Set it full blast; it will be very effective! ~> **Warning!** ~> One may not wake up to music; make your selection accordingly.

🐾 Fill ice cube trays by pouring from a pitcher of water; it's easier and you'll waste less water than the traditional method of holding the tray under the faucet. When there is extra space in your freezer, keep a supply of these multi-purpose wonders. An empty freezer uses more electricity than a full one, so the ice will cause the freezer to work more efficiently. And you never know when you may want to chill soup, or apply to a bite, bump, burn or swelling. Once you have a supply of extra ice, you'll find other uses for it; you might even enjoy a cool drink!

🐾 When freezing liquids, such as soups or drinks, don't forget they will expand. Allow space for this; do not fill the container.

🐾 Fill a bottle halfway with water and place it in the freezer on a slant, ensuring that the opening will not become blocked by ice as it freezes. When you want a really cold drink, simply remove the bottle and fill it with water. Within seconds you will have a delicious, refreshing drink.

🐾 Glass or plastic ware looking scummy? Pour undiluted bleach into a large container; soak the items. Check periodically; I have found these kitchen utensils need about thirty minutes or more. Continue to soak other pieces; when all done, refresh your drain or toilet with the leftover bleach.

🐾 Need a set of dishes for everyday use? Consider buying just bowls instead of a full set with flat plates. Requires less storage, and really all foods can be eaten in bowls.

🐾 Ironing a sleeve or some circular area? Roll up some towels or use a roll of paper towels and insert inside the sleeve; remove some towels for narrower sleeves.

🐾 Can't find time for mending that can be done by hand? Keep all necessary accessories in one bag; add torn items as you come across them. Grab the bag before a long phone call, an outing to the park or when hosting a visitor who cheerfully allows you to multitask. Catch up on repairs when traveling. A firm container for your sewing supplies can prevent accidental jabbing and loss.

🐾 Irreparable tights? Slice them, to create useful bands.

🐾 Falling asleep when trying to say *Shema* or *Tehillim*? Try pacing while you daven; it will keep you awake.

🐾 Don't leave rechargers and transformers plugged in when not in use; most are drawing electricity the entire time.

🐾 When accessing the bottom of the refrigerator, oven or any low area, have pity on your back. Sit on a low step stool.

Prepare a chair nearby from which to transfer items. Climb onto this same step stool to access high areas. It will ease your task, and you'll avoid stretching situations which tend to pull up shirts.

Nursing – It's a Natural 🐾

Nursing my children was a wonderful experience for me. Although I had problems here and there, especially initially, I was so eager to feed my baby naturally that I was determined to put up with anything! As I matured and heard about all kinds of difficulties others experienced, I had to thank *HaShem* all over again for the time I spent with my babies and the relatively mild issues I had to overcome. I hope it is safe to say that while you may encounter problems here and there, it can be mostly smooth sailing.

See if these ideas can help you; *Mazal Tov* and enjoy!

🐾 Relish every moment. Once you triumph over the hurdles, you will enjoy a period of unparalleled bonding. While nursing your baby, relax and admire him; perhaps catch up with some conversations or reading. It's a unique stage, there is truly nothing like it. Unfortunately, it is not endless.

🐾 Don't worry about how long your baby nurses. Some thrive on a feeding that takes about five minutes, others enjoy over half an hour. If you have the time, fine, but know that your baby gets most of what is needed after just a few minutes.

🐾 Of course, you need to triumph over the hurdles! Check out this list, consult with friends and read books. If necessary, go to a professional. It is well worth whatever it costs. If nothing else, you'll recoup any fees just by saving on formula!

🐾 Adequate rest is a must. A friend of mine once related the following to me. We were comparing nursing experiences, and she told me that she was able to feed her baby every day without a problem, except on Fridays. She simply did so much on that day, of course, *l'kavod Shabbos*, that she was exhausted and had nothing left for her baby. So prioritize: put sleep ahead of a fancy menu and a spic and span house.

🐾 Drink plenty of water; six to eight cups a day will probably be adequate. Try a cup before and after each feeding. Eat well.

🐾 Set up a basket with anything you might need while you are with your baby. Baby items, tissues, reading material and a water bottle are some things to include; you'll figure it out as you go along. When your baby needs you, grab your supplies and baby and get comfortable. Hang a "do not disturb" sign on the door; just make sure to remove it when done.

🐾 Don't want interruptions during this interlude? Ensure your answering machine is on or unplug the phone.

🐾 Decide how you feel about frequency of feedings. Some use the "on-demand" system, others want to know they can get out a bit, and make an effort to space the feedings a couple of hours apart. Still others like to offer occasional bottles. Try to figure out what will work for you, but stay flexible. Although many advise giving a baby one bottle a day to prevent starvation in the event of an emergency, beware! Some nursing consultants claim that just **one** bottle **one** time can jeopardize your nursing. Perhaps that is an exaggeration, but consider carefully before deciding. Just for the record, it is possible to never give your baby a bottle, and still get out to run errands and even work a few hours. I did, *B"H*, with all my children, so I know it can be done.

🐾 If you have a baby that cries more than you would like – mine all did – put on your detective hat. I found that I had to avoid certain foods for the first six months or so. Most commonly troublesome foods include milk, chocolate, citrus fruits, most vegetables and beans – all of which I faithfully avoided; it made a big difference to my babies. But there are no rules; I had a baby who wouldn't let me eat – of all things – sweet potatoes! Hard to believe, but I experimented a few times. So I had to manage without them. I also discovered, by trial and error, that some foods were okay as long as I didn't overdo it; one bowl of pea soup was okay, three sent my baby into a tizzy! If you are ready to try this system, start out by restricting your meals for a day or two to foods generally recognized as safe. Based on my experiences, that would be limited to chicken, meat, eggs, potatoes and rice. Or consider what you have eaten on days when your baby was calm; those are obviously fine as well. If your baby is content with this diet, then you have established two facts. One, you now have an acceptable group of foods that you can safely eat. Two, some items that you usually eat are making your baby cry. Every day, try out one or two new foods; just proceed gradually. Your baby will let you know right away when you eat something that disagrees with her. Keeping an accurate food diary will help you determine which foods or quantities are the culprits. A friend of mine cannot eat chocolate until she weans her baby. She can't understand why friends tell her she is such a nice, sacrificing mother. "I do it for myself!" she admits. "Who wants to deal with a screaming baby!?"

🐾 Be creative. For example, a change in position or location can help if your baby balks during feedings. Try rocking, cooing or singing.

🐾 Plan to nurse your baby long-term? Designate a code word such as "din-din" or "munchies" to refer to feeding time; that way you will not be embarrassed when she becomes verbal and is hungry in a group setting!

🐾 Need to occupy little ones while you feed your baby? You have a unique opportunity to multi-process. "Pick out a book," I would instruct the older siblings. We would settle down on the couch, and they would take turns holding the book and turning the pages as I nursed and read. It reached the point where they would beg me, "Feed the baby!" What they really wanted was story time! Alternatively, have some good toys available only during feeding time. Just don't neglect to remove them when the session is done, so that they maintain their special status.

🐾 Remember that nursing has been the way to feed babies for thousands of years. It may seem inconvenient at times, but don't get scared off; you'll have plenty of time later to do the things you have to compromise on to maintain a successful nursing relationship... And this special time with **this** baby will never come again.

Paper Towels/Wipes 🐾

🐾 Cut some paper towels into halves or quarters; you will have a choice readily available for your next need. Of course, leave some full size! Prepare a pile for *Shabbos*, but you will find them handy during the week as well.

🐾 They are also the perfect germ-free solution to drying dishes. If you allow the dishes to drain for a few minutes before wiping, one towel can dry lots of dishes. Don't discard the towel when done! It's perfect for wiping down the table and chairs.

🐾 Baby wipes are so much sturdier than tissues and can be used for all sorts of minor cleaning tasks. Try them on bathroom sinks, faucets and light switches. They even work wonderfully when cleaning away an ant invasion.

🐾 ~> **Bonus!** ~> It's fun and easy for children to clean with them! Even toddlers can! They will be thrilled to see how dirty the wipe becomes as they clean. It's quite safe and mess-free; nothing to spill, and economical! Although the children will be tempted to discard them after a swipe or two, they can be used much more than that.

🐾 Don't discard unused dried-up wipes; they will renew easily when moistened, suitable for baby or cleaning.

🐾 Baby wipes are also great to have when traveling. If you do not have a travel pack, simply put a few in a zip-loc bag, and seal well. They will retain their moisture for a few days or even more.

Razor Blades 🐾

Until I inherited razor blades, I never missed them. My benefactor assured me, however, that I would discover a multiplicity of uses for them; she was right! Here are some warnings, and a few uses we found.

🐾 First rule: Store and handle with care!

🐾 Second rule: They do get dull rather quickly, so when you have trouble cutting or scraping, it's time to replace the blade.

🐾 Sewing – They are wonderful for opening seams, and can remove buttons and zippers easily. Use minimal pressure and only the threads are cut. Do exercise caution to avoid cutting material!

🐾 Scraping – If there is a bit of stuck-on dirt, part of a label on an item or old burnt build-up on pots try the blade. It's also fantastic for removing rust, such as on an iron. Use carefully if you do not want any scratches to show.

🐾 Construct a container out of a water or soda bottle. Cut off the top narrow part, which is done more easily with a blade. Since there is no lid, you may prefer to line it with a plastic bag.

🐾 Create a sand toy out of a bottle. Start by cutting off the top; the bottom is your pail. Next, cut away part of the top half on an angle, along the side, toward the neck. Voila! A shovel! Although this cutting can be done with a scissors or knife, it is easier with a blade.

🐾 When you need to cut Styrofoam or something rather thick such as cardboard or plastic, try a blade. Just remember, with care!

🐾 Sharp blades can cut deeply, so it is worth repeating: Make sure to put them away when done!

Shabbos Kodesh

🐾 Prominently post a list of everything that needs doing *erev Shabbos*. Let your personal experiences guide you as you compile the list.

🐾 Make a separate list of do-at-the-last-minute-tasks as well. Have an alarm ring about thirty minutes before you plan to light as a reminder to review this list.

🐾 When removing *muktza* objects, why not put not-for-*Shabbos* toys out of sight at the same time? Although it may not be *ossur* for very young children to play with them, the *muktza* toys will probably not be missed. This will result in a more *Shabbos-dik* atmosphere, without unnecessary temptation or inadvertent handling of *muktza* for older children and adults. You'll also avoid *sheilos*.

🐾 Speaking of which, how about some toys just for *Shabbos*? Gives the little ones something extra to enjoy, so they will not feel deprived of their *muktza* toys.

🐾 Cover light switches. Making cover-ups can be a nice craft project for children. We recently discovered that thin metallic paper (found in art stores) cut it into strips, fit right into our light switch and makes a very nice miniature fence around it. Looks lovely, fits in quickly, and is quite effective for a reminder or to prevent accidental turning on or off. Be creative and see what works for your switches. If you wish to guard the switch from determined tots, get a small box or some such item and tape it over the switch. Alternatively, consider unscrewing the light bulb, unplugging the appliance or even pulling the fuse if you do not need it on *Shabbos*.

🐾 Judaica shops have a variety of *Parsha* question-and-answer material. These cards and books can greatly enrich a *Shabbos* table.

🐾 Open all packages *erev Shabbos,* even if you would open them on *Shabbos* anyway; this will help you avoid tearing letters and other problems. Look at it this way; done *erev Shabbos* it is a fun job, especially for children. When done on *Shabbos*, it can be very annoying to do all kinds of acrobatics to open it in a permissible way.

🐾 Do you have a household with children or adults, each on their own schedule? Prepare a few notes, such as "Wake me up at 4:00"; "Went to visit the Cohen's"; "Will be back for *Seuda Shlishis*." Keep them accessible in a specified place; perhaps near the candlesticks. This enables everyone to make last-minute plans without leaving anyone wondering or disturbing anyone's sleep.

Sholom Bayis 🐾

This is a topic I really hesitate to touch, but I have a few thoughts to share that can really help strengthen or even change a relationship. I do not mean to minimize anyone's challenges and will stress that these ideas should help those with normal ups and downs. For serious problems, be in touch with a qualified (don't make any assumptions) *Rav*.

These are simply ideas that have helped many and I hope they will do the same for you. Incidentally, most really apply to any relationship; use them to strengthen personal ties with everyone in your life!

🐾 Step one is always the same. Start out with heartfelt concentration as you *daven* for *hatzlacha*.

🐾 Even if you didn't begin married life with this mindset, it is never too late. Treat your husband as you (hopefully) did during *Sheva Brachos*. Make his word **the** word. As Rabbi Avigdor Miller says, "There can be only one captain of a ship!"

We are so far removed from the concept of respect, however, that we may not know where to begin. Before any interaction with your husband try to think, "How would I handle this if he were not my husband, but rather my father? My grandfather? My *Rav*?" Would you argue with any of them about taking out the trash? Picking up their socks? How they left the bathroom? Swallow those trivial annoyances and feel *HaShem*'s love for you. You are not being a *shmatte*; you are behaving in the most elevated manner. Remember *HaShem* sends each of us **everything** we need, help and otherwise. Make believe you are honored with custodian duty in the *Bais HaMikdash* – since in reality, you are. An extra shoe to put away is another chance to do your holy *avoda*.

🐾 You can also create some free-wheeling associations with little annoyances; let your imagination fly. Tissues left around? Make believe they are little love notes. You just have to compose them yourself. Books and papers can be cash. Dirty dishes left around become jewelry. Make up a few of these associations according to what you have to deal with and giggle as you take care of them. Watch your mood lift, little by little; enjoy the pleasant atmosphere.

🐾 Refer to the guidelines in **How to be a Loveable Child** and apply them to your husband when possible. Respectful behavior and **Ascribing Positive Motives** will move mountains and allow you to build a strong Torah-*dik* relationship. It will also provide a wonderful paradigm for your children to follow in respecting you, your husband and their future spouse.

🐾 Reframe. Everything can be looked at from two sides. Does your husband noisily awaken you when getting up to learn or *daven*? Be delighted he is going. Does he leave the table without clearing off his dishes? Be glad he comes home to eat. Did he leave you without a key to the car? Remind yourself that you could have made the extra key copy as well. And how fortunate you are to have a car altogether.

🐾 Do your utmost to prevent issues from escalating and snowballing. A stitch in time really saves nine.

🐾 Facing challenges? Speak to an experienced *Rav* or *Rebbetzin*, not your parents. Parents mean well, but lack objectivity and know-how; unfortunately, they may cause more harm than good. And they have long memories. Any helpful suggestions or hints coming from them or any well-meaning family members or friends should be discussed with your mentor. If deemed irrelevant, relegate to the circular file as soon as possible; it's rubbish!

🐾 When you **do** decide to clear up an issue, be solution oriented. Lay ground rules – no dredging up the past, unless absolutely necessary to clarify a problem. Remind your spouse and yourself that you would like a respectful discussion. Try saying, "I feel motivated to change when…" or "I find it difficult when… Do you have any ideas on how we can change?" If your spouse cannot come up with any suggestions, offer your solutions in a non-controlling manner. Make it clear that you are asking, not telling, and want input, to arrive at a solution that works for both of you.

🐾 Feel you married below yourself? Hmmm… *HaShem* thought very highly of your spouse to gift you to him.

🐾 Be an actress – go for an Oscar. Maintain good cheer and change the ambiance in your home; you are sure to notice an ever-widening ripple effect. Tell a joke or funny story, sing a song; help everyone lighten up – yourself included.

🐾 Be an Olympic gold medal winner – in the category of "Fastest Forgetter." When it comes to any errors on your spouse's part, make believe he apologized and said all the beautiful words you wish he would say. Then move on.

🐾 Conversation not proceeding pleasantly? Beg off, excuse yourself to freshen up, change the focus. Chances are the topic won't surface again or you will be more prepared when it does.

🐾 In general, avoid arguments. It's particularly pathetic to get into one over an issue that is not really related to either of you directly. How your relatives vacation or how your neighbor shops is **their** business. You needn't work on solving or understanding their issues! Actually, these types of topics should be avoided altogether, unless it's part of a discussion aimed at clarifying your *hashkafos*. If that is your goal, don't forget to keep in mind *shmiras haloshon* guidelines. Unfortunately, getting into arguments due to such concerns is not as uncommon as we might hope, yet it is truly inane.

🐾 Don't compare. When reading about great marriages, concentrate on how to modify and improve your behavior; don't think about all the marvelous things your spouse could do. Avoid these types of conversations with family and friends; they are poisonous for all concerned.

🐾 If you are contemplating divorce, picture in detail how your life would continue afterwards. There are plenty of articles and (unfortunately) examples in every community. It is not fun. Be certain you have done all you could and that divorcing would really improve your life – and your children's, if there are any.

🐾 Try this reframe: Picture yourself as a single parent with children, finally ending your difficulties by marrying this fellow (your husband)! Imagine how grateful you would feel for anything he does on behalf of your children. How happy you would be to have a man in the house.

🐾 Remind yourself of what it is like to be looking for a spouse. Consider the bitter plight of singles you know. Passing around a resume, revealing your hopes, background and more to so many people. Loneliness. Waiting for *Shabbos* invitations and other such legacies of single living. It's harder for divorcees, since people tend to hesitate to start a relationship with them; sorry, that's reality. And think about your spouse, too; try to feel empathy for the situation you would foist upon him or her.

🐾 Try this: Make a list of your spouse's good qualities, as if you were a *shadchan*. Surprised at what you came up with? Now, list your shortcomings. Be realistic, as you assess each of you. Could be it's not such a bad deal, everything considered. Having made this list, use it! Compliment your spouse as often as you can; be sure to express yourself with sincerity and pride. And feel free to work on your weaknesses.

🐾 Concentrate on fulfilling "Love your neighbor as yourself." It really applies in a marriage relationship, and for the rest of your family, while you are at it. Think of the aggravation divorce would cause to all involved: in-laws, relatives and all associated individuals.

🐾 Remember – rather be righteous than right!

Shopping Successfully 🐾

🐾 Shopping can take a lot of time. When you are running short on that valuable commodity, you may want to get a delivery or hire someone, possibly a capable young girl, to shop for you. Although you may be sacrificing quality, exactness and preferred selection, look at the bright side. Getting an order will force you to cut down on impulse shopping, and thereby probably lower your food bill. Keep reminding yourself that you are trading for time to be spent on other higher priority tasks.

🐾 When on a tight budget, write up a shopping list. Don't forget to check your stock-on-hand to avoid duplicates! Unless there is a special sale that replaces an item you need, stick to your list.

🐾 If you feel that you have got to go to a specialty store for certain items, try to trade off with friends who shop there or see if it makes sense to get a few weeks' worth at a time. Be wary when stocking up, however. If you are not able to police or cleverly conceal, you may just end up going through three jars of pickles in a week instead of one!

🐾 When you do go out to shop, try to leave the children at home. They will invariably talk you into buying more, and you'll end up spending more time at the store as well. You may decide that this is a great way to spend time with them; just realize it isn't free. Better to play with them, and shop while they are in school. They may be initially disappointed, but upon inspecting the bounty, will quickly recover.

🐾 Comparing prices takes time, but the savings can be significant. Try it for a few weeks and see. At the very least, be flexible in your menu and shopping list. Try to work your recipes around the lower priced foods. We enjoy a variety of fruit, but shop according to the store's special. One week the refrigerator is full of pears; the following week, apples.

🐾 When comparing various food choices, don't forget to evaluate according to the portion size normally used in your household. For example, notice the difference in sizes of fruits. If the peaches are large, and the nectarines are small, even though the nectarines may cost somewhat more per pound, you will probably get fifteen nectarines for the price of ten peaches. Each is a portion. Do the **real** math.

🐾 You may find it easier to shop with a standard shopping list. If so, consider varying recipes with the same ingredients. For example, ground meat can be hamburgers, meat loaf, meat balls and sloppy-joe. Tuna can be made into casseroles, salads and so on. Potatoes, rice and other grains can be prepared in many different ways.

🐾 Inspect your receipt. Errors often occur, ranging from a few cents to a few dollars. Cashiers key in the wrong quantity, leave off items, charge for kiwis instead of onions and commit other innovative errors. It's understandable as they are very pressured both by their employer and shoppers. Make sure to speak kindly when investigating any error, and remember: you may be mistaken!

🐾 When buying items sold by weight, take a second to verify that the scale is set to zero when empty. True, it usually is, but more than once I found that it wasn't, and my order had to be redone!

🐾 Check dates carefully when purchasing perishables such as dairy products. Many times, I have found a variety of dates in the refrigerated section. May as well buy the freshest! And don't neglect to rotate your stock!

🐾 Overspending? Shop only with cash. You are done when it is.

Simply Superb Simcha 🐾

🐾 The Torah admonishes us that we will be held accountable for not performing *mitzvos* with *simcha*.

🐾 Our body works better when we maintain an optimistic, cheerful mood. As an example, Rabbi Twerski tells of a man who received a dreadful diagnosis. His doctor had given him 18 months to live, *lo aleinu*. When he told Rabbi Twerski that he was scared and depressed, Rabbi Twerski hypnotized him and told him to recall a joyous event. Rabbi Twerski further instructed him to store this idea in his head and recall it any time at will, simply by saying the word *simcha*. The man did this throughout his ordeal… Forty years later, he was still alive, *B"H*. In another amazing story, Norman Cousins (author of *Anatomy of an Illness* and other books) was declared "terminal" and in great pain. He found that twenty minutes of laughter brought him two hours of pain-relief!

🐾 Make the most of that idea. Gladden yourself with your imagination; picture all kinds of scenarios. Relive your *chasuna*, your birthing experiences (whatever aspect you **did** enjoy) or some such blessed event, loving moments with your family or friends, outings. You can even sing! Anything that cheers you up, makes you smile or laugh is fair game.

🐾 Put yourself in a *simcha* mood by laughing, with or without a joke! Clap your hands and chuckle or stamp your feet and giggle; whatever works. Just laugh.

🐾 Humor, an aspect of *simcha*, saves marriages, children, relationships. As you feel your temper rising, recall "*simcha!*" Reprimands and rebukes can always be administered later if need be. First try to lighten up and put things in perspective.

🐾 Are you faced with situations that either do not require your input or where experience has show that it simply won't help? Leave it to *HaShem*, daven and trust in Him and rejoice in that relationship. Direct your energies to areas where you **can** accomplish.

🐾 Depressing thoughts intruding upon you? Set a timer for five minutes in which you allow yourself to wallow in sorrow. Ding! That's it. Move on to cheerful thoughts.

🐾 So much can be accomplished through *simcha*. The *Arizal*, a *Gadol* of the 16th century, said he only accomplished what he did through *simcha*.

🐾 *Chazal* say: *HaShem* says if we do a *mitzva* with *simcha*, His heavenly court will come to greet us and even *HaShem* Himself will come and welcome us. Wow!

🐾 In the *sefer Ruach Chaim*, Rabbi Chaim Volozhin writes that the amount of learning that can be done in one hour with *simcha* is equal to many hours of learning without.

🐾 Remember that we perform *mitzvos* not as a "tax," but rather as a privilege. Exult in that thought.

🐾 Play a game. Think about an event that you did not enjoy and challenge yourself to come up with five happy thoughts concerning that event. Not three or four, but five. Do ten for extra credit!

🐾 Play a different game. Exaggerate your aggravations. Think – or say out loud or sing, whatever works for you – I'm glad she hung up on me; I wish everyone would. I'm so happy I can't afford what I need; I hope I will manage with even less. I'm delighted my mother criticized me; I hope she will again soon… Try to laugh. When more calm, reassess your situation.

🐾 Or this game: Get yourself deliriously happy when you hear or see someone else's good fortune or *simcha*. This game can reap exponential happiness. After all, most things in life are limited. How much chocolate can we eat? How many *simchos* can we make/attend? How many prizes can we win? But when we decide to be happy for others, the opportunities are boundless!

🐾 Take some time to consider other people's challenges, now and throughout the ages; in all likelihood, you'll want to grab your burden and gleefully run away.

🐾 Remember, our difficulties can all be thought of as *kaparas avonos*, a chance to have our sins wiped away; a wonderful gift. And after all, Who is behind each challenge in your life? So, delight in the knowledge that your loving Father is paying detailed attention to you.

Sleep Aids 🐾

🐾 Make sure everyone gets enough sleep! I read of a young girl who had been taking medication for a few years, enabling her to sit still in school. At about the age of ten, her parents increased her hours of sleep by an hour or two, and were able to take her off medication! Read this again!

🐾 Dr. Sleep is the first specialist I patronize for any problems. Flu, colds, stomach ache, bad mood... Try some additional sleep. It often works! It's the cheapest and best cure.

🐾 Can't fall asleep quickly? The *Gemara* recommends repeating *shema* or a *pasuk* from *shema*. When used consistently, this idea can really speed up your falling-asleep time. In any event, don't lie in bed reviewing your day or planning tomorrow's schedule; that will just make you more alert than ever. Keep your thoughts boring!

🐾 Recruit your *yetzer hora*: Recite *pesukim*, *Tehillim* and/or *daven* to *HaShem*. Your evil inclination will not care for that and will quickly put you to sleep.

🐾 If your schedule allows, get a short nap during the day. Set an alarm, so that you do not overdo it; 45 minutes is the amount of time recommended by experts. Longer than that a person tends to fall into a very deep sleep. Alternatively, I once read about a busy executive who occasionally needed a really short nap to refresh. He would hold a spoon while he sat at his desk closing his eyes; as he fell asleep, the spoon dropped onto the desk; that noise woke him up. With that, he was sufficiently energized to work a few more hours.

Speech Therapy

🐾 Speech therapists can really accomplish a lot. While taking children is pretty standard, here is a reminder that it's never too late; adults can get help. Think you speak clearly? Check with a good friend. Many people lisp or have other easily fixed speech impediments; surprisingly, even lecturers. Cooperative, motivated adults may be helped with relatively few sessions.

🐾 Can you help yourself? Doesn't hurt to try. Once your mispronunciation is pointed out to you, see if you are able to speak correctly when concentrating; using a mirror or recording device can be very helpful. Practice speaking properly a few minutes a day and note improvement.

🐾 Mispronouncing the "s" sound is fairly common. Try this: Bite down or close your teeth; say "s." Did it sound better? If so, practice until you have formed a new habit.

🐾 If you are unable to properly produce the desired sound, see a professional.

🐾 Hoarse? Speak slower, speak less, raise your tone of voice. Relaxation exercises can be very beneficial; try tensing, then relaxing groups of muscles. Breathe into your abdomen and use that air to speak. Enunciate well; open your lips and push out the air as you speak. Irrigate yourself by taking at least a sip of water every half hour. Pantomime and practice the art of silence when possible.

🐾 Save screaming and whispering for emergencies; they are each big strains on your vocal chords.

🐾 Some foods, such as those containing caffeine, dairy products and dry crackers and pretzels can be irritating to your throat and cause hoarseness. Try managing without them and see if it makes a difference.

Teenage Trials

So many fantastic, information-packed books fill the book stores' shelves. These are some of my favorites, which have helped me out in so many ways.

- *Chinuch in Turbulent Times* by Rabbi Dov Brezak
- *Raising Roses among the Thorns* by Rabbi Noach Orlowek
- *Raising Loveable Children* by Sarah Chana Radcliffe
- *With Hearts Full of Love* by Rabbi Mattisyahu Salomon

Although such books can be borrowed, when you find one that truly speaks to you, purchase it. Highlight or bookmark the behavior that you really want to instill into yourself. Find a few minutes to read as little as a section or two every day. It's a good idea to refresh right before the difficult times; morning, coming home from school, bedtime. Those few invested minutes can yield great results.

- Number one is always to *daven*. Ask *HaShem* for help as you recite *tefillos* or *Tehillim*; use your own words when you have a chance. Select a *perek* or *pasuk* that gives you *chizuk* and memorize it for a quick *tefilla*. Check out chapter 119 for a *pasuk* that resonates within you.

- Take a long-term view. If your children are generally well behaved, don't analyze and agonize over every lapse in conduct; we ourselves probably wouldn't do so well thus scrutinized! Whenever possible, just ignore, ignore, ignore. Create a healthy distance by regarding your child as your niece or nephew, and interact accordingly.

- As children enter the teenage years, you may find that they do not express their thoughts as much as they used to or you may feel that they are not really listening to you. These are the years to increase your warmth, say less and look away. They have heard your parenting for at least ten years; some may enjoy hearing your advice and directives, many will not. On the other hand, it is a good time to build your relationship. Try to share your day with your teen, go for walks, play games or do puzzles and projects together. Your goal is to provide a pleasant ambiance.

🐾 At this stage more than ever, your teen is watching you. Modeling good *middos* is your best way of delivering the message. Be enthusiastic about *Yiddishkeit* and life in general. Be loving, honest, helpful, kind and warm.

🐾 Time is a great problem-solver. We all have heard lots of expressions about time; "Time heals all wounds" and "That which [fill in the blank] cannot do, time can do" are two good examples. There is much truth to them. The old joke, where the twenty-year-old comments, "I can't believe how much my parents have matured and changed in the past few years!" can be a reality. Be patient.

🐾 As with any relationship, but here so much more so, think well before responding to just about anything! Your knee-jerk reaction may get you into a lot of hot water. If you feel you absolutely must argue some issue, in most cases it can be done later. Train yourself to say, "Hmm, I'd like to think that over" or "I need to discuss that with your father" or the like. Calm yourself down and make an effort to see their point of view. Use this as an opportunity to practice *dan l'kaf zechus* (judging favorably) and **Ascribe Positive Motives**.

🐾 Before responding to anything, consider; must you respond? What will be the perceived intent of your words? Was a question asked? Questions should get a response eventually. Statements don't have to. Even if it **is** a question, just providing some information may be enough of a response; it's not always necessary or even beneficial to give a complete dissertation. At times it can be downright detrimental. Consider well and give it your best shot.

🐾 Confrontations can be avoided by giving in at the beginning. Before entering the foray, do a mental check: When was the last argument? Is this the right time to feud? Is this issue really important? What will you lose if you give in? If it is your pride, worry about neighbors' reactions or an archaic principle, say *"gam zu l'tova"* or *"zuhl zahn azoy"*; acquiesce graciously. In most cases, your child will outgrow a lot of oppositional behavior, and if you have avoided the potential minefields, your relationship can emerge stronger than ever.

🐾 Often the real cause behind difficult behavior is hunger, exhaustion or both! Don't react; stay calm and pleasant. Offer some food and strongly encourage adequate sleep. And treat yourself to the same. Filling those two needs may yield a calm and manageable teenager – and parent.

🐾 Remember that teens value their friends' opinions very much, more than those of their parents'. They also have strong privacy needs. Despite the difficulties engendered, we need to remember this as we interact with our adolescents.

🐾 When helping your teen deal with a challenge in her life, acknowledge her pain and frustration and encourage her to find a solution. Only if asked, attempt to help; do not assume ownership of the problem.

🐾 Never let any age child hear you say you cannot handle him, or that she is driving you insane. It's one of the most counter-productive messages imaginable.

Recipes

These recipes have all been chosen with care
Firstly, they're quite easy to prepare
Next I tried to cut sugar and fat
But still have taste – imagine that!
Where I could, I sneaked in whole grain
So that getting fiber would not be a pain
I included some treats for special times
and tried to keep them in these guidelines
Hope you'll try them; do your family a favor
They may actually come to savor the flavor!

Let's start with ideas that save time, effort and sometimes even food! While working in the kitchen, I always try to improve my methods and thus have concocted quite a variety of useful techniques. I collect ideas wherever I can as well, so included are my thanks to many forgotten sources. Of course, a great strategy for one may be disastrous for another. Some of these ideas will work for you; others will start your creative juices flowing. You'll generate your own systems!

Build clean-up and energy conservation into your work system. When you have a lot of fruits and/or vegetables to prepare, wash or soak them as needed, and then prepare to work at a table. Cut open a garbage or shopping bag and spread it out. Gather all of your supplies: peeler, knife, cutting board, containers. Now pull up a chair and get to work. When done, throw out the plastic with all the peels. Use the same idea when making cookies, *knaidlach*, meatballs; gather all supplies, and work seated at the table. It may be an adjustment to work in a sitting position, but you will become accustomed to it. You may even feel rested afterwards – your legs certainly will, especially when there are lots to do in the kitchen.

When beginning projects in the kitchen, try to figure out how much time you have; don't forget to account for cleaning up, if that is a priority for you. Although you may think it will be efficient to make a few things at a time, consider carefully. While working "en masse" can save time in some areas, the overhead result may not be worth it.

When there is a lot more food, people may tend to eat more; not really a good idea. Minimize this by putting the finished product away as soon as possible – perhaps even storing it with a neighbor! Occasionally, one forgets about the food and it becomes inedible. Or it simply didn't come out just right this time and now you are stuck with tons of it! Experiment and you will determine what works for you. Of course, it is not a one-time decision; during each phase of life, you can reassess.

Remember to keep the dough or ingredients you are not currently using covered or refrigerated, especially if you are working with large quantities.

When you have time or when the vegetables are well priced, buy, prepare and freeze for future use:

- Sautéed onion (sauté them with water or wine, or a small – or generous – amount of oil; any way will work, just depends on how healthy and tasty you want them to be)
- Sliced mushrooms (sautéed or raw)
- Raw bell pepper strips

❧ Raw tomato chunks

❧ Raw zucchini, butternut squash, sweet potato, carrots, eggplant chunks (try French fry cutter on food processor!) or shredded

Place the vegetables in individual small bags according to the amount you use at a time. Alternatively, fill a large bag and when frozen, break off the amount you need. Whichever way you choose, for optimum results squeeze out air and flatten out the bag of vegetables so that it's not more than half an inch thick. It will be very easy to snap off the amount you need, and will defrost in a jiffy.

Cook a few cups of white beans. They are great to use for soup thickener and simple to prepare. Just take a cup of beans; soak them in three cups of hot water for about an hour or in the refrigerator overnight. When done, water your plants or discard the water. Next add three cups of fresh water; boiling water will speed up the process. Bring water with beans to a boil. Lower heat to simmer – just make sure it is still bubbling a bit – and cook for about an hour. Prick with fork; when the beans are soft, you are done. Cool, grind and freeze flat; add chunks to vegetable soups for extra nutrition and thickening.

Save yourself some time and work by re-using pots and baking dishes when you are making a few things at a time. Putting food away in the fridge? Slip the pot you just cooked it in or the container/pot you will use to re-heat or serve into a plastic bag and refrigerate. Making cookies and then a cake? Even when making **very** different varieties, no need to wash up in between recipes. Keep this principle in mind as you work in the kitchen and you will engender many such short cuts.

Do you prepare a frequently-used recipe that calls for a variety of spices? Prepare your own spice blend. Multiply each spice by four, ten or any convenient number. Combine the spices in one container and calculate the total amount of spice required. For example, if your recipe calls for ¼ tsp pepper, 1 tsp salt, 1 tsp onion powder and ½ tsp garlic powder, multiply by 8, since that makes the pepper simple to calculate. Put 2 tsp pepper, 8 tsp each salt and onion powder and 4 tsp garlic powder in a container; mix well. Total the original amounts; for this recipe use 2¾ tsp (a little less than a tablespoon) of mix. Don't forget to label the container!

Deciding on which cookies or cake to bake? Although many factors go into this decision, let one of those be the amount of sugar. Since recipe sizes vary, don't just look at the quantity of sugar. Instead, compare the proportion of sugar to flour. Many baked goods have equal amounts of flour and sugar, so I tend to think of that ratio as the base line. More sugar than that is really sweet. Less than that is almost healthy! Notice the chocolate chip cookie recipe, with 3 cups of sugar to 4 ½ cups of flour. Not so bad, but it depends on how many chocolate chips you use! Oat Bars are made with three cups of oats, one of flour and only one cup of sugar. Again, we must not forget about those chocolate chips, but still these recipes are lower than the standard baked goods offered. The best I have seen is Cocush Cake. Seven cups of flour, yet only $2/3$ cup of sugar. Include the cup of chocolate mix, which contains about another $2/3$ cup of sugar. That adds up to a mere $1^1/3$ cups sugar for seven cups of flour!

Margarine is another ingredient to minimize. Try cutting out a quarter of the margarine and substituting oil; that is, if a recipe calls for a cup of margarine, use only ¾ of a cup and ¼ cup of oil. If no one notices, next time do half and half and keep going… You may be able to do a total substitution. Chances of success are best with cakes; less for cookies and even less with a crust or crispy, flaky dough. Be alert; you may need a slightly smaller amount of oil altogether.

Use the same idea to cut down on the total amount of oil and sugar in any recipe; leave out a little and see if anyone can tell the difference. Many recipes are eaten just as happily despite minimizing these unhealthy ingredients. Although I thought most of my recipes were cut pretty much to the bone, friends have told me that they were able to reduce even further! So, blaze your own path, and enjoy!

One final 'minimizing' tip – serve smaller portions! Make slightly smaller cookies; cut kugels, cakes or meatloaf into smaller pieces. Be brave and prepare a little less. Use a small ice cream scoop! People usually eat a portion as served, and over the years portions sizes have grown by leaps and bounds. Do yourself and your loved ones a favor – downsize.

While cutting down on the unhealthful ingredients, try to include whole grains and vegetables that are not usually sought out; just work gradually. Add spices, sesame seeds and vary quantities to find the flavor blend that works for you, especially as you cut down on oil, salt or sugar. Many recipes that call for regular white flour can tolerate up to half whole wheat, for example. ~> *Hint!* ~> sifting flour? It will go quicker with a larger sifter! Two knives shaking around inside will speed it up a bit more.

Soups are undervalued in terms of their vital impact. All I can say is make a lot – often! They're so nutritious, inexpensive and filling! And those frozen prepared vegetables mentioned above make prep time a snap. Sneak in grains such as barley, millet and/or quinoa; they do not detract from the taste at all and contain nutrients that you might miss otherwise! Find them in your regular market or health food stores. Add frozen peas ae high in fiber and other nutrients to cool off quickly; great for children and everyone else!

Double – or even triple – your oven usage by inverting a baking pan on the bottom of the oven and using that pan as a shelf. Naturally, check to make sure that everything gets done properly! If your oven does not bake so evenly, turn around the baking pans, and/or rotate the items from shelf to shelf.

A countdown timer can prevent the agony of burnt food. Keep one in the kitchen and use it; save yourself aggravation, wasted food and difficult clean ups, as well as gas or electricity. Warming food or cooking for a while? To avoid burning or overcooking, place a "heat disperser" under the pot. Found in most shops in *Eretz Yisroel,* this fantastic adjunct costs a couple of dollars. Elsewhere, perhaps some specialty shops carry them.

For those that haven't seen such an item, it looks like a small, rimless frying pan with lots of small holes. For more food related ideas and tips, see **Reuse with Relish**, and **Health and Hygiene Tips**.

Unless otherwise stated, these recipes are to be baked for 30 minutes at 350° Fahrenheit, about 180° Centigrade; a normal oven temperature. Use a 9 x 13 baking pan (23cm x 33cm) or similar size. Be alert when following a recipe the first few times; adjust baking time, temperature and pan size according to your oven and taste. Notate the recipe right away, before you forget.

In recipes calling for baking powder or baking soda, it is always best to combine those with the flour and mix well before adding other ingredients.

Read through the entire recipe, including instructions, before beginning. Ensure you have everything you need.

When using a rolling pin, no need to wash it when done if you place baking paper on the dough. Else, roll the rolling pin in some flour scattered on the work surface to prevent sticking. Haven't got a rolling pin? Use a straight-sided mug.

~> *Tip!* ~> Cookie sheets without sides are super easy to roll out onto! Or prepare your dough on a baking sheet; roll, score and then transfer to baking pan.

~> *Reminder!* ~> before beginning any work in the kitchen, even just setting the table, wash your hands. Even so, do not unnecessarily handle food or anything the food will touch. For example, when setting the table, hold the handle, not the part that will come in contact with food. Hold the bottom of the glass or cup, etc. Train everyone to do the same!

~> ***Note:*** ~> * indicates kosher for *Pesach*
Tsp = teaspoon
Tblsp = tablespoon = 3 tsps
Half kilo = a little more than a pound = 16 ounces/454 grams
1/2 inch = approx. 1 cm.
. That's enough info; let's get in the kitchen! *B'taiavon*!

Challah

5 lb (=2½ kilo =18 cups) flour
2 Tbs yeast
2 Tbs salt

²/₃ cup sugar
1 cup oil
6 cups warm water

Throughout many years of baking challos *erev Shabbos*, I have suffered a few snafus with the ingredients. My solution? During the week, prepare a container with the proper amount of salt, sugar and yeast. I have not had any problems despite allowing salt and dry yeast to mix. Store in the fridge; it's ready when you are. No more forgetting or discovering that you are out of yeast! Saves a minute on a busy *erev Shabbos*.

~> ***Tip!*** ~> Prepare warm water easily. Combine 5 cups of room temperature water with 1 cup of boiling water.

Once you get used to it, this mixes quickly by hand. I have experimented with many types of flour, mostly with the same results. In the beginning of my challah-baking career, my challos invariably came out heavy. A few years down the line, they came out light! So all I can say is – stick to it!

Use a large bowl and work at a table rather than at a counter; it's a more comfortable height. Combine all dry ingredients, stir for half a minute then add liquids. Mix by inserting your hand or hands into plastic gloves or even a bag; makes it easier to knead by hand. Do not squeeze dough; it will ruin the texture. Just keep punching and turning over. If you are a beginner, be patient and persevere; after a few times you won't believe how quick and simple it is! It takes about fifteen minutes from start to finish, when I don't get side-tracked!

If the dough is very sticky, add a bit of flour; if that doesn't help, add a bit of oil. Too much flour will make it heavy. Too dry? Add a bit of water at a time, or again, some oil. Once it becomes dough with a nice feel and appearance, you are finished! Cover the dough by inserting the entire bowl into a fresh garbage bag. Let rise for about an hour, until double in bulk. You may let it rise for a longer period of time, but not too much as it may develop a yeasty taste. Separate challah with a *bracha*. Burn it, then *daven* – you have been transported to the Western Wall!

Punch down; divide into four equal parts; each part can make either two medium-sized challos, or 12 – 16 small rolls. Braid, brush with 1 egg yolk mixed with a Tbs of water, sprinkle with sesame seeds. Strips of baking paper can be placed between the challos to prevent them from joining together as they rise. You can probably trim a 2-inch strip off the paper you plan to bake them on and use that as a separator.

~> ***Bal tachshis tip!*** ~> Plan on using the leftover egg, if any. If you are making kugels or some such dish earlier in the day, simply reserve an egg yolk; cover to prevent it's drying out. If you have leftover egg and are no longer baking, consider making *knaidlach* dough which can be frozen, frying omelets or dropping dollops of it into your chicken soup.

When the braiding is almost completed, pre-heat the oven to 325°. Wait five minutes, turn off the oven; let challos rise in the hot oven and they will be ready to bake in about ten minutes. Bake at 350° for 45 minutes; rolls need only 30 minutes. (Baking time and temperature will vary according to your oven, so watch carefully for the first few times!) Traveling with hot challos or rolls? Use a pillowcase; plastic bags may cause them to 'sweat' and can be unhealthy.

Challos (or rolls) shaping ideas:

❧ Braid together three or six ropes. Method of braiding with six: Connect six ropes at one end. Grasp the two rightmost ropes, one in each hand. Swing both hands toward the left, dropping the rope in your right hand to the middle of the four ropes on the board. Your left hand continues holding its rope. With the now-empty right hand, pick up the leftmost rope. Swing both hands back toward the right, dropping the rope in your left hand to the middle of the four ropes on the table. Your right hand continues holding its rope. With your left hand, pick up the rightmost rope, swing back towards the left. Continue swinging and dropping back and forth. Pinch the ropes together at the end when done, tuck under a bit if desired. You may want to practice this with some rope; it is easier than it sounds, and comes out beautiful.

🐾 Easiest and quickest – roll out a rope; hold one end and coil the other end around, snail fashion. Tuck the end under so that it doesn't pop open.

🐾 Make a rope and knot it; if you bring the bottom end up through the little hole formed by the knot, it looks even nicer.

🐾 Flatten the rope, so that you have a piece of dough shaped like a ruler. Using a sharp knife, make cuts spaced a finger apart along the length of the dough, half the width of the dough; make sure to cut through the dough all the way down to the board. Roll it up along the length of the "ruler" and you have a fancy rose! Fabulous for crust-lovers!

🐾 For beautiful, *Rosh Hashanah* style challos, make six ropes; form a tic-tac-toe board with four of them and put the last two on top, one in each direction, cutting the center square into four. You will have four groups of three "tails." Just braid each group of tails and tuck in the end. Very pretty and easy!

🐾 Although I make fresh challos *erev Shabbos*, they didn't taste as delicious during the day meals as they did Friday night. This lapse of quality was resolved by freezing the challos; they tasted as good as fresh when thus preserved.

~> ***Tip!*** ~> Use this dough to make frank-n-blanks. Cut hotdogs in half so that you have two short pieces. Take a piece of dough – about the size of an egg – and wrap it around the hotdog. No need to be fancy, it will puff out and look pretty no matter what! Let rise a few minutes then bake for 25 minutes.

~> ***Bonus tip!*** ~> Freeze dough for pita. Take an egg-size piece of dough, place it in a plastic sandwich bag, flatten into a circle with a hole in the middle – like a CD – close and freeze; it's quick and easy to churn out a pile of them. To enjoy, remove from bag while frozen. Bake as is, or make a mini-pizza. Top with tomato sauce – or chopped tomatoes – and cheese; microwave for a minute. Don't forget about them in the freezer! They do not retain their consistency for long.

Amazing Croutons

1 challah or loaf of bread
½ Tbs salt

4 tsp paprika
1-2 Tbs

Optional: onion powder, garlic powder, dried parsley, etc.

    For the best results, use white bread or challos, but any bread will do, even defrosted or somewhat stale bread or whole wheat.

    Heat oven to 350°. Slice the bread; take four slices at a time and dice them. If the bread is not so soft, you may have luck with a food processor; try the french-fry cutter attachment. Although the croutons made in this way were quickly consumed, they don't look very attractive!

    Place the cubes on a cookie sheet, but do not pile them. This is a toasted product! One regular sized challah will fill two cookie sheets with croutons. If your oven is large enough, bake them at the same time on two different shelves. Although I provided amounts, it can be done without measuring; you will get the idea of it after a few times. Sprinkle with spices. Drizzle lightly with oil and using one hand (why get two dirty?) grasp clusters so they all get coated. Bake them for 15-20 minutes; turn off the oven, leaving croutons in for about an hour.

    Check them. If the croutons crumble when squeezed, they are toasty enough. Otherwise, bake a few minutes more; just check on them to ensure they don't burn! Great on salads or for a *nosh*, but we didn't care for them in soup – they get soggy quickly. Children just love these!

~> ***Alert!*** ~> The *bracha* is *hamotzi*!

Israeli Salad*

6 tomatoes
1 small onion
6 small cucumbers

a few leaves of lettuce
1 carrot
1 pepper

Dressing:
1 Tbs oil
3 Tbs vinegar

¾ tsp salt
¼ tsp pepper

Shred the carrot and pepper or use a vegetable peeler to make very thin slices. Dice everything else and combine. Cut the lettuce with a plastic knife, as a metal knife removes some nutrients. We have not been happy with food processor salad, but if your family likes it and you need the processor for other things as well, it will save time; try that french fry blade.

To dress, drizzle oil onto salad. Sprinkle on salt, pepper and pour in some vinegar. Although I have provided amounts for those that like to measure, if you just pour it on, it's easier; you will get the idea after doing it a few times. Dress it as close to serving time as possible.

~> *Tip!* ~> If your oil bottle has no flow-restricter, try to keep the cap partially on or transfer it: Wash out a ketchup container and fill it with oil; you'll be able to dispense a small stream easily.

~> *Tip!* ~> Try these additions instead of the dressing to add flavor to your salad: chopped walnuts, tuna fish, **Techina**, chummus, cheese, avocado chunks or **Amazing Croutons**. Serves between 5-10, depending on what else you are serving and how much everyone likes salad!

~> *Tip!* ~> Take a liter or quart bottle of vinegar and, using a funnel, pour in one tablespoon of pepper and 3 tablespoons of salt. When dressing salad, use this mixture and just add oil.

Techina Dressing

2 cups 100% ground techina
3 cups of water
1½ tsp salt

2 Tbs lemon juice
5 garlic cloves (or more)

    Combine everything in food processor. Scrape sides, blend well. Taste and adjust seasonings, and recipe! A bit watery, it will thicken overnight. Pour into individual cups, it freezes very well and defrosts quickly; just place in a cup of hot water for about 30 minutes. Nutritious and delicious!

~> **Warning!** ~> Lasts only a few days in the refrigerator.

Falafel Balls – Dietetic

2 cups raw chickpeas
coriander (or parsley or celery) leaves
¼ cup prepared Techina

2 Tbs cumin
5-10 garlic cloves
1-2 onions
1 tsp salt

About 2 Tblsp of oil for greasing scoop – or more!

Optional – flour, bread crumbs, baking soda, water, oil.

    Soak peas overnight; grind everything. Refrigerating a few hours will solidify the mixture. Form balls by using a small scoop; a two-tablespoon measuring size is perfect. Drip a bit of oil into the scoop; fill with mixture, deposit onto baking sheet. Place the balls as close as possible; they do not spread. Re-oil the scoop after forming three or four balls; or more often. Be generous; you'll clearly use much less oil compared to frying. Bake at 350° for 30 minutes. Freezes well.

Spicy Tomato Dip* 🖐

5-10 garlic cloves
1 chili pepper, any type
4-5 tomatoes

1-2 Tbs vinegar
1-2 Tbs oil
1 tsp salt

Blend and taste; adjust seasonings. If you are shot on tomatoes, use some tomato sauce/paste, and water according to taste. Appetizing with **Techina**, and assorted vegetables, chips or crackers. For a blander version, simply use less chili pepper or omit it entirely. ~> ***Warning!*** ~> Chili peppers can cause coughing or other reactions. Use cautiously and wash hands with soap after handling or wear gloves. You may want to prepare a few peppers at a time. Clean, cut and freeze; they will retain their sharpness.

Ketchup* 🖐

Experiment with this, but it has a pretty good taste. If you don't want it for a steady diet, you may appreciate it when you run out of ketchup and must improvise.

½ cup tomato paste
¼ cup water
2 Tbp sugar

4 tsp vinegar
¼ tsp salt

Mix well, taste and adjust seasonings; refrigerate leftovers for up to a couple of weeks.

Oven Baked French Fries*

8 medium potatoes
Or 4 sweet potatoes
1 tsp salt
2 Tbs oil

    Scrub and cut into French fry shape; no need to peel. Coat with salt and oil. Spread on a cookie sheet; if there is extra room, add more. Bake at 350° for 45 minutes, or broil for about 15 minutes. Scrumptious and much healthier than real fries! If you prefer a richer taste, simply add more oil.

Doughless Potato Knishes

8-10 potatoes
4 onions, sliced or chopped
¾ cup oil
1-2 shredded zucchini
4 eggs
2½ cups flour
1 Tbs salt
1 tsp pepper

    Boil and mash the potatoes; let cool a bit, for easy handling. Or grate potatoes and use raw. Different taste, both work! Optional: saute onions. Combine potatoes with remaining ingredients. Optional: Reserve one egg yolk and brush on top; sprinkle sesame seeds. Bake 1 hour at 350° in 9"x13".

    This recipe freezes and re-heats easily. To defrost, put in fridge overnight. Bake covered, at 350° for about 30 minutes, then uncover and bake an additional 15 minutes; times will vary depending on how frozen it is and how your oven works. Cut into individual knishes. Savory and filling

Kishka Kugel

Bottom layer:
2 carrots
1 onion
1 celery stalk
¾ cup oil
1½ cups flour
1 potato
1 tsp salt
1 tsp paprika
¼ tsp pepper

Grate vegetables and combine with remaining ingredients; press into standard baking pan.

Top layer:
4 medium zucchini
1 Tbs mayonnaise
2 eggs
1 tsp onion powder
1 Tbs dried onion
½ tsp salt

Slice and boil the zucchini for about ten minutes, until soft. Drain and combine with remaining ingredients. Pour onto bottom layer. (Drained water is perfect for any soup!)

Bake at 350° for an hour. Beautiful and delicious, hot or cold. Appeals more to adults than children.

Pickle-y or Spicy Eggplant*

2 large eggplants, sliced
1 pepper
1 tsp oil
5 garlic cloves
½ tsp salt

Option A:
¾ cup boiling water
¾ cup vinegar

Option B:
3 tomatoes, ground

    Place eggplant slices into a container and sprinkle liberally with salt to remove its bitter taste. Let stand at least half an hour. You may want to periodically drain the liquid that collects. Rinse eggplant and squeeze to remove excess water.

    Cook eggplant for about a half hour in a pot with oil; more oil will make it tastier, but a small amount is enough. Use a low flame, stirring every few minutes, as you remember or keep resetting a timer. When the eggplant is soft and done, add the pepper and garlic; cook five more minutes. Taste before adding additional salt; depending on how well you rinsed the eggplant, you may not need any.

Option A:
    Add the water and vinegar, turn off the flame, mix and refrigerate.

Option B:
    Add the tomatoes, cook about 5 minutes more.

    Quickie version: slice an eggplant; salt as explained above if desired. Top each slice with tomato sauce and cheese, any kind will do. Bake in a toaster oven for about 15 minutes or microwave a few for about 5 minutes. ~> ***Tip!*** ~> Prepare and freeze eggplant slices, with or without topping. No need to defrost; just bake and serve.

    Healthy and dietetic, eggplant is fantastic with many foods; potatoes, rice, fish or salad. Or try cottage cheese!

Beans in Tomato Sauce

(aka vegetarian cholent)

2 cups white beans, any type
4 large onions, chopped
1-2 large peppers, sliced
3 tomatoes, chopped
2-3 zucchini, sliced
1 cup tomato paste
6-8 cups of water
Optional: eggplant slices.

1 Tbs dry mustard/paprika
1 tsp ground cumin
1 tsp chili powder
1 tsp unsweetened cocoa
½ tsp cinnamon
1 tsp salt (if there is none in the tomato paste)

If you plan to serve this often, prepare the spice mix as described in the hints section. In this case, 2 Tablespoons of combined spice will suffice.

Quantities of vegetables can vary according to stock on hand; it will come out wonderful regardless! Check and soak beans overnight or in boiling water for about an hour. Boil beans for about an hour then add the rest of the ingredients. Cook for another hour. Add more water if bean mixture appears dry. Tastes fantastic with shredded lettuce, fresh chopped tomatoes, grated cheese or as-is.

Cabbage Salad*

4 cups shredded cabbage
1 Tbs oil
3 Tbs vinegar

½ tsp salt
½ tsp pepper
2 Tbs sugar

Optional: shredded carrot, radish, butternut squash, onion – according to taste.

Combine well; wait twenty minutes and taste. Adjust seasonings and enjoy! Goes well with toasted almonds, sesame salt, Chinese Noodles or croutons.

String Beans 🐾

1 package of frozen string beans, 800 grams ~ 2 pounds
1 onion, chopped
¼ cup oil (approximately)
1-2 Tbs sesame seeds
1 tsp salt, to your taste

    Allow beans to defrost while you chop and sauté the onion in oil until golden brown. Add string beans and continue to cook, stirring occasionally. When the beans are soft, after about five minutes, add sesame seeds and salt. Using untoasted sesame seeds? Sauté them with the onions. Seeds leftover from pretzels? Omit/decrease salt. Avoid burning by using a low flame. It will take longer, and will be a softer texture, but will get done. Delicious fresh, hot or cold; great for *seuda shlishis*.

Beet Salad* 🐾

2 raw beets, peeled, shredded
4 cloves garlic, minced
¼ cup oil
¼ cup vinegar
1 tsp salt, to taste
½ tsp pepper

Optional: add some sugar and/or shredded onion, cabbage, kohlrabi

    Mix, chill, taste and adjust. Stays fresh for a week or more. Unusual, colorful, healthy and tasty. Try it!

Tuna Quiche*

Crust: See recipe for **Spinach Pie** crust, or omit.

3 cans of tuna ~ 500 grams
1 tsp salt
¼ tsp pepper

4 eggs, beaten
1 cup solid part of vegetable soup

Optional: Add about half a cup of any combination of grated potato, zucchini, bread crumbs, matzo meal, corn flakes, oats.

If using tuna in oil, discard some of the oil and mix the rest into the quiche. When using tuna in water, include the water if you prefer a moister *kugel*; you may want to add a few tablespoons of oil for a better taste. Mix everything well and put on top of crust, if using. Bake at 350° for 45 minutes.

Gregarious Grains

For a healthy side dish or even main course, consider cooking grains. Brown rice, kasha, lentils or oats – and even millet and quinoa, combined or alone – are full of fiber, protein and more; all you need to do is add various flavor enhancers. When cooking grains, turn off the flame while just a bit of liquid remains. The mostly cooked grains will absorb the remaining water, and you will avoid burnt or dried out grains while retaining more nutrients.

To cook rice or kasha, combine 1 cup with 2 cups (boiling) water; bring to a boil and simmer for about 45 minutes. For lentils, millet and quinoa use three or four cups of water with one cup of grains, and follow the same cooking directions. ~>
Suggestion! ~> Prepare the grains in a *pareve* pot and go either way serving time.

Standard oatmeal calls for twice as much water as oats. This recipe is named **Inside-Out Oats** due to its requiring **half** as much. Use the same recipe for medium cut kasha. There are a few varieties; use any type. We prefer old-fashioned oats.

3 cups oats/med cut kasha	1½ cups boiling water
1 egg	½ tsp salt

Combine oats or kasha with egg and toast in a frying pan or pot set on a medium flame; start with some oil if you prefer. After it is a bit toasty – not more than five minutes – pour on the boiling water. Stir, cover and cook for about five minutes. Turn off the flame, and wait about ten minutes for the water to be completely absorbed. Cook a few minutes more if it's still watery, but it shouldn't be.

Try any of the following additives with any of these grains; you never know who will enjoy what, and you will have a new healthy item on your family's menu!

Milk (and craisins) go(es) well with rice
Cheese – melted cheese makes just about everything yummy!
Cottage cheese is a close second
Tuna, ketchup or sautéed onions (and mushrooms…)
Salt, oil and pepper or
Browned ground beef, diced meat or chicken
Sauce; can be leftovers from meatballs, stews, etc. Prepare ahead – when available, freeze flat for such recipes.

Tried, but it just didn't go? Freeze any leftovers. Add those raw or cooked frozen grains to cholent or to soups in small amounts. Little by little, you will use them up.

Mixed Vegetable Soup *

(When using this recipe for *Pesach*, omit the beans and grains)

8 cups of water
1 zucchini
1 sweet potato
1 carrot
1 chunk pumpkin
1 chunk butternut squash
1 celery stalk, thinly sliced
1 onion, chopped
Optional: a few tablespoons of soup mix

2 or more potatoes
2 tsp salt
¼ tsp pepper
1 cup ground beans
2 Tbs barley
2 Tbs millet
2 Tbs quinoa

Shred or chop vegetables or leave vegetables in chunks; blend when done cooking. Or, dice onion and celery, quarter remaining vegetables. Mash when done. This last option is quickest, and looks great; all taste delicious. Feel free to vary the vegetables and quantities. Cook about an hour until vegetables are soft. Mashing vegetables after about 15 minutes of cooking will speed up the process and make blending easier.

~> *Tip!* ~> Reminder: frozen peas added straight into the bowl will quickly, nutritiously and deliciously cool the soup.

Tomato Soup *

1 can (15 oz) tomato sauce
(we prefer sugar-free)
Optional: raw/cooked rice

1 sliced zucchini
1 diced onion
2 cups water

Cook about twenty minutes. Add milk to cool it off a bit. Season to taste; depends on brand of sauce – they really vary!

Onion Soup* 🐾

6 onions, sliced
2 tsp salt
1 tsp pepper
½ cup dry red wine

8 cups boiling water
2-4 Tbs oil
2 Tbs flour/oat bran (on
Pesach use potato starch)

Optional: ¼ cup onion/mushroom soup mix

    Sauté onions until golden; add salt, pepper, flour and soup mix and sauté a few more minutes. Add wine and water; cook thirty minutes more.
    Serve with croutons and/or grated cheese.

Lentil Soup 🐾

2 cups brown lentils or
1 cup pink lentils

1 cup shredded zucchini
6-8 cups of water

Optional: ½ cup sweet potato
Optional additions with brown lentils: 1 cup tomato sauce and vegetables; see **Beans in Tomato Sauce** for ideas.

Pink lentils require about 45 minutes cooking time; a very easy, quickest and healthy soup. No need to cut the sweet potato, it will fall apart easily when fully cooked. If you have a masher, no need to grate the zucchini either. And a surprise awaits you when preparing this soup the first time. It will turn a lovely shade of green! Brown lentils need about 90 minutes; it's a very thick soup that is delectable with shredded cheese.

Mushroom-Barley Soup

8 cups water
1 cup ground beans
8 oz mushrooms or soup mix

1 large onion
¼ cup barley
2 tsp salt
¼ tsp pepper

Sauté onion and mushrooms in water or oil; use more or less according to your taste. Next add water and barley. Cook about half an hour, add remainder and cook an additional half hour. Alternatively, cook all at once, for an hour. It's simpler, and there is no great loss in overcooking the beans.

Chicken and Potatoes*

Easy and scrumptious, although not so healthy

1 chicken – whole or parts
6 potatoes, sliced
Or 3/4 cup raw brown rice

1 onion, sliced opt.
1-2 cups of water
2-3 Tbs paprika

~> *Tip!* ~> try sweet potato and eggplant cubed, about a cup of each – delicious! Do not add any water.

Layer onions if using, then vegetables or rice in baking pan. Sprinkle paprika as desired. When baking a whole chicken, cut only as needed so that it lies flat; it is so much easier to cut when baked! With potatoes, add a cup of water; for rice, add two cups; check while baking to avoid dried potatoes or rice. Bake about two or three hours at 325°. The chicken gets delightfully crispy; the potatoes/rice with the chicken drippings taste heavenly. Alternatively, use chicken from chicken soup. Although it will not taste as yummy, it will be healthier with fewer calories!

Chicken Soup*

1 chicken or various parts. The more, the merrier!
2 carrots, sliced
2 stalks of celery, sliced
Celery leaves, chopped or whole
2 zucchini, sliced

1 onion, chopped
4 garlic cloves, quartered
1 cup butternut squash or pumpkin pieces
6 quarts water

Optional: quartered white potatoes; makes a full meal!

Bring water and chicken to boil, cook for about half an hour on a very low flame. Just make sure it is bubbling! If your family enjoys boiled chicken, just add vegetables, sliced and chopped as you prefer. Cook at least another hour. If you like a stronger taste, keep cooking. Experiment and adjust quantities.

Your family prefers baked chicken? Remove the chicken from the soup after half an hour; longer will result in a bland taste. Refrigerate for later or bake with or without spices. Consider adding more chicken or other parts, which can be similarly handled, or leave in a few pieces.

Here are some methods to cool down the soup as quickly as possible to avoid growth of bacteria: Pour soup into a large, shallow baking pan and immerse it into a larger container full of cold/icy water. Wait a few minutes, then dump out the warm/hot water, and refill with cold; re-immerse the soup pan. Put ice cubes in a baking bag and place the bag in the soup; replace ice as it melts. Repeat as time allows. Refrigerate; remove fat before reheating.

Optional: Reheat and cook for 20-30 minutes with fresh vegetables; you can probably add some water if needed.

~> *Tip!* ~> freeze clean whole celery leaves, crush when frozen and add to soup as desired. Crushing the frozen leaves can be a fun reward for a cooperating child!

Knaidlach*

1 cup matzo meal   ½ tsp pepper
1 tsp salt   4 eggs
½ cup seltzer or soup; fine to take from the top, better with some *schmaltz* (chicken fat) in it!

Combine dry ingredients; add liquids and mix well. If the mixture is too soft, a brief stay in the refrigerator will firm it.

When you are ready to cook them, prepare a small bowl of water. Dip in fingers, then take about 2 Tablespoon of the dough and form into a ball. Re-wet fingers after every two or three balls. Drop balls into a large pot with about 8 cups boiling water; cook for about twenty minutes. Remove balls with a slotted spoon; use remaining water to make soup or cholent!

When warming soup for *Shabbos*, add *knaidlach* after the soup comes to a boil. It doesn't pay to cook them in the soup, as they soak up quite a bit of it without enhancing their taste. They are an excellent side dish for during the week too!

Zucchini Kugel

8 zucchini   5 eggs
1 butternut squash   4 tsp salt
½ cup of quinoa/pink lentils   1 tsp pepper

Shred vegetables, combine all ingredients. Bake at 350° for an hour. This is a healthy and tasty alternative to starchy kugels. Fat free, you may want to offer *techina* or sour cream as a delicious topping.

Chicken Salad*

Fantastic for *Shabbos* lunch and/or for using leftovers.

1 piece of baked chicken breast or schnitzel, cubed
1-2 tomatoes, cubed
1 small onion, chopped
4 cups shredded lettuce
¼ tsp pepper

½ tsp salt
Or 2 tsp sesame salt
1 Tbs oil
2 Tbs vinegar
1 Tbs sugar

Combine well shortly before serving. Taste and adjust seasonings. Delightful with **Amazing Croutons**.

Hamburgers/Meatballs*

3 pounds ground meat
4 eggs
¼ cup tomato sauce/ketchup

1 chopped onion, tomato
1 shredded zucchini
1 cup filler

~> *Tip!* ~> Use any combination of turkey, chicken and beef

Vary vegetables and filler ingredients according to taste and what's on hand. Select any combination of bread or crouton crumbs, matzo meal, potato starch, mashed potatoes or mashed vegetable soup. Combine all ingredients and shape as desired. For hamburgers, this mixture fills two trays. Bake at 350° for about thirty minutes. For meatballs, bring 1 cup of tomato sauce and 5 cups of water to a boil; add balls. Cook for about an hour stirring occasionally. Goes well with rice or pasta. Leftovers freeze beautifully, but if you want to have any, you may have to remove them before serving…

Cholent

5-6 quartered potatoes
1½ cup beans
1½ cup barley
1 Tbs salt

½ tsp pepper
3 Tbs paprika
1 pound (one kilo) meat

Optional: sliced onion, whole zucchini and/or butternut squash

Check beans and barley; soak in boiling water or overnight in refrigerator. I have experimented many times and the onions are really optional.

Place all ingredients into a heavy 6-8 quart pot, first vegetables, then grains; add seasonings. At this point, the pot and contents can be refrigerated.

Erev Shabbos, add 10 cups of (boiling) water and bring to a boil. Add meat, slices of chicken breast, kishke as desired. Lower flame to a simmer and cook for a couple of hours.

~> **Tip!** ~> You can cook slices of chicken, they will be ready in about a half hour. Remove and add more if you like. This is the easiest way to prepare chicken which can be frozen for future meals. It enhances the *chulent* taste with little or no extra work or cost.

Check water level before placing on *blech* or hot plate; if it looks dry, add a cup or two of water.

Please do not simply dispose of any leftovers. It's good food! If there is no more meat, serve with **Sloppy Joe**. It can also be frozen flat; use as a delicious side dish.

I have even heard of freezing *chulent* in a pot and placing it on the *blech* a week later. No one guessed! If no one in your family will touch it, find someone who will. You'll be surprised, just ask around.

Goulash/Stew* 🐾

2 pounds (1 kilo) meat cubes
2 onions, chopped
Few cloves garlic, chopped
1 or 2 of each: bell peppers,
 carrots and zucchini, sliced
15 potatoes, quartered

½ cup tomato paste
Or 1 cup tomato sauce
2 tsp salt
1 tsp pepper
1 Tbs paprika
6 cups (boiling) water

    Clearly, you can play around with this. If the meat is good, it will be tasty. You can brown the meat and sauté onions and vegetables, but it is delicious without those extra steps. Throw it all in, bring to a boil, lower the flame to the smallest, as long as it is still bubbling and cook three or four hours. A *Yom Tov* treat! And a wonderful *Pesach* cholent!

Sloppy-Joe* 🐾

1 pound (500 grams) ground
turkey, chicken or beef
2 onions, chopped
2 tomatoes, chopped

1 pepper, chopped
1 zucchini, chopped
3 Tbs tomato paste/sauce

    No need to defrost; this can still be quickly prepared. Place the meat in the pan on a low-medium flame; after a few minutes invert it. The cooked layer will easily scrape off into the pan. Continue inverting and scraping. Remove meat when fully cooked. Sauté vegetables, add tomato paste or sauce and cook for about twenty minutes. Add browned meat, and serve with your choice of **Gregarious Grains**.

Pizza

Dough:
8 cups flour – use half or all whole-wheat	2 Tbs sugar
	2 Tbs oil
1 Tbs yeast	2 cups warm water
2 tsp salt	½ cup tomato sauce

2 cups shredded cheese or cottage cheese – use more or less according to your taste and budget!

Optional: sautéed onions, sliced olives and/or mushrooms. Add pizza spices, garlic powder and/or chili peppers as well.

Any challah dough recipe will do; it will simply be a richer dough than needed, so you may want to use less oil and sugar.

Prepare as with challah **dough**. Bake right away or let rise an hour or so. Yield: two pizzas.

Use baking paper or sprinkle cookie sheet with a bit of oil or flour. Roll out dough. Spread with tomato sauce; top with any grated cheese. Alternatively, mix cottage cheese into the sauce and spread onto dough. Add spices and toppings as desired. Bake at 400° for twenty minutes; when done, remove quickly from oven and enjoy.

Tomato sauce recipe: you can make your own by taking 2-3 Tablespoons tomato paste and adding water to get half a cup. Ketchup or canned tomato sauce can also be watered down, just proceed gradually until you reach the desired consistency and taste. Add salt, sugar and spices as desired.

Pizza Wheels

Dough:
3 cups of flour
1 tsp baking powder
½ cup of oil

1 cup soft white cheese or plain yogurt with ½ tsp salt

Filling:

1 cup cottage cheese
2 Tbs tomato paste/sauce
¼ cup chopped olives

1 tsp oregano
½ tsp salt

    Combine dough ingredients; divide into 3 balls. Roll out a ball until it is about a 10-inch square. Combine filling ingredients, and spread about a third on each flattened dough ball. Roll up dough jelly roll style, and cut 1-inch slices. Arrange slices on baking dish; repeat with remaining dough. Bake at 350° for about thirty minutes.

Spinach Pie*

Pie Crust: (*omit on *Pesach* or substitute mashed potatoes)

4 cups flour, okay to use half whole-wheat
1 egg
½ cup water

1 Tbs vinegar
1 Tbs sugar
1 tsp salt
1¼ cup oil

    Combines easily by hand, right in baking pan. Makes enough dough for two 9"x13" pans; freeze half of the dough for future use.

Or try this healthy and simple "piecrust":

2 cups of plain cooked brown rice	$1/3$ cup oil
	1 tsp salt

Mix well. With either type of pie crust, just press into baking dish. Voila! You can even skip the crust, but it adds a nice taste and helps make this a one dish meal.

Filling:

2 pounds grated spinach	1 cup cottage cheese
1-2 cups grated vegetables	1 cup grated yellow cheese
2 eggs	

Reminder: a pound = 454 grams. No need to be exact, go according to package size. Best way to defrost is to place the spinach into a colander in a leak proof container. Refrigerate 24-36 hours before needed. Alternatively, leave the colander in the sink for a few hours; either way, no need to cook the spinach! Squeeze the spinach to remove most of the water. You can add ¼ cup quinoa or red lentils to absorb the liquid if you prefer not to squeeze so much. You will thereby add nutrition which will somewhat affect the appearance but not the taste. Some Rabbonim say that checked spinach should be ground in a food processor to avoid any insect concerns.

Experiment and add your choice of grated vegetable(s). I have tried zucchini, but have gotten better reviews with butternut squash. Onion goes well here also; it all depends on what you have vegetable and time-wise, what your family likes, and how much you want to stretch out the spinach. Combine filling well, press onto piecrust if using or straight into baking pan. Bake at 375° for about an hour.

~> *Tip!* ~> Add sautéed onion and mushroom for a fancier dish; mix in and/or place on top as a garnish

Tomato Quiche*

Use any pie crust; rice fits very well here see **Spinach Pie**.

3 eggs
1 onion, chopped
½ cup milk
2 tomatoes, sliced

pinch pepper
¼ tsp oregano
¼ cup shredded cheese

Press pie crust dough into round pie plate. Combine eggs, onion, milk and spices, pour onto pie crust. Top with tomatoes and shredded cheese. Bake for 45 minutes in a 350° oven.

Cornflake Quiche*

3 Tbs oil
1 onion, chopped
1 cup cottage cheese

1½ cups cornflakes
2 eggs
½ tsp salt

On *Pesach*, use any *Pesach-dik* cereal.

Combine all into a round pie plate. Bake for 45 minutes in a 350° oven. This actually tastes very delicious!
~> *Tip!* ~> Easily hide shredded zucchini in these quiches!

These quiches can bake together. If you have a large enough oven, bake some **Oven-Baked French Fries** at the same time. A complete delicious dinner.

Easy Lasagna

1 cup grated cheese
1 cup cottage cheese
1 zucchini, shredded
1 lb (400-500 grams) pasta
2 cups of tomato sauce and 3 cups of water
Or 1 cup tomato paste and 4 cups of water
Optional: Add spices such as oregano, garlic or onion powder

Use more or less tomato sauce/paste according to taste; mix sauce with zucchini and cheese. Layer sauce with **uncooked** lasagna pasta; yields about four or five layers. Bigger short cut: Substitute any pasta for lasagna, just mix everything well, cover and bake! If watery when done, wait a bit; the sauce will become absorbed into the mixture.

It's actually quite simple to make **lasagna shaped pasta**. Mix a cup of flour with ½ a cup of water and knead. Add a bit more flour or water as needed to make a smooth dough. Sprinkle flour on your work surface, and flour the rolling pin as well by rolling it in the flour. Roll out the dough as thin as possible, aiming for a large rectangular shape; cut out rectangles, approximately 2.5"x10", just like the ones in the store! Although you could make any pasta with this recipe, it is very tedious to cut out small pieces. The pasta needs to dry out, so put it on racks or cookie sheets. The lasagna should be done within a day or so; speed up the process by putting them in a warm oven or by a fan. Even when only mostly dry, they are ready. Use as directed above. They can even be frozen as is and used for a future lasagna dish!

Bake covered for about 2 hours at 225° – a low oven. Great to put in oven and leave home, return hours later and walk into dinner! Check occasionally during baking process to determine exact time and temperature that will work with your oven.

Lo-Cal Cheese Cake*

Crust: (omit for *Pesach* – or use *Pesach* cookie dough)
½ cup butter or oil
6 Tbs sugar
2 cups flour
2 eggs
1 tsp baking powder

Mix; pat into baking dish. Bake at 350° for about twenty minutes while preparing the filling

Filling:
6 cups cheese and yogurt
¼ cup sugar
Optional: juice of one lemon
½ cup milk
3 eggs

Use any combination of cheese and yogurt. Blend or mix by hand, pour onto pie crust, bake at 350° for an hour. Leave cake in oven until cool or until you just can't wait!
~> *Note!* ~> This is so healthy, serve it as part of a meal!

Cheese Danishes

Dough: Use recipe for **Cocush Cake**.

Filling: 2 cups cottage cheese   2 packages vanilla sugar

Combine cheese and sugar; add more sugar if desired. Take an egg-size piece of dough; flatten to about 5"x5" (12 cm) Place a spoonful of cheese mixture in the center. Fold all corners or sides of the dough toward the center. The cheese may be partially or completely covered. Let rise for fifteen minutes. Bake for twenty minutes. Delicious and freezes well.

Pancakes

2 cups flour
1 tsp baking powder
2 Tbs of sugar
Oil for frying; about ¼ cup
pinch salt
2 eggs
2 cups of milk

Optional: Add pineapple pieces or cottage cheese.

Combine dry ingredients; add remainder. Mix well by hand; no need to break up every single clump of flour, but do try to get most. They will actually disappear in the frying pan! Or use a blender.

These can be made in a non-stick pan without oil, but they will not taste the same. To make them tasty, pour about a tablespoon of oil into the frying pan. Use a spatula (plastic, if you are using a Teflon pan) to coat the pan with oil, and wait about a minute for it to heat up. Find a measuring cup or ladle that makes the size pancake you like and use it to pour out the batter. Fill the pan; drizzle oil around the sides so that it runs onto the edges of the pancakes. Wait about 90 seconds; turn the pancakes over. Again, drizzle oil along the sides of the pan, wait another minute and transfer the pancakes to a plate. Re-oil and continue.

~> **Warning!** ~> Wandering away from your frying pan runs a great risk of burning your hard-worked-on pancakes! If you absolutely must drift away for a few minutes, lower the flame and/or set a timer; you might get away with it. Don't forget to raise the flame again upon your return!

Although most – especially children – enjoy them with all kinds of syrups or sugar, I shake on a bit of salt. Tastes delicious!

If a few drops of batter drip into the frying pan, your children will love them; call them baby pancakes!

Banana Ice Cream *

Freeze six very ripe, peeled bananas until firm or up to several months. Defrost for only five or ten minutes; if they get mushy, the ice cream loses its consistency. Select a flavor by adding one of the following:

    1 cup crushed pineapple (our favorite)
    1 cup fresh squeezed orange juice with pulp
    1 cup fresh squeezed lemon juice with pulp – you may want to add some sugar to this
    1 cup kiwi – about 6-8 fruits

Or one of these, with a scant cup of water:
    ½ cup pineapple pieces
    1 1/4 cup unsweetened cocoa
    ¼ cup peanut butter (another favorite)
    ¼ cup techina paste (for halva flavor!)
    2 Tbs coffee granules, dissolve first

Use a mixer or food processor with a strong motor; to ease blending process, slice bananas first. When using an open-top mixer, use a flour guard will stop bananas from flying out. Mix bananas and flavorings for a couple of minutes. You may want to stop the machine and break down chunks or reposition them. The mixture will become creamy, like soft ice cream. Depending on the size of the bananas and your consistency preference, you may be able to add more water.

Tastes best when fresh, but it is fine to freeze; do so in a large flat container, for quicker defrosting and easy dispensing! Since the ice cream hardens when frozen, transfer from freezer to refrigerator about an hour before serving.

Perfect Popsicles *

Orange juice concentrate   Water

Do not omit reading this recipe! The techniques here have taken literally decades to perfect; yes, there is a science to it. Read on to make the easiest and most delicious cool treat!

Start by preparing the juice. Skimp on the water; reconstitute the concentrate with about 80% of their recommended amount of water. That is, if it calls for a cup of concentrate to three cups of water, use just two and a half cups of water. Adjust according to taste, and mark a container for regular use; easy to measure accurately each time.

Next, fill your ice cube trays with this orange juice; make a few at a time. You may find it easier to fill the trays when pouring from a cup rather than from the container. To avoid spills, stack the trays in a clean plastic container; any spillage will be limited to the container. Actually, those drops will freeze as well and you'll have a little treat on the bottom of the container. You'll also forestall a messy clean up. No need to insert spoons, sticks and the like.

Don't search out freezer space while holding the container; it's too risky. Free up space in the freezer, then get the container and insert it. Your perfect popsicles will be ready within hours; actual time depends on your freezer.

Be efficient; remove the popsicles and store in a container. Now you can serve them quickly when desired; you can also immediately re-fill the trays. To serve, put a few in a plastic disposable cup. Simply squeeze the cup, forcing the cubes to the top, and take a bite. Motivate your children to dispose of cups properly by offering a chocolate chip as a reward for their return. Save even more clean-up time; either make more popsicles immediately or store the trays in the freezer.

~> *Fun!* ~> Use interestingly shaped ice cubes trays!
~> *Warning!* ~> Frozen plastic is brittle. Handle with care!

Jello Sherbet

1 pkg any flavor red jello
(¼ cup powder)
1 cup boiling water

1 cup orange juice
¼ cup sugar
1 cup pineapple juice

You can substitute juices, but this is the recommended combination. For pineapple juice, open a can of pineapple pieces in juice; it contains a cup of juice. Put a few pieces of pineapple in the jello or freeze for a separate treat.

Combine jello with boiling water; add the remaining ingredients. Pour into a shallow pan and freeze. When frozen, break it into chunks and blend in a food processor. Scrape down the sides as you work. It turns into a lovely color and consistency. Refreeze in a container or pretty mold. Luscious and very attractive!

Egg Kichels

7 eggs
2½ cups flour
¾ cup oil

¼ cup sugar
pinch salt
¼ cup water

Lighten the flour by sifting or stirring. Mix all ingredients, for at least **five** minutes in mixer or food processor – not less or you will not achieve desired texture in these light-as-air *kichels*! If your mixer does not work well with thick dough, add the flour at the end and mix for just one more minute. Using two soup spoons, spoon out batter onto cookie sheet, leaving a space of two fingers between each *kichel*. This should make 24; line them up and they'll all fit on one cookie sheet. Preheat oven and bake at 350° for 45 minutes. Enjoy this tasty, low sugar, old-fashioned treat.

Mandelbroit

3 cups flour
1 tsp baking powder
⅓ cup sugar

4 eggs
½ cup oil
½ cup chopped nuts

Mix dough by hand, divide into two loaves, about 10 inches by 2 inches and about ½ inch high. Bake at 350° for about 30 minutes. Remove from oven; wait 15 minutes until cool enough to handle, or anytime thereafter. Slice into ½ inch slices. Lay slices on their side and bake a few minutes more.

Crackers

1 cup quick oats
1 cup any flour
¼ cup sesame seeds
½ tsp baking soda

½ tsp salt
¼ cup oil
¾ cups water

Optional: coriander seed, crushed or chopped garlic or onion.

Combine all ingredients; if sticky, add flour, oats or oil. For a tastier cracker, increase the oil and use less water. Total liquid must be a cup. Roll dough out on a rimless cookie sheet or baking paper. If you delay, the dough hardens and becomes very difficult to roll out. Cover the sheet completely; the dough must be thin.

Score with a pizza wheel or knife before baking, cutting the dough into cracker size shapes. Bake at 350° for 35 minutes. Break apart into individual crackers when cool.

Scones

(High fiber, low sugar cookie)

¼ cups of oats, any type
2¼ cups flour
¼ cup sugar
2 tsp baking powder
2 eggs

1 cup oil
²/₃ cup liquid (juice, soy milk or beer)
²/₃ cup sesame seeds, ground nuts or coconut

    Combine by hand. Shape into curved logs, about 3 inches x 1 inch, by squeezing the dough into shape; yields about 30. Or make bars; roll out dough to fill the cookie sheet. It may be a bit sticky; if so, sprinkle with flour or potato starch. Score into pieces while still raw with a pizza wheel or knife. Bake at 350° for thirty minutes. If you like them toasty, remove the well done pieces from the edges and bake the rest for an extra few minutes. Delicous fresh or frozen.

Oat Bars

3 cups oats, any type
1 cup flour
1 scant cup sugar
1 tsp baking powder

2 eggs
½ cup chocolate chips
1 scant cup oil

    Mixes easily by hand; stir dry ingredients, then add liquids. Insert your hand into a sandwich bag and use it first to spread the oil, then to pat in the dough. Skimp on chocolate chips by placing them on top, spaced out well. Bake at 350° for 30 minutes. Cut as soon as cool since it hardens quickly. Great tasting, quick to make, and quite nutritious! For variety, try baking in an extra-large pan. Crispy and light!

Cocush Cake

7 cups flour
¾ cup oil
3 eggs
½ tsp salt

1 Tbs dry yeast
⅔ cup sugar
1⅓ cups warm liquid (juice or soy milk

Reserve an egg yolk if you wish to paint the rolls of cake before baking. Prepare as challah dough. Ignore for hours or use as soon as doubled in size. Divide into three balls. Roll out a ball of dough, as thin as you have patience for!

Filling for each roll:
⅓ cup chocolate-milk mix   1-2 Tbs oil
Or 4 Tbs sugar and 2 Tbs cocoa

This is the minimum; be more generous if you like. Sprinkle oil, followed by chocolate powder on dough; spread evenly with a pastry brush. Roll up the dough, and put into baking dish, seam side down.

All three rolls will fit in a large baking pan. Put baking paper between rolls if you want to keep them from joining together. Alternatively, make four rolls instead of three and bake them two at a time – four will probably be too tight in the baking pan.

Mix reserved egg yolk with approximately 1 Tablespoon of water; brush onto rolls. Let rise about 30 minutes; the rolls will grow more effectively if placed in a warm or even a hot turned-off oven. Bake at the same temperature and time as challah. Compared to other cakes, this is a low sugar choice, and very attractive, tasty and filling.

1-2-3-4 Cookies

Another low-sugar favorite)

1 cup sugar   300 grams/12 oz margarine
2 eggs   4 cups flour
~> **Optional Substitution** ~> $2/3$ cup oil and 3-4 Tbs juice!

Cream sugar and margarine, add eggs and flour. Roll out part of the dough – depending on the size of your work surface – until about a quarter inch thick.

Moon shaped cookies are easily made using a round cookie cutter or a glass. The first cookie will be a complete circle, but for the rest, simply lower the cookie cutter about halfway from the first cut – you can quickly form a pretty moon! If you choose to use cookie cutters, save a bit of time with the following method. Cut cookies as close as possible to each other, then bake those odd shapes of dough leftover after cookie cutters no longer fit. The larger ones can be cut. Children have fun naming the shapes!

Bake the cookies for about 10-15 minutes at 350°. Watch them, as they go from being not-yet-done to getting burnt very quickly. When done, melt chocolate and dip in the cookies, partially or however much you choose. Decorate further with chopped nuts or sprinkles; add them quickly before the chocolate hardens. This entire project is a fun and useful way to entertain children! Or try this…

Chocolate Icing:
2 cup confectionary sugar   Boiling water
½ cup cocoa

Combine ingredients; use enough water to make the desired consistency. When cool enough to handle, but before it hardens, put into a plastic bag. Cut out a small hole and draw funny faces on the cookies. A real hit!

Cookie-Cutter Cookies

4 eggs
1 cup oil
1¼ cups sugar

5½ cups flour
1 Tbs baking powder
Pinch salt

These cookies are almost as good as the 1-2-3-4 Cookies, and have no margarine. Beat all ingredients together, except for flour. Add flour gradually. See previous page for instructions.

Apple Crumble

12 apples, peeled and diced
1 tsp cinnamon

¾ cup sugar
1½ Tbs flour

Mix and put into a 9"x13" baking pan.

2 cup flour
2 cup oats, any type
1 cup brown sugar

1 cup oil
1 tsp baking powder
¼ tsp baking soda

Combine and spread out on top of apple mixture. Bake at 350° for about an hour. Optional: Halve the dough; it will still come out mouth-watering!

Chocolate Chip Cookies

300 grams/12 oz margarine
½ cup oil
1½ cups white sugar
1½ cups brown sugar

4 eggs
4½ cups flour
½ tsp baking powder
½ tsp baking soda
1 cup chocolate chips

No-Marg Chocolate Chip Cookies

4 cups flour
2¾ cups brown sugar
1 cup oil
3 eggs

1 tsp baking powder
1 tsp baking soda
3 Tbs hot water
1 cup chocolate chips

Cream (margarine and) oil with sugar(s); add combined flour and baking soda/powder. Mix with remaining ingredients. Drop by teaspoonful, and leave some space; they will flatten as they bake. Bake at 375° for 10 minutes in a preheated oven. Remove quickly before they harden. Hide in the freezer as quickly as possible! ☺

Biscuits

3 cups flour
⅓ cup sugar
⅓ cup oil

1 Tbs baking powder
1 cup juice or soy milk
Pinch salt

Mixes easily by hand. Divide into 8 or 12 balls. Bake at 400° for 15 – 20 minutes. Scrumptious with butter.

Pesach-dik Cookies *

2 eggs
1 cup oil
1 scant cup sugar
2 cups potato starch
1 cup (or less) coconut or ground nuts

Optional: few Tbs cocoa, raisins, or chocolate chips

Combine all by hand. Preheat oven. Use two spoons to form into balls. Bake at 350° for 15 minutes; makes 20 cookies.

To use as a pie crust, reduce the sugar and coconuts/nuts according to taste, to about ¼ cup, or omit. Flatten into pie plate and bake for a few minutes. Remember, it is a *Pesach* substitute, and will not taste like a regular crust!

Bubby's Oatmeal Cookies

1 cup flour
1 tsp baking powder
½ cup brown sugar
3 eggs
½ cup oil
Scant ½ cup apple juice
3½ cups oats, any type

Combine flour, baking powder and sugar well; add liquids and mix. Lastly add the oats – use more if needed – and mix well. Preheat oven. Form into flattish balls, they will not spread out. Bake at 350° for 15 minutes; makes 35 cookies. A healthy favorite! Thank you, Bubby!

Dedication
Reflections on the Life of My Father

I sat at the *levayah* of my father, R' Shmuel ben Yehuda Dovid *z"l*, with many emotions coursing through me. Shock – his *petirah* was so sudden. Sorrow, grief, and misery – never mind that I needed to be thankful for his *arichas yomim*, long life. How would I go on without his regular warm greeting, "*mine tiere kind* – my precious child" and twinkle-y smile? Curious – what would each speaker have to say? I was hopeful that I would hear words that would be an everlasting comfort to me, my dear mother, my husband, children and to all the precious friends and relatives who had gathered together on such short notice.

The first speaker, a cousin, *Rav* Herschel Fried *Shlit"a*, spoke about my father's love of Torah, and the great happiness he had in learning and sharing Torah thoughts. Rabbi Kornfeld *Shlit"a*, the *Rav* of the *shul* in which my father *davened*, brought out how inspiring it was having my father *daven* there, with his great *mesiras nefesh* for performing *mitzvos*. My son, R' Yosef Younger, talked about how much his Zaidy meant to him and his siblings, and how special he was. These were themes that would be repeated by many of the comforters we were fortunate to have during the *shiva*.

My father's love of Torah and *Yiddishkeit* was implanted in his youth. He was born in Rzeszow, Poland, in 1923, into a *Chassidish* family. Rzeszow's pre-war population was fifty percent Jewish, with a strong *frum* community. He studied in the *cheder*, as did most of the boys there, and did quite well. That was despite the lack of amenities which would have been conducive to better absorption of the lessons. Often, as I was growing up, he regaled me with anecdotes of the *cheder*. He described the lack of heat, space and light and adequate well-printed *sefarim*; all kinds of things we take for granted today. He often marveled upon visiting my spacious, modern classrooms throughout my school years, reminding me how fortunate I was. However, we are adjured in *Pirkei Avos* that the way to learn Torah is with dry bread and minimal water. So perhaps his situation was superior to ours...

Rabbi Levine, an important *Rav* of the Galicia area, chose my father, together with one other *bachur*, from among all the *chedorim* in the area, to be tested for the famed *Yeshivas Chachmei Lublin*. He advised them that they needed to know 250 *blatt Gemara*, with all the questions and answers involved, referred to as *shakla v'tarye*, but might get by with 200. In the summer of '39 my father passed the entrance exam... but his dreams of *shteiging* were crushed by the outbreak of WWII. *HaShem* had other plans for him.

My father saw a lot of *hashgachas HaShem* in his life; he was saved from death many times. As a young boy, he once tried to fix a cigarette lighter. In those days, it was a small container filled with kerosene, with a bit of cotton and some type of flint attached. He didn't realize that while he was working on it, he was getting drops of kerosene on himself. With his clever mind and capable hands, he was able to ignite it; but when he did, he himself burst into flames. *B'hashgacha*, his mother *a"h* was nearby and knew just what to do; she swiftly wrapped a quilt around him and pushed him onto the floor, smothering the flames. *B"H*, he wasn't hurt.

Any survivor of the war has at least one or two stories to tell, of how *HaShem* saved him. "Two from a family, one from a town or city," see *Yirmiyahu* 3:14. My father actually had a few such *nissim* happen. At one point in one of the camps he was in, there was a call for all able-bodied men. Everyone was certain that whoever was not included would be killed off or at the very least, that the stronger men would receive better treatment or working conditions. My father joined that line of men hoping to be included, but was told to go back, as he was too weak. Determined to join, he tried once more to pass the selection; again, no luck. To the horror of all the inmates, the selected group of strong men were taken and murdered! My father's life had been spared.

One night my father was climbing into his bunk bed, trying to maneuver himself past the others. Conditions were very crowded, and the fellow in the lower berth didn't appreciate the disturbance. He pulled a knife out and slashed my father in the knee. My father tried to stop the bleeding and care for it on his own, but infection set in and he was frightened. Afraid to enter the hospital, and afraid not to. Everyone knew that going to the hospital was often a one-way trip. Only very desperate people went in. As the condition of his knee became worse, he decided to go in. To his great relief, the nurse greeted him warmly. "Shmulik! You are here? Don't worry; I was a good friend of your mother. I'll take care of you and keep you here for a while until you regain your strength!"

The next miracle that occurred came in a hidden way; initially, he didn't know what had happened. He was standing among a group of prisoners, and his number was called. He went to join the group he was directed to, not knowing what he had been selected for. He saw someone he recognized and inquired, "What is to become of us? Where are we being transferred to?"

"You don't know?" his friend was taken aback. "We have been selected to work for Oscar Schindler. Didn't you pay to get here?" My father found out that others had bribed, fought, pushed themselves – done whatever was possible and more, to get in to the now famous 'Schindler's List'. But for him, his number had just been called. To quote my father, "I was selected from out of 25,000 people! *Mamash* (literally) a miracle."

Amazingly, Schindler personally saved my father's life. One

day, my father and a few inmates were sighted committing a "crime" – cooking some potatoes. A Nazi guard came over, and all managed to escape – except for my father. The Nazi began to beat him, when suddenly Schindler saw and quickly called the Nazi over. Reluctantly the Nazi stopped, promising my father that he'd return and "finish him off." *Baruch HaShem*, he never did.

After the liberation, my father was snatched from death one more time. He returned to Rzeszow with some friends to see if any Jews were left. A kindly neighbor saw him, and exclaimed, "What are you doing? There are no Jews here! They'll kill you if they see you! Run away!" That answered his question, and he now knew what to do. He and his friends headed for Krakow, thinking that in the big city matters were under control. Admittedly, they appeared to be; the group was given a house, albeit a dilapidated one.

Shabbos morning, after *davening*, they heard shouts and screams. The building was surrounded by what seemed like thousands of Poles; men, women, and children. They were screaming out murderously, "You gassed all the Polish people in Auschwitz – now you have returned for our children's blood for your matzos! We'll slaughter all of you!"

My father was in shock. "Did I survive the war, only to be killed here?" He and his friends ran up to the top floor, as the crowd threw bricks and rocks, and prepared to storm the house. This time, *HaShem*'s life-saving messengers were the Russian soldiers. They came with guns and dispersed the crowd. The soldiers continued to guard the house for the next few weeks, after which my father and his comrades made it across the border to the safety of the American-controlled side. To his good fortune, he was able to be in the DP camp of the Klausenberger Rebbe. All his life he retained fond memories of the time he spent there, and how it had lifted his mood and outlook, restoring his spirits.

At this point in time, my father's aunt, Necha Pak *a"h*, woke up one morning, quite shaken. She told her husband, R'

Moshe *z"l*, that she had been visited by her dead sister in her dreams. It was my father's mother, who had come to ask her, "Please take care of my only son!"

Uncle Moshe was not impressed. "You keep thinking about the entire family, so you had such a dream. It's nothing."

Imagine their great happiness and surprise when they received a letter from my father a few days later! They wanted to take him in, but at that time it was very hard for refugees to enter Belgium, where the aunt and uncle were residing. A very clever woman, Tanta Necha contacted a smuggler, and told him, "I cannot afford to pay you cash to bring in my nephew, but I can give you names of former residents of Belgium to use in your smuggling operations." A deal was struck, and my father was brought in. He was welcomed into their home, but the first thing Uncle Moshe did was inspect my father's suitcase. Tanta Necha was embarrassed, "What are you doing?" she cried out.

"It's fine; I found what I was looking for. Shmuel has *tefillin*!" Uncle Moshe and my father happily embraced.

Finally, my father's years of suffering were over, but he never forgot them, and never forgot the memory of the family he lost, all so brutally murdered. Unfortunately, in the aftermath of the holocaust, there was a lot of misunderstanding. People who had not lived through the horrors just couldn't understand how the victims had "let such a thing happen." My father took great offense at this line of thinking and tried to convey the facts. Over the years, mindsets were changed and the general population came to realize that they could not have done any better under the circumstances.

He also felt it was important to emphasize that although atrocities against different groups of people have been committed through the ages and still are, the holocaust was unique in three ways:

- No demands of any kind were made by the Jewish people; neither land, money nor jobs. Nor were the Jews trying to overthrow the government in any way. It was merely their existence that the Nazis and their cohorts could not tolerate.

- Although killing large groups of people is nothing new, historically speaking, no nation or group ever built crematoria,

railroad tracks, and all related mechanisms to annihilate an entire people.
- During the entire process – nearly five years – not one country came to protect the Jews. It would have been relatively simple to bomb the railroad tracks used for transporting the Jews to the death camps; but no one did.

Despite all he went through, his deeply ingrained faith in *HaShem* stayed firm. This faith actually gave him the strength to survive, and rebuild his life afterwards.

A few years later, a *shadchan* introduced my father to my mother; they married and settled in Belgium. It was my father's fervent desire to move from there to *Eretz Yisroel*. For some reason, however, when he had to fill out a form concerning his planned destination, he wrote America. A while later they were notified that they had permission to move to the United States. What to do? Life in *Eretz Yisroel* was very hard in those days. "Go to America, earn a few dollars, and after that you'll be able to settle in *Eretz Yisroel*," they were advised.

My father agonized over this decision, staying up all night. In the morning he told my mother very reluctantly, "I guess we have to go to America." This was a typical example of his shouldering responsibility for his family. He never wanted to depend on others, despite all he had gone through. He knew he had to provide, and did not consider handouts, solicited or not. Even when they received a gift from the *Agudas Yisroel* – a *Hagada* for *Pesach* – he told my mother, "Do you think this is for free? We must send them a donation." They weren't able to send in much at the time, but looked forward to donating more in the future.

They arrived in Newark N.J. in 1952, and subsequently my brother and I were born. My parents were overjoyed at having a family, and felt particularly *bentched* in that they had a son and a daughter. They raised us with care and devotion. Always very involved in our lives, they continuously helped and advised us.

My father, very skillful and clever, was a diamond cleaver, and knew his craft well, but there were no jobs in diamonds. He changed gears and sought any sort of work, finally taking a job in a leather coat factory. The foreman later said, "I knew you didn't really know how to operate a machine and sew, but I saw you were a capable person." Sure enough, after a short time, he was producing very fine work.

He considered opening such a factory on his own, but my mother's brother spoke very realistically with him. "Opening up such a business will run over a hundred thousand dollars. Where will you get that kind of money? Work for me in my butcher store. You'll pick up the necessary skills in no time. Then you can open your own store, for just two thousand dollars." My parents understood the wisdom of this suggestion, and decided to accept my uncle's offer.

My father worked long, hard hours as a butcher for close to forty years. He had to rise daily at about five in the morning, and twice a week an hour earlier, in order to go to the slaughterhouse to select meat. Remarkably, he never needed an alarm clock!

In his business, alone or with a partner, he always had smooth relations with his suppliers, customers, and employees. People liked him, and appreciated his friendly, easy-going nature. His faithful customers claimed that his meat was the finest to be had; truthfully, there is a skill to choosing good meat and trimming and cutting it properly. One time, he was at the slaughter-house selecting various cuts of meat for his shop. A fellow butcher who had been in the business long before my father, came to consult with him, as to which was the superior choice. My father simply had a knack for doing things properly.

One of my strongest memories of spending time with my father was our weekly *Shabbos* walk to *shul*. I used to love to get up early and go with him, hearing stories and riddles, with a few math problems thrown in. He loved talking to me and "*kvelled*" – really enjoyed – my responses, which he considered to be so clever. One time he asked me to spell the word "door," and I guess I needed to stall for time to think. "Is that a closed door or an open door?" I asked. He loved that line! I remember my father leading the *davening*; how he especially enjoyed the role of *chazzan* for the *Rosh Chodesh bentching*. My brother also shares my warm memories of those *Shabbosim*, and recalls how my father would comment at the end of a *Yom Tov*, "We won't have this type of *davening* again for a while." Every *tefilla* was precious to him.

Another important aspect of his *shul* attendance was supporting the *shul*. In West Orange, he *davened* at one *shul* Friday nights, and another *Shabbos* mornings. He maintained membership in both. He also appreciated getting an *aliyah*. Keeping with the time-honored method of gratitude for such a privilege, he always gave a donation, and usually brought it over as soon as possible. Years later, whenever my parents would visit us in *Kiryat Sefer*, my father would leave a check or cash with my husband – a contribution for his *aliyah*. Once he decided to give money, be it *tzedaka*, a gift to his children or for any purpose at all, he just had to take care of it as soon as possible; he didn't want to delay. To him it was an unpaid debt. What an exemplary *middah*, well worth emulating.

Although my father was in a very *balabatisha* surrounding, and *shiurim* were not as popular as they are today, he became part of a *chevra shas*; a group that gathered *Shabbos* afternoons to learn *Gemara*. As people began moving out of Newark, the group disbanded. My father made sure to restart it in the city he moved to, West Orange. There, Rabbi Witkin *zt"l*, a local *talmid chochom*, gave the *shiur*. My father had a lot of satisfaction from the *shiur*, and made sure it continued on a regular basis. Interestingly, my father was *niftar* on Rabbi Witkin's *yahrzeit*.

As the years flew by, my father, along with my mother, *yblct"a* was kept busy with work and raising my brother and me. *Baruch HaShem*, we each married, and I moved to Los Angeles, where my husband's family lived. When my oldest daughter married, she and her husband decided to live in *Eretz Yisroel*. Surprisingly, when it came time for her brother to find a *shidduch*, he told us he wanted to do the same! When my third child's wedding took place in *Yerushalayim* as well, we decided to stop dreaming about *Eretz Yisroel*, and just move there! My parents were very enthusiastic about our decision and told us, "You go, and we will follow!"

In *Elul* 5765, September 2005, they surprised everyone when they fulfilled their dreams and actually moved to *Eretz Yisroel*. No one had believed that they would really do it! Friends heard that they were planning to move to Ramat Beit Shemesh, and tried to dissuade them. "It's such a young community. You won't fit in," they were told.

"Why would we want to live with a bunch of old folks?" my mother retorted, and off to RBS they went.

To say they never regretted their decision would be putting it mildly. If a king and queen had moved in, I cannot believe they would have merited a more honorable reception. The community took an immediate liking to my parents, and this feeling was mutual. I would dare say that the relationship was the epitome of an ideal friendship. My parents were constantly greeted, offered rides, and welcomed in many ways.

In turn, the community was inspired with the friendliness, warmth, and dedication to *Yiddishkeit* so apparent in my parents. They were further enriched by the togetherness they witnessed, and in general benefited from the total image of special people from the pre-war generation.

My mother and I were so grateful and overwhelmed at the *shiva*; so many came to share their many happy memories and meaningful anecdotes in which my father had played a major role. A warm smile, kind greeting and inquiry, of course a *vort* or insight into a *Yiddishe hashkafa*; it seems like he had interacted in a warm and caring way with so many and left an indelible mark on them.

In RBS, my father was careful to come to *shul* for *minyan* three times a day. That and his *daf yomi shiur* became the mainstays of his life, and gave him tremendous satisfaction. The other *shul*-goers were so motivated by his regularity. It instilled in them a greater *cheshek* for their own learning. They were also amazed at his knowledge. A few weeks before his *petirah*, he was in the *Bais Medrash* while some *avreichim* were struggling with a *tosafos*, commentary found in *Gemara*. He approached them, looked over the material, and proceeded to explain it. "This was one of the hardest *tosafos* I learned for the entrance exam to the Lubliner *yeshiva*. I haven't forgotten it!"

Leading the *davening* and *laining* the *parsha* in *shul* were other precious *mitzvos* to my father. He was surprised and disappointed when my older boys *lained* "only" the *maftir* at their bar mitzvas. A couple of years ago when we were planning another bar mitzva, my father asked, "Can't I hear my grandson *lain* the entire *Parsha*?" My husband apologized, explaining that such a thing was just not done. In the *shul* my husband *daven*s at, the *Rav* is very strict about having a proper *laining*, and does not want to risk hearing a possibly improper rendition of a bar mitzva boy.

A few weeks later, my parents were visiting for *Shabbos*, and I encouraged my father, "Why don't you just ask the *Rav* yourself?" My father went to do just that, and returned mildly disappointed. "I had an entire speech planned, but as soon as I began, '*Rav*, please, I survived the war and would like to hear my grandson *lain* the entire *Parsha*…' the *Rav* kindly responded, 'no problem.'" To further motivate my son, my father offered to pay him each time he would *lain*. After searching all around, my son found a very early *minyan* which would allow him to *lain*. For a few years, he made an effort to be there whenever he could, waking up very early to be there on time. What a lasting legacy.

My father constantly thanked my mother for encouraging him to make the move, and was so grateful for each day. He loved watching apartment houses spring up, viewing the rebuilding of *Eretz Yisroel*. When he heard the sound of construction, he would tell my mother, "I just have to go outside and watch. I love to see how our country is being re-established!" On one of my visits to their apartment in RBS, he drew me over to the window, and showed me the building behind which the sun would set. "See the shadows? Every few days, you can see the progress, as the days get longer," he seriously explained. This was something most of us would not think about or notice. To him it was part of his love of *Eretz Yisroel*.

My father loved people of all ages, and he loved to share his knowledge. He had a unique ability to be able to size up a person; I think because he really listened to others and focused on who they were. Subsequently, he was able to treat them to the appropriate *vort, d'var Torah* or riddle. Every stranger with a friendly face was just someone he hadn't yet met; my father along with my mother *yblct"a* were real people-collectors! They loved to travel on the bus, where they enjoyed a panoramic view of the countryside and plenty of opportunities to meet more people.

My father loved giving children candy, and liked to get his favorites from New York, through various travelers. My mother reassured him that the children would enjoy regular local candy, but he just had to give them what he enjoyed. Amazingly, he was very sensitive to my health concerns; I cannot remember him ever bringing candy for my children. He came up with a good alternative, however. He would stand across from them, individually, and toss coins to them. If they caught the money, they could keep it. If they couldn't, he handed it to them after a few tries. They just loved that game!

My parents had a very unique relationship. For nearly sixty years, they were not just a husband and wife; they were each other's mother and father, sister and brother. They did almost everything together. Everything was discussed; they were very open with each other and often had a lively exchange of ideas. My mother took her role as a caring wife very seriously; it was manifested in many ways. When it came to food preparation, there was no such thing as grabbing a sandwich. Every meal was painstakingly prepared with attention to every detail. And eaten together.

My mother wanted to make sure that my father's mind would stay lucid. She thought of a great activity; every night they had to play a couple of games of Rummykub. They called it their brain sharpener!

On *Shabbos*, when they would walk home from *shul*, they would stop and sit on a park bench for a few minutes to take a little rest. How many couples and families saw them each week, and were strengthened in their own family ties? My parents were once out shopping, and met a woman my mother knew from before the war. In the course of the conversation, she mentioned that her husband was getting depressed. "Why did you leave him home when you went out shopping? I would never do that to my husband!" The woman looked at my mother, astonished. Such an idea had never occurred to her.

In 2007, my father was diagnosed with a heart problem; together we mapped out his personal *refuah* plan. Always a contributor to various causes, he agreed to help out a few hard-pressed families that I had met. The extra *shekels* each month would make a difference in their lives. He started saying *Tehillim* daily with my mother, another shared activity from which they derived immense satisfaction. My brother began learning with him daily on the phone; a true source of *nachas* which our father thoroughly enjoyed. I studied the *sefer Chofetz Chaim* with him. He was a unique *chavrusa*. Although he was much more learned than I, he always wanted me to read, and even called me his *Rebbi*! He followed each word in his *sefer*, and took the learning to heart, as indicated by some of his comments. "Oy! We had better not talk so much!" "I think the *sefer* could be made a lot shorter; just write what may be said!" The time was so special for us, I am so grateful that we enriched our daily conversations with the lessons from the *sefer*. Perhaps in the merit of all this, we were *zochim* to two additional years.

These aspects to my father's persona were brought out over and over again during the *shiva*. Each visit was a big source of encouragement to my mother and me. Through the entire ordeal, however, a phrase kept wandering around in my head – about the scotch tape…one of the *hespedim*… during the *levayah*.

The scotch tape speaker had spoken so emotionally, that

although he addressed us in English it was difficult to follow. How he mourned my father! And how delighted I was to hear the beautiful tidbit he shared with us, a practice of my father that I had known nothing about. "Mr. Stimler always had scotch tape in his pocket. After *davening* or when a *shiur* was finished, if he noticed any page of any *sefer* needing repair, he took care of it immediately." In his humble, unassuming way, he was involved with upkeep of the *shul* on a daily basis. Certainly it was a small thing. That was my father – always with a twinkle in his eye and forever seeking to improve things; to warm up a person's heart through his pleasant countenance and good cheer; a person's mind, through his wit and wisdom and yes, even *sefarim*, with scotch tape.

Anyone could do any of these things. And I hope that many will take it upon themselves to do so, *l'ilui nishmas avi mori*, as a merit for my father's *neshama*, R' Shmuel ben Yehuda Dovid z"l. *Yehi zichro baruch,* may his memory be a blessing.

Dedication
My Children's Bubby A"H
Extraordinary Mesiras Nefesh

I was young when I met my mother-in-law for the first time. I knew she was a survivor – well, so were my parents and most of my aunts and uncles, and many other adults I knew. I also knew she was an *almana* – the father-in-law I never met succumbed to illness before my husband's bar mitzvah. That was a new situation for me, one that I could not identify with. I only saw a friendly, charming, intelligent, strong yet giving person. She was gracious, and served a lovely meal which she said was all leftovers from *Shabbos*! It was quite a spread; I was very impressed. She allowed me to help serve and clear off, and I felt confident that we would get along… *B"H* we did.

When we got married, we were certain LA would be a great place to visit when possible, but that was it! Hashem had different plans in mind for us. Four years later we relocated to the West Coast. Although we did not live in her neighborhood, it took us only about twenty minutes to drive over, and we visited regularly. We even walked there on some *Yomim Tovim* – an enjoyable one hour plus excursion.

She was a model grandmother. She loved each one, and couldn't wait to see them. She was especially close with my oldest daughter, and loved baking with her, helping her with her homework, having her sleep over; they had a very special relationship. When we all came for Shabbos, she had all sorts of delicious delights, and I was so very glad to get the leftovers, usually enough for a couple of meals.

I recall her inviting us for a visit one Sunday afternoon. I had so much to do, I tried to beg off. "We were just there on Thursday…" I explained. "So what?" was her immediate response; "that was last week!" Of course we drove over. She kept a large freezer near the back door where we usually entered, making it very convenient to enjoy a few of her delicious oatmeal cookies. Although the family business was wholesale candy, chocolates and wafers, she respected my no-sugar rule. Truly, I did not appreciate how hard that must have been for her, I was however pleased with her cooperation.

Unfortunately, our time together was cut short. About five years after our move she suffered a heart attack from which she never really recovered. Towards the end, as weak as she was, she was still determined to help me. I cannot forget how she lay in her hospital bed, assuring me that she would come out and host me for Pesach. True, she had little to clean, as it was always neat and sparkling by her, and she had help in the house… but would we really be able to go? We were not *zochim*; she was *niftar* before Pesach.

I only began to value her extraordinary behavior years later. One day I contemplated how much I owed this woman who although all alone, allowed my husband to study in Yeshiva in Eretz Yisroel for a few years. Of course she valued Torah study, having been raised in such a home, but how did she continue it, and how did she personally make that great sacrifice?

In those days, and in that area, extended *Gemara* learning was unheard of. She was a true trailblazer, allowing her firstborn son to learn in Lakewood and her youngest to fly halfway across the world to learn in *Yerushalayim*.

She was home alone. She did not make them stay home to keep her company; although she suffered from post-holocaust nightmares, she toughed it out herself. She did not keep them home to help run her business; she chose to work long hours instead. She did not keep them home due to her dislocated hips and the pain she endured. She did not hold them back due to the expenses involved.

As I considered all these angles, I was filled with deep regret. I had never thought to ask her how she had the *mesiras nefesh* to make such sacrifices, nor to thank her. This was due, at least in part, to the fact that I hardly recall her speaking about her hardships, and certainly not complaining. This is a *midda* we can certainly try to emulate, *l'ilui nishmas chamasi*, as a merit for my mother-in-law's *neshama*, Faiga bas Ephraim *a"h*. *Yehi zichra baruch,* may her memory be a blessing.

And it is never too late. Thank you, my dear mother-in-law. I am sure you are watching down on us from a beautiful place. Having *nachas*, seeing how your investment paid off big time. May we not be tested as you were, but please help us be strong in our challenges, and continue pulling the strings for us up in *Shomayim*. I am certain you are.

Appreciation
Thank You, Mommy!

"We have to look for opportunities to try to do as much *chessed* as we can. That's what I always notice in a person; when I see someone involved in *chessed*, I know that he/she is a good person."

"Be considerate. Think of the other person. Don't ask others to do something that is hard for them. Refrain from inconveniencing others; if they offer, that's nice!"

"We are all *Yenem*-ites! (Play on words – we are from *Yenem* – them in Yiddish; sounds like Yemen, the country.) We go to *shiurim* and learn about proper behavior, but don't take it to heart; we think it is meant for them, our neighbor; not us. We need to analyze, think deeply; can this *mussar* apply to me?"

"Feeling down? Get busy! Bake a cake for someone, wash your floor, go for a walk. You'll feel good and be energized."

"Clean your house yourself. Just tell yourself as you work, 'I'm exercising!' Save gym-membership money at the same time."

"Eat healthy food; you'll get used to it. When I hear that a particular food is good for me, I incorporate it into my diet. My husband *z"l* laughed when I told him, 'I have developed a taste for the tasteless!' Afterwards, I saw that the Rambam advises people to accustom themselves to eating healthy food, and once they get used to it, they'll like it. It's true! Honestly, I thoroughly enjoy preparing and eating my meals."

"The key to a happy home? Home cooked food. Your

husband and children will thrive on the attention, and you'll feel fulfilled knowing you are providing nutritious meals."

"It's easier said than done, but the best advice is to trust in *HaShem* and do good. Doing good for others will make you feel good, too!"

"Don't be jealous of what others have. From my long years, *B"H*, I have learned it doesn't pay. You have exactly what *HaShem* wants you to have, and so do they. You don't know what they are lacking. You could make yourself sick, and it will prevent you from enjoying what *HaShem* has allocated to you! Just thank *HaShem* for what you have, and enjoy."

"Missing your children or grandchildren living far away? All *Yiddishe* children are sweet. Enjoy any of them; it won't cost you a thing. And they will really appreciate and love you!"

These are just some of the concepts that my mother promotes and shares with others when she can. Although many have profited from her *hadracha*, I am certainly the foremost beneficiary of her cheery, determined outlook, with numerous anecdotes to back up every insight. My mother's extraordinary memory allows her to access all kinds of interactions she personally experienced, heard or read about; she has a knack of matching the right story for each message.

How does my mother, a holocaust survivor, who had a difficult life, maintain such a positive attitude? I would like to share her story as inspiration for all of us struggling with our own personal tests. I believe we can learn and improve our lives through her example.

My mother grew up in Romania/Hungary in a very small town, Ruskava; the youngest of a large *chassidish* family. Outside observers may surmise that people who live in such locales tend to be uneducated and simple minded. My mother stresses that such an assumption is totally incorrect; all kinds of people live in all kinds of places. As an example, she was blessed with a mother that taught her a lot about life through example and explanation despite her lack of formal education.

One of my mother's earliest memories is of her mother

asking her to take milk to some neighbors. The town was a rather poor one, and my mother's family was considered wealthy, as they owned livestock, as well as forests and land. They didn't have much cash or possessions, but they had food and real-estate, something many of the others didn't have. Although my mother went cheerfully to most homes, there was one family that made her uncomfortable. When she tried to beg off, her mother would remind her that if she didn't go, that family would have no milk at all. My mother didn't need to hear another word; she took the milk and ran off to deliver it. A typical example of the *chessed* she grew up with.

My mother still marvels at her mother's wisdom in so many areas. My Bubby *a"h* taught my mother about hygiene, nutrition and other general knowledge. There were no toothbrushes in Ruskava. My Bubby taught my mother to clean her teeth with her finger. Years later, my mother heard from a dentist that massaging one's gums is the best thing for teeth. Home economics and *middos tovos* weren't taught, they were caught; my mother lived and breathed them. In later years, after the war, she took a cooking class in school. After a test was graded, the teacher expressed her annoyance with the class. Why did only one student know how to bake bread properly? That one student was my mother, who explained, "They didn't know, because you didn't teach it. I simply wrote what I had observed at home."

When the Second World War broke out and continued to rage for years, my mother and her family thought they were safe, since Hungary stayed out of the war. Unfortunately, despite the fact that Hitler, *yimach shemo v'zichro*, was not doing well on the battlefront after nearly five years of war, he did not slow his diabolical plan. He was more determined than ever to annihilate the Jews. First came various decrees. At one point, oil, the main source of lighting, was purposely made available for sale only on *Shabbos*. My Zaidy *z"l* was firm in his response. "I don't care what anyone else does. We will sit in the dark. We will not get oil on *Shabbos*."

The situation quickly moved from bad to worse; Hungarian

Jews were rounded up, gathered from cities and small towns, and placed in ghettos; my mother's family among them. A month later, they were transported to Auschwitz. My mother, fourteen years old at the time, clung to her mother and would have been gassed with her, had her mother not run back to the train for some cookies she had baked to give the children. During those few minutes that my mother was left alone, she was chased to march on; she never saw her mother again. Those cookies had truly saved her life; had my Bubby been there, my mother would never have separated from her.

It wasn't just the cookies; Bubby's wisdom saved her as well. My mother remembers her mother comforting her sister who was left pregnant when her husband was taken away. "Don't aggravate yourself. From aggravation you can get yourself sick." This was something my mother told her other sister when they first arrived in Auschwitz. "Let's not aggravate ourselves; Mamma said it'll make us sick if we do."

Always scrawny and weak, my mother didn't think she would survive. As she stood for hours in thin clothing during all kinds of rain and freezing temperatures, she was certain she would catch a cold or even pneumonia, but she never did. *HaShem* was watching over her.

A few weeks later, selections began; workers were chosen from among the inmates. My mother despaired as she was rejected twice. At the third selection, the infamous Mengele grabbed her hand and asked her age. It was the only time she lied spontaneously. "I am sixteen years old," she replied. She was tall for her age and he believed her. She was finally sent to the workers' group, luckily with one companion; an older friend from her hometown. They clung together.

One morning as they stood at attention, this friend said, "You look so skinny! If only I could get a job in the kitchen, I'd get you extra food!"

"How can you? You don't stand a chance." my mother answered. "We're newcomers. Such good jobs are all taken already by those who arrived in the transports ahead of ours.

Even if they need more workers, they'll just choose from amongst their relatives or friends!"

"With *HaShem*'s help, everything is possible," her friend confidently assured her. Sure enough, she acquired her kitchen job, and brought my mother extra food and comfort regularly; my mother feels certain that this friend was *HaShem*'s messenger, sent to help her survive.

After the war, my mother traveled to her older brother *z"l* living in England at the time. He took her into his home, and there she stayed until her marriage. He thought he would have to re-strengthen her *Yiddishkeit* after all she had been through; but it was not necessary. She made *brachos* on the first meal served. He also thought he would need to educate her to general ethics; he feared she might feel entitled to help herself to compensation, due to the horrors she had lived through. The first time they went to a store, he warned her, "Don't take a thing without paying. True, you lost your home and parents, but it's not the shopkeeper's fault."

She looked at him in amazement. Such an idea would have never occurred to her.

Although he sent her to school, she wanted to be somewhat independent, so that she could buy clothing and other personal items. She left school and took a job, glad to be productive and able to take care of her own needs.

My mother managed to deal with various challenges throughout life, and although she did very well, she always missed her mother. When I married, she told me, "After this, everything is extra. I brought you to the *chuppa*. How I wish I could have had my mother do the same for me." That encapsulates her view of the role of a mother.

My mother wasn't able to learn seriously until Artscroll and Feldheim began publishing a great variety of Judaica. From that time, until today, this has become her favorite pastime – reading about *Gedolim*, learning the meaning of *Tehillim* and other parts of *Tanach*, and reviewing the *Parsha*. Although her faith in *HaShem* was and continues to be rock solid, through all these *sefarim* she completes her education. She is so appreciative of the publishers and authors.

At this point in her life, my mother delights in whatever she can do, for herself and others. Learning, baking for her friends, giving advice, and speaking for groups occasionally, fills her life and gives her great satisfaction. She takes her responsibility for her health very seriously, eating carefully – adhering to the Rambam's diet as much as possible. My mother is continuously grateful to *HaShem* for each of His many gifts and *daven*s for His constant help. She attributes her successes to Him, and to her mother and father who were very righteous people and gave her a proper upbringing. And to her relatives and ancestors, including the saintly genius, Rabbi Eliyahu Kramer, better known as the *Vilna Gaon*.

That is her life in a nutshell. Always learning and always teaching. And always caring. May *HaShem* grant my dear mother many more fulfilling years, and may we be *zochim* to follow her inspiring examples. Together, may we and all of *Klall Yisroel* merit *bias goel tzedek*, the arrival of the righteous redeemer, speedily and in our days, together.

Count and Save Your Words

Conceal identities and shun all types of gossip
Open by asking for *HaShem*'s help in conversation
Utter your words slowly, there is no rush
Now and then express your gratitude and admiration
Think before speaking, take your time

Always encouragingly, share inspiration that's *Torah-dik*
Nicer to ask, rather than tell, when applicable
Don't be judgmental, arrogant, condescending, sarcastic

Speak in a slow, clear tone that's easily understood
Aim for your listener to feel superb and wonderful
Verify that it is a convenient place and time
Exercise consideration, with your response be careful

You'll benefit by reviewing this before conversation
Only speak for *HaShem*'s sake as you planned
Undermine or deflate their narrative? – never!
Revealing any confidential matters is strictly banned

Wrangle, quarrel, argue only with your *yetzer hara*
Obliterate interruptions, their thoughts breaking
Respect must emanate through your words
Don't lose track of your true goal – giving not taking
Speak sparsely – you'll pay for every improper word

~~~ *B'hatzlacha in all you say!* ~~~

Sing a Song

You call a manufacturer, seeking information and are informed that estimated wait time is seven minutes. Now you are their captive audience and must listen to their drivel until an operator becomes available. You are waiting in a lounge, perhaps the airport, with seemingly continuous announcements, kidnapping your thinking time. You are sitting on the dentist's chair, mouth wide open, bracing yourself for the pain. You are in bed, but cannot fall asleep.

In all of these instances, you cannot really concentrate; the stimulus is uninteresting, yet relentless. You feel frustrated, trapped in a prison, unable to extricate yourself and utilize your time profitably.

I discovered an escape route. It is a song; but not just any song. True, any song can allow you to think and perhaps be entertained and/or inspired, but with this song, you can earn amazing *mitzvos*, exercise your mind, distract yourself, and yes, even put yourself to sleep. And I will not have to sing my song to you, because you can create your own. Follow these easy steps, and enrich your life! Use your song in the ways indicated above, and to overcome countless other challenges.

Choose a tune. I like "Ninety-Nine Bottles of Beer on the Wall" but any tune you enjoy can work.

Select a refrain. I chose a brief rendition of the six constant *mitzvos*; if you do the same, you will not only earn *mitzvos* whenever you sing, you will truly improve your mindset. The

English version could be, Believe in Hashem, not another, know He is ONE – love Him, fear Him, do not roam. Try it and see – the words fit – they even almost rhyme!

The final step is to pick a verse or expression or part of a *tefilla*, or phrase from *Pirkei Avos*, or anywhere that inspires and/or thrills you. Pick one for each letter of the *aleph-bais*. Again, it can be in any language. Some of my selections include:

Aleph – If I am not for myself, who am I? (Pirkei Avos)

Mem – How goodly are your tents (Bamidbar 24:5)

Taf – The *Torah* was commanded to us by Moshe (Devarim 33:4)
(Contact me for complete list)

Now you are ready to sing. Sing the refrain, then the *aleph* verse. The refrain, then the *bais* verse. And so on, all the way to *taf*. Write your selections down for easy reference, but after a few renditions, you will know your song by heart. Of course, this is **your** song. Feel free to select just a few verses, spell out your name if you like, be creative! And don't worry if you skip or repeat any while singing, it will still be very effective.

Now you are forever prepared. Selecting fruits? Strolling or exercising? Dwelling on depressing thoughts? Trying to catch a nap? Sing **your** song. You may even enjoy singing it backwards. Sing it to yourself, and find endless opportunities to grow, exercise your brain, and truly delight with your life.

You could almost call it the song of songs!

The Dreidel's Message

Nothing in Judaism is trivial, no matter how apparently minor.

A *Torah* Jew believes that **every** element of the *Torah* is laden with significance beyond our understanding. A letter in the *sefer Torah*, a *mitzva*, laws enacted by our Rabbis; a lifetime of study will not be enough to reveal all of their meanings. Our customs are also significant, with multiple explanations for many of the foods we eat, clothing we wear and other practices.

But what about a game such as the *Chanukah dreidel*? Yes, even that has profound meaning.

Playing with a *dreidel* on *Chanukah* is a well-known tradition. The *dreidel* has actually become a symbol for *Chanukah* and even Judaism. It reminds us of how *Yidden* had to hide their *Torah* learning from the Greek soldiers thousands of years ago, when *Torah* study was punishable by death. When soldiers approached their hiding places, *sefarim* were hidden, and the *dreidels* began to spin. Could such a toy have deep significance? Its association with *Chanukah* portends that it cannot be arbitrary. Let's examine this spinning top and see what we can expound.

The four letters on the *dreidel* are found in only one word in the entire *Torah*, in *Bereshith* 46:28, in the *Torah* reading that almost always follows *Chanukah*, *Parshas Vayigash*. There it states that Yehuda went "to Goshen," using the term גשנה, *Goshna*. This is a very significant match, since the purpose of going to Goshen was to establish a *Bais Medrash*.

Rashi elsewhere explains that the last letter of the word, *hei*, performs the job of a *lamed* at the beginning of a word; therefore, גשנה means לגשן, **to** Goshen. Combining the two versions, the written and implied, yields us לגשנה. With this, we have the letter *lamed* in two forms: an actual one at the beginning of the word and a symbolic one at its end. Now, the very name of this letter means learning, so we seem to be looking at two kinds of learning, one more real than the other. Their placement reminds us of our sages' reference to those who learn *Torah*. Those who do so with proper intentions are considered to be approaching *Torah* from the **right.** This is in contrast to those who learn for personal gain, who are said to be approaching from the **left**. מיימינים בה משמאילים בה.

As we refer to the order of the letters in לגשנה, we can see that the *dreidel* game and its rules connote exquisite depth. The letter *gimel*, positioned next to the *lamed*, the true *talmid chochom*, is sure to benefit thereby. Perhaps it even indicates that the *gimel*, cognate to *gomel* (to give), is also supporting *Torah* learning. In any case, it is easy to see why he is a winner. The *hei* however, being involved in lower-class learning, takes only half. This clarifies the inadequacy of his efforts, while at the same time shows how amazing *Torah* learning truly is. Yes, even in this form, it yields rich rewards. The 'nun', neighbor to the *hei*, cannot expect very much. It is enough that he is protected from loss. The 'shin' is neither learning, nor close to one who is. His fate is therefore clear; he must lose.

One may object. The *hei* symbolizes one who **is** actually learning *Torah*, albeit without the best of intentions. The *gimel* is merely **next** to one who learns. Shouldn't the *hei* win more? The answer is revealed in a *Mishna*. In *Pirkei Avos* (4:1) we are taught: Better to be a tail of lion than the head of a fox.

Unequivocally, the primacy of learning *Torah* is displayed!

But what about the winnings of the *lamed*? How did something that ought to be the biggest winner of all wind up with nothing? True, the *gimel* already gets everything, so it might be hard to reward the *lamed* adequately. Nevertheless, he should somehow get more; perhaps this pot and the next. But the answer is obvious, revealing the undisputed truth. Nothing is assigned to the *lamed*, because there is no way to express, in earthly terms, the reward reserved for the true *Torah* student. No mortal can perceive it; only *HaShem* alone.

Even the game's omission speaks volumes!

There is still one point to clarify. Where on the *dreidel* **can** the *lamed* be found? How was he left off, when all the other letters are prominently displayed? His reward may be beyond description, but why don't we at least see him?!

In actuality, it is not his absence, but rather our nearsightedness that should confound us. Upon inspection, a *dreidel* actually resembles two *lameds* opposing each other (ל׳ל). So, in reality, the entire *dreidel* is composed of many *lameds*, each facing the center. Wonder of wonders; the letter we couldn't find is all over! Moreover, it occupies three dimensions, not like the puny flat surfaces that show each of the other four. The entire *dreidel* is composed of *lameds*!

There's more. As the game is played and the *dreidel* spins, the letters are obscured; except for the *lameds*. Still it goes unnoticed. All wait impatiently for the twirling to stop, so that they can see the letter that counts. Then a flurry of activity ensues – which letter? Who spun it? Take, pay! As for the *lamed*? He carries the letters, does all the work, runs the whole show... but literally no one knows he exists. Interesting, isn't it?

Dear reader, it is not just **interesting**. It's a parable to nothing less than the world itself. Ask anyone, "Who is important? Who or what makes things go?" The answer will be, "Those who have made it big financially, politically, or socially, of course!" Ask further, "What about those who study *Torah*?" the answer may range from, "What? Those parasites?" to "Well, we need them, too."

The world was created for *Torah*. Everything that goes on here is determined by how *Torah* has been learned and kept until now, and what the needs for its continuation dictate. The ultimate factor guiding world events is the learning that is for the sake of *HaShem*, performed by the true *talmid chochom*, unnoticed as he may be.

In *Hands-on How-to's for the Home and Heart,* my sister has put together a wealth of ideas, all with one purpose; to help us each in our *Avodas HaShem*. Because the sustaining of the *Torah*, its study and observance of its laws, is our true purpose in this world. Each chapter and thought is "spinning" around this central theme.

May all readers merit to improve their *Avodas HaShem*, and thus raise the level of spirituality of their families and communities. And may we all merit to understand the lesson of the *dreidel*, and to see "The raising of the glory of *Torah*, speedily and in our days."

Rabbi Dovid Stimler
Telzstone

Glossary

a"h; aleha hashalom – may she rest in peace; see *z"l*

aguna – commonly: a woman who cannot obtain a divorce from her husband, and therefore cannot remarry

ahavas Yisroel – love toward fellow Jews

ais ratzon – auspicious time

akeida – binding; refers to the binding of Isaac as a sacrificial offering

aleph-bais – Hebrew alphabet

almana – widow

asher yatzar – prayer said after relieving oneself

Ashrei – chapter 145 in *Tehillim*; an alphabetically arranged prayer recited thrice daily

aveira/aveiros – transgression/s or sin/s

avoda; avodas HaShem – literally work; herein refers to our "service of the heart" as in prayer or other spiritual pursuits

avos – the Patriarchs: Abraham, Isaac, and Jacob

avreich/avreichim – man/men learning *Torah* in *kollel*

Avrohom Avinu – Abraham, our forefather

ba'al teshuva – Jew that has returned to Torah observance

ba'alei simcha – people celebrating their joyous event

Bais Medrash – *Torah* study hall

Bais HaMikdash – Holy Temple

Bais Yaakov – educational system for Orthodox girls

bal tashchis – wastefulness, wanton destruction

balabatisha – associated with working people as opposed to rabbinical students and teachers

B"H; Baruch HaShem – Thank G-d

bentch – to bless; often refers to reciting 'grace after meals'

Birkas HaMazon – grace after meals

Birchos HaShachar – blessings recited at morning prayers

bisli – fried, spicy flour snack for children

blech – metal sheet covering a fire on *Shabbos*; food placed upon it before *Shabbos* may continue cooking

bracha/brachos – blessing/s

bracha achrona – blessing recited after eating

bris – circumcision; literally, covenant

b'dieved – according to a lower, yet acceptable, standard, usually referring to an aspect of *mitzva* observance that can or will no longer be done in the preferred manner

b'taiavon – hearty appetite; *bon appétit*

challah – special braided loaves of bread for *Shabbos* meals; also refers to the small portion of dough separated off and burnt when making a dough with at least 8 cups of flour; check with Rav for exact amounts and procedure.

chas v'shalom – G-d forbid

chassidim/chassidish – literally 'pious ones'; sometimes refers to sect of Orthodox Jews

chassan – bridegroom, title used from time of engagement

chasuna – wedding

chatzos – *halachic* middle of day or night; close to noon and midnight; not exactly 12:00

chavrusa – study partner

chazzan – cantor

Chazal – acronym referring to sages of Talmudic times, of blessed memory

Chazon Ish – book by Rabbi Avrohom Yeshaya Karelitz (1878-1953); the author became known by the book's name, a common appellation

cheder/chadorim – literally a room/s; refers usually to classroom of boys learning Torah, especially as was found in Eastern Europe and now in *frum* communities

cheshek – desire

chessed/chassadim – loving-kindness; such act(s)

chillul Shabbos – desecration of *Shabbos*

chizuk – encouragement

Chofetz Chaim – literally, 'desires life'; book written by Rabbi Yisroel Meir Kagan (1839-1933), concerning the laws of proper speech; the author is known by the name of his book

Chol HaMoed – intermediate days of *Pesach* and *Succos*; they are part of the holiday, but have fewer restrictions

Chovos Halevovos – Duties of the Heart; book of ethics written by Rabbi Bachya ibn Pakuda, circa 1200's

chometz – bread or any type of leavened product, such as beer and pretzels, all forbidden to be eaten or in our possession during *Pesach*

cholent – a stew typically made with meat, vegetables and beans; prepared before *Shabbos* and left cooking until *Shabbos* lunch when it is appropriate to enjoy a hot meal (see recipe section)

Chumash – the five books of Moses

chuppa – marriage canopy and ceremony

daf yomi – system of studying *Gemara* where one learns a folio, two sides of a page, daily

daven – pray

Da'as Torah – statements made based exclusively on Torah knowledge

derech eretz – manners

-dik – suffix similar to -ish; for/like/with

d'var Torah – Torah thought; **divrei** – plural

Elul – the month before the Jewish New Year

Eretz Yisroel – the Land of Israel

erev – literally evening; usually refers to the day before a holiday such as *Shabbos* or *Pesach*

frum – strictly observant Jew

Gadol hador – Torah giant of a generation

gam zu l'tova – this too is for the best

Gedolim – Torah leaders of the generation

gemach; gemillas chassadim – organization or place for performing kindnesses of varying types, especially cash loans

Gemara – Oral law, Talmud; **blatt Gemara** – a page of *Gemara*

gematriah – numerical value of Hebrew letters

hadracha – mentoring, ethical instruction

Hagada for Pesach – formalized guide for the S*eder* that details the evening's proceedings and traditions, commemorating the Jews leaving slavery in Egypt and becoming a nation

hakaras hatov – acknowledgement and appreciation of a benefit received

halacha/halochos – Jewish law/s

hamapil – *bracha* said with bedtime *Shema*, after which no speaking or activity is permitted

hamotzi – blessing said before eating bread

Har Sinai – mountain where the Torah was given

HaShem – G-d

hashgacha/s – special attention, such as that given to kashrus surveillance; herein refers to the way *HaShem* supervises every detail of our lives

hashkafa – Jewish thought and outlook

hatzlacha; B'hatzlacha – success; with success – good luck

hechsher – kosher certification

hesped/hespedim – eulogy/eulogies

heter – lenient ruling or special dispensation to do an action that would normally appear to be forbidden, but is permitted under particular circumstances; this is decided by a *Rav*

hishtadlus – effort, tempered with realization that HaShem runs the world

Igeress HaRamban – an ethical letter written by Nahmanides for his son, still studied by many, circa 1200's

Kaddish – herein refers to prayer said by mourners for sanctification of G-d's name; as a merit for the soul

kallah – bride, title used from time of engagement

kashrus – having to do with kosher – Jewish dietary laws

kavana – focus, intention especially in davening and *mitzva* performance

kavod – respect

Kiddush – prayer prior to the first two *Shabbos* meals, preferably performed with a cup of wine

kittel – white garment worn by men on *Yom Kippur*, during the marriage ceremony, at the *Seder* and lastly as burial shrouds

kivrei Tzaddikim – graves of righteous individuals

knaidlach – matzo balls, usually enjoyed with chicken soup

kollel – institution of men involved in Torah studies

korban – offering brought to *HaShem*, mostly during the era of the *Bais HaMikdash*

kodesh – divine, holy

kugel – side dish usually baked with eggs, vegetables or noodles, and more – a typical *Shabbos* or *Yom Tov* dish

lain – to read the Torah portion in *shul* for the congregation

levayah – funeral

licht – candles (Yiddish)

loshon hora – derogatory communiqué or one that hurts another in any way

lo aleinu – may it not happen to us

l'chatchila – according to the highest level of performance, usually a *mitzva*

l'havdil – to separate due to its elevated level, not to compare

l'tova – for good

Maftir – last section of *parsha* read in *shul*

Mazal Tov – congratulations

mechanech/mechanchim – Torah educator/s

mechutonim – refers to parents of one's son-in-law or daughter-in-law

Melave Malka – meal eaten Saturday night, after *Shabbos* is over, as a farewell to the *Shabbos* Queen

Mesilos Yesharim – Path of the Just, book of ethics written by Rabbi Luzzatto, circa 1700's

mesiras nefesh – self sacrifice

mevater – give in, yield

middah/middos – character trait/s

Midrashim – information originally passed on orally, extra- Talmudic Rabbinic literature

milchig/fleishig – dairy/meat; basic division of a kosher kitchen

Mishna/yos – section/s from *Mishna*, central text of the Talmud

mitzva/mitzvos – commandment/s

Modeh Ani – 'I thank you' – the first prayer, uttered upon arising

Moshe Rabbeinu – Moses our teacher, leader of the Jews when redeemed from Egypt and formed into a nation

Motzei Shabbos – Saturday evening, after *Shabbos* has ended

muktza – items forbidden to move on *Shabbos*

mussar – studies in ethical behavior; hence, admonishment, rebuke

nachas – contentment and satisfaction, usually from children for parents

nebby – unfortunate, pitiful

neila – closing prayer on Yom Kippur

neshama yesaira – extra soul, given to *Shabbos* observers just for the duration of *Shabbos*

niftar – deceased

nissim – miracles

nosh – snack

Olam Haba – world-to-come, place of ultimate reward: closeness to *HaShem*

ossur – forbidden

Oz Yashir – section of prayer taken from Exodus chapter 15, praising G-d for the splitting of the sea

pareve – neither meat nor dairy; usually refers to status of food and dishes

parsha – section of Torah; one *parsha* is read each week for a yearly cycle

pasuk/pesukim – verse/s of Torah, Prophets or Writings

Pesach – Passover, the springtime holiday celebrating our delivery from Egyptian bondage; its observance is mainly defined by totally ridding our homes of all leavened products and eating matzos

petirah – death

Pirkei Avos – Ethics of the Fathers, a *mishna* traditionally studied *Shabbos* afternoons from *Pesach* through *Succos*

posek/poskim – Rabbi/s capable of rendering legal decision in Jewish law

Purim – joyous holiday, celebrated with reading the book of Esther, gifts of food, charity and a festive meal; takes place a month before *Pesach*

p'sak – *halachic* decision

p'shat – simple explanation of any kind of Torah related text

Rashi – a principal commentator on the Torah, circa 1200's

Rav, Rebbe, Rebbi, Rabbonim – Torah scholar, leader or teacher (s)

Rebbetzin – wife of a *Rav* or *Rebbe*, typically involved with the community

refuah shleima – complete recovery

retzei – extra paragraph recited when *bentching* on *Shabbos*

Rosh Chodesh – the start of the new month, a minor holiday

Rosh Yeshiva – head of a Torah academy

Seder – literally order; tradition laden sequence of events enacted Passover evening; see *Hagada*

sefer – Jewish book – including *Tanach*, *siddur*, *halacha* and related topics

sefiras haomer – counting seven full weeks between Passover and *Shavuos* (the next holiday)

seuda – festive meal, usually for *Shabbos,* holiday, *bris*, bar mitzva, wedding or *siyum*

Seuda Shlishis – third *Shabbos* meal

Shabbos – the Sabbath; proper observance of it defines us as observant Jews

shadchan/shadchanim – matchmaker/s

shalom – peace

shalom zocher – open house celebration held by parents of newborn boy on the first Friday night following his birth

shehakol – blessing made before eating foods other than bread, wine, baked goods, fruits or vegetables

sheila/sheilos – question/s involving proper *mitzva* observance

shekel – Israeli currency

Shema – daily prayer, morning and evening, declaring oneness of *HaShem*

Shemoneh Esrei – main section of prayers, consisting of nineteen blessings recited daily; three times on weekdays, four on *Shabbos* and holidays, five on *Yom Kippur*

sheva brachos – celebratory dinners, often fancy, in honor of the new couple held first week following the wedding

shidduch/shidduchim – match/es arranged for the purpose of marriage

Shir HaShirim – Song of Songs, part of the *Tanach*

shiur/shiurim – Torah lecture/s

shiva – seven-day mourning period following the death of a parent, spouse, child or sibling

shkia – sunset

Shlit"a – blessing for a long and happy life, appended to name of a Rabbi

shmatte – rag

shmira – the act of guarding or observation

shmiras haloshon – guarding one's tongue; referring to laws of proper speech

shmooze – herein light conversation, chit-chat

shomayim – the upper world, Heaven

shteig – to grow in Torah knowledge through serious diligent study (Yiddish)

shul – house of worship (Yiddish)

shva – a vowel in the Hebrew alphabet

siddur – prayer book

simcha/simchos – happiness; often refers to a joyous occasion such as a wedding or *bar mitzva*

Simchas Chosson V'Kallah – herein a dessert reception held toward the end of a wedding, usually at the time of the second dance after the *chuppa*, to which one invites guests who were not invited for the meal

siyata dishmaya – literally, help from heaven; refers to *HaShem*'s guidance

Siyum HaShas – completion of study of oral Torah, often celebrated with a festive meal and guests

Succah – small temporary dwelling used for living quarters during the week-long, fall holiday of *Succos*

Talmid/im – student/s

Talmid/ei chochom/im – Torah scholar/s

Tanach – an acronym referring to the collected writings of the Torah, Prophets and Writings

tefilla – prayer

tefillin – phylacteries; worn by men during prayer

Tehillim – Psalms

teshuva – repentance

Tu B'Shevat – New Year for trees, observed a month before Purim

Tzaddik – a meticulous *mitzva* observer

tzedaka – charity

tznius – modesty in dress and behavior

v'ahavta l'reacha kamocha – the *mitzva* to love your friend as yourself

vort – literally 'word' usually refers to an engagement party or Torah thought

v'sein tal u'matar – prayer for rain, inserted in *Shemoneh Esrei* wintertime

yasher koach – congratulations on a job well done

yblct"a – acronym of a blessing added to a name of a living person when referenced with someone who has died

Yehudah – the fourth of the twelve tribes of Israel (Jacob's children)

Yehudim – Jews

yenem – them (Yiddish)

yeshiva/s – academy/s of Torah study

yesurim – troubles, difficult situations

yetzer hara – evil inclination

Yid/Yidden – Jew/s (Yiddish)

Yiddishe – Jewish (Yiddish)

Yiddishkeit – Judaism (Yiddish)

yimach shemo v'zichro – may his name and memory be erased

Yom/im Tov/im – Jewish holiday/s

zechus – merit; to be worthy or deserving of

zoche/zochim – person/people worthy of merit

zuhl zahn azoy – let it be like this (Yiddish)

z"l; zicrono l'vracha – a blessing added to a name of a person who has passed on, meaning 'his memory should be for a blessing'

zt"l; zecher Tzaddik l'vracha – same as *z"l*, but for a righteous person

www.ingramcontent.com/pod-product-compliance
Lightning Source LLC
Chambersburg PA
CBHW070530010526
44118CB00012B/1093